Law and Society
Volume 6

A Dialogical Framework for Analogy in Legal Reasoning
The Ratio Legis and Precedent Case Models

Volume 1
Criminological Theory. Just the Basics
Robert Heiner

Volume 2
Is Legal Reasoning Irrational? An Introduction to the Epistemology of Law
John Woods

Volume 3
The Law's Flaws. Rethinking Trials and Errors?
Larry Laudan

Volume 4
Logical Concepts in Legal Positivism. Legal Norms from a Philosophical Perspective
Juliele Maria Sievers

Volume 5
Chinese Legal Theory and Human Rights. Rearticulating Marxism, Liberalism, and the Classical Legal Tradition
Elena Consiglio

Volume 6
A Dialogical Framework for Analogy in Legal Reasoning. The Ratio Legis and Precedent Case Models
Hans Christian Nordtveit Kvernenes

Law and Society Series Editors
Robert L. Heiner
John Woods

rheiner@plymouth.edu
john.woods@ubc.ca

A Dialogical Framework for Analogy in Legal Reasoning
The Ratio Legis and Precedent Case Models

Hans Christian Nordtveit Kvernenes

© Individual author and College Publications 2022
All rights reserved.

ISBN 978-1-84890-391-3

College Publications, London
Scientific Director: Dov Gabbay
Managing Director: Jane Spurr

http://www.collegepublications.co.uk

Original cover design by Laraine Welch

All rights reserved. No part of this publication may be reproduced, stored in a retrieval system or transmitted in any form, or by any means, electronic, mechanical, photocopying, recording or otherwise without prior permission, in writing, from the publisher.

First, I would like to thank Shahid Rahman for introducing me to the dialogical approach to logic and for supervising the writing of my dissertation that now has been extended and turned into a book. In addition, I would like to thank the laboratory STL for being particularly accommodating of my special demands. The Institute of philosophy at UiT also deserves a large amount of gratitude for including me in their scientific activities, providing me with a suitable workplace and for giving me an opportunity for a lecturing position while at the same time providing time and support for finishing this book. I would like to thank the associates of the institute, and in particular Michael Morreau for introducing me to problems of similarity. Last, I would like to give special thanks to Mariette and Emil for their continuous support and encouragement for finishing this book.

Contents

Introduction   1
   Background 1
   Structure of book 7
   Intention, motivation and goal 9

I   What is analogy?   15

1   Preliminary remarks   17
   1.1   Civil Law 19
   1.2   Common Law 23
   1.3   Analogical arguments of two forms 26

2   Theories of analogy   29
   2.1   Categorising theories 29
   2.2   Schema-based approaches 30
         Brewer's notion of analogical reasoning 30
         Alchourrón's arguments a fortiori and a pari 43
         John Woods' notion of a GS 49
   2.3   Inference-based approaches 57
         Bartha's notion of analogical reasoning 57
         Prakken and Sartor's model of legal reasoning . . . 78
         Rahman and Iqbal's theory of co-relational inference   100

3 Comparison of contemporary theories — 107
3.1 Horizontal relations 107
3.2 Vertical relations 110
3.3 Multiple analogies 114

II Formal and informal background — 119

4 Constructive type theory — 121
4.1 Judgments 121
    Categorical judgments 121
    Propositions 124
    Hypothetical judgments 125
4.2 Rules in CTT 128
    Cartesian product of a family of sets 129
    Disjoint union of a family of sets 134
    Disjoint union of two sets 137
4.3 Specification and contexts 140
    Modality 140
    Contexts in possible worlds 140
    Specification by context 142

5 Immanent reasoning — 145
5.1 Preliminary notions of dialogical logic 145
    Particle rules 146
    Structural rules 147
    General definitions of the dialogical language . . . 148
5.2 Standard dialogical logic 149
    Rules of dialogical logic 149
    Equality and example of a play 158
    Extensive forms and strategies 163
5.3 Dialogues with play objects 177
    The local and the global level 178
    Strategy level and example 195
    Example of dialogue in immanent reasoning 197

6 Imperatives, precedents and relations — 201
6.1 Implementing imperatives — 201
Heteronomous imperatives — 202
Logical analysis of heteronomous imperatives — 208
Conditionals and heteronomous imperatives — 213
6.2 Capturing the notion of precedent — 217
A model of analogy — 217
The notion of a case — 218
Initial conditions — 221
6.3 Explaining relations — 223
Horizontal relations — 223
Vertical relations — 226
Other relations? — 228

III Analysing analogy — 235

7 CTT analysis — 237
7.1 General precedent-based reasoning — 240
Performing analogical reasoning — 240
Representing source cases — 249
Representing the analogical procedure in CTT — 252
7.2 Precedent-based reasoning with imperatives — 260
Performing analogical reasoning — 260
Representing source cases — 265
Representing the analogical procedure in CTT — 269
7.3 Steamboat example — 275
Assumptions and description of example — 275
Informal analysis — 276
Formal analysis — 280

8 Dialogical implementation — **289**
8.1 Precedent-based reasoning 289
Terminology 289
Challenge rules 292
Explanation rules 296
8.2 Explaining and extending the analysis 309
Explanation of the dialogical approach 309
Formation plays and permitted analogies 315
Introducing heteronomous imperatives 318
8.3 Dialogical example 319
Steamboat example 319
Mortgage loan example 325
Results 345

9 Theoretical considerations — **359**
9.1 Logical, actual and real assumptions 359
Potentiality and actuality 360
Propositions 364
Assumptions, possibility and actuality 365
9.2 Distinction of steps and future contingency 370
Characteristics of a conditional right 371
There will be a sea-battle tomorrow 374
CTT and moral conditionals 379
9.3 Performance and deontic qualification 386
Good Shoemakers 386
CTT and hypotheticals 391
Deontic logic and hypotheticals 395

Conclusion — **399**
Project 399
Results 400
Further research 401

Bibliography — **403**

Introduction

Background

The present project is twofold. First, it gives a thorough representation of the concept of analogical reasoning in law by introducing and comparing contemporary theories regarding the subject. Second, it provides an independent analysis of analogical reasoning in the framework of immanent reasoning.

The first part provides explanations and comparison of six contemporary theories of analogical reasoning in law. These theories are categorised into schema-based theories and inference-based theories. Schema-based theories of analogical reasoning capture the notion of analogy by a description of a rule or schema. Inference-based theories on the other hand explain analogical reasoning as a distinct way of reasoning. Based on this distinction, the project compares the theories by how they handle the notions of horizontal and vertical relations and by how they analyse multiple competing analogies.

The second part of the project provides an independent analysis of analogies by utilising the framework of immanent reasoning. Immanent reasoning is described, together with an explanation of other notions that are relevant for the given analysis. The project then introduces two kinds of analogical reasoning, general precedent-based reasoning and precedent-based reasoning with heteronomous imperatives. These kinds are first analysed in the general formulation of constructive type theory (CTT) and is then given an alternative formulation in its dialogical interpretation. Following this, we introduce a discussion on the advantages of utilising this framework for analysing legal reasoning in general and analogical reasoning in particular.

Based on a variant of the principle of proportionality, the present project provides a new analysis of analogical arguments in the framework of immanent reasoning. By utilising the formalisation of moral conditionals, we show how we can achieve an analysis of analogical reasoning. Because of the particular notion of dependent types in CTT, this approach also allows for formalising initial conditions and thereby an explicit notion of permitted analogy. The dialogical interpretation takes this one step further as this allows for representing this feature as an individual condition for the particular form of the introduced analogy.

The inclusion of initial conditions is a new feature not known to have been previously introduced in any other contemporary analyses of analogy and the particularity of this project is that it provides further meaning explanations of analogical reasoning that includes an initial permission in a simple and natural way, closely related to actual legal practice.

Contemporary theories of analogy

Problems of analysing analogical reasoning have received much attention in Antiquity and Middle Ages, notably by Aristotle's analysis of *proportionality*. And in recent years, these questions started again to receive attention. In the scientific context, this modern attention to questions about analogy can be traced back to Hesse's (1965) *Models and Analogies in Science*, where she provided a thorough analysis regarding the use of analogies in different scientific contexts. Somehow distinct from this tradition, another contemporary interest in such questions stemming from legal theory also emerged.

In the context of law, the use of analogies is widespread and theoretical problems regarding their analysis have the last 30 years received attention from researchers across multiple disciplines, such as philosophy, legal theory and computer science. Theorists have from different perspectives tried to analyse the notion of analogy and its use in legal argumentation. Some theorists attempt to unite theories about analogy coming from both the legal and the scientific contexts, while others try to apprehend it only as a legal phenomena. Theorists also differ in what they consider to be the object of their analyses. Some take the perspective of a particular legal framework, while others intend to have a more general scope.

Broadly, we might distinguish between theories that explain analogical arguments as regular deductive arguments with some particular premises and theories that explain these arguments as a distinct form of reasoning. We will call the first kind *schema-based* theories and the second kind *inference-based* theories. In the schema-based theories the goal is to identify a *schema* or *rule* that enables us to consider the analogical argument as a valid deduction. In the inference-based theories, the goal is to identify analogical reasoning as a particular form of *reasoning* or *inference*.

Brewer (1996), Alchourrón (1991) and Woods (2015) describe three important schema-based theories. In «Exemplary Reasoning: Semantics, Pragmatics, and the Rational Force of Legal Argument by Analogy», Brewer provides a theory of analogical reasoning that became widely influential in the debate about the use of analogies in contemporary Common Law, particularly in the Anglo-American tradition. Even earlier, Alchourrón wrote a paper called «Los Argumentos Juridicos a fortiori y a pari» that provided a logical analysis of two kinds of analogical arguments. This paper became very influential in the Spanish-speaking (and to some extent German-speaking) academical debate, though since the paper never has been translated to English, its influence in the English-speaking context has unfortunately been marginal. The book *Is Legal Reasoning Irrational?: An Introduction to the Epistemology of Law* by Woods is a very recent work that attempts to analyse the legal understanding of analogy in light of insights stemming from the theory of science.

Bartha (2010), Prakken and Sartor (1996) and Rahman and Iqbal (2018) provide three important inference-based theories. In *By Parallel Reasoning: The Construction and Evaluation of Analogical Arguments*, Bartha provides a formal model for analogical reasoning in a wide range of areas, from mathematics to everyday reasoning, including legal arguments. It has recently shown to be a very influential general approach to questions of analogy. Prakken and Sartor develop in multiple papers a particular dialogical theory that comes from a computer scientific perspective on legal argumentation generally. Rahman and Iqbal provide in the paper «Unfolding Parallel Reasoning in Islamic Jurisprudence (I) epistemic and dialectical meaning in Abu Ishaq al-Shirazi's system of co-relational inferences of the occasioning factor» a contemporary logical analysis of analogical reasoning stemming from the often neglected, but rich tradition of Islamic legal theory.

The different theories do indeed share many aspects, though there are also important differences, both between the schema-based theories and the inference-based theories, and across the individual theories. Some differences can be explained by the point that some theories reduce the notion of analogy to a schema, while others considers them as a particular kind of inference. A noticeable point is however how the different theories deal with multiple, competing analogies. In this aspect, the theories varies greatly. Some reject that this should be a part of the formal framework. Some introduce a particular formal concept to create a systemised hierarchy, while some consider that the competing analogies should be decided by the use of an analogical argument in itself.

The framework of Immanent reasoning

Constructive type theory was developed by Martin-Löf (1984) in order to have a language to reason constructively both about and with mathematics. The idea is to have a system where you do not distinguish between syntax and semantics in the same way as it is traditionally done. This enables us to keep meaning and form on the same level and therefore also interact with each other in a way that is explicit in the language itself.

Dialogical logic should not be considered a logical system by itself, but rather a framework where we can interpret different logical systems. It may be considered as a general approach to meaning, and we can therefore use it to develop and compare different logical systems. The idea is to consider meaning as being constituted in the argumentative interaction between two agents. We may trace this idea back to later Wittgenstein and his notion of *meaning as use*. The interpretation of constructive type theory in the dialogical approach is what is called 'immanent reasoning', where its most recent version has been developed by Rahman, McConaughey, et al. (2018).

The connection between CTT and dialogical logic seems to be strong. Again, we can refer to Wittgenstein and his claim that we should not position ourselves outside language when trying to determine meaning. In CTT we do not consider syntax and semantics to be distinguished in a similar way as in classical logic. For propositions, we have inference rules and not distinct syntactical rules that describe when a proposition can be formed. In the dialogical approach, the meaning is determined by how it is used in interaction. Because of this, we may consider dialogical logic to be a pragmatical approach to meaning and semantics. If we link CTT to the dialogical approach, we do only consider syntax to be a kind of semantics, but that both actually belong to the pragmatics. What we end up with is a system where we do not distinguish syntax, semantics and pragmatics as separate domains. Syntax, semantics and pragmatics are all essentially related to interaction and their meaning should be understood in terms of a normative obligation of interaction between the players, which in turn is a moral notion. In this sense, logic is considered to be a result of the moral obligation of interacting. It is not something essentially fundamental, but rather found in the investigation of ethics.

The dialogical approach describes a dialogue between two players. These players may be called the 'Opponent' and the 'Proponent'. The two players argue on a thesis. A thesis is a statement that is subject for the dialogue. The Proponent begins by stating the thesis and the Opponent will try to challenge it. The Proponent will again try to defend this thesis from the Opponents attacks. The notions of challenging and defending is then used to establish the dialogical understanding of meaning.

Structure for formalising analogy in immanent reasoning

In immanent reasoning there is a distinction between formation rules and particle rules. In order to represent analogies in this framework, we will use this distinction and consider the formation rules to represent initial conditions that might be imposed on the analogy and particle rules to represent a principle coming from Aristotle's notion of proportionality. This proposal of the implementation of analogies in immanent reasoning will be an essential part of this project.

In this part we will first analyse analogical reasoning by providing two different kinds of conditions that need to be satisfied. The first kind of condition describes a permission for the utilisation of analogical argumentation in this precise case. In many situations the use of analogies in the legal argumentation process is restricted. This can be for several reasons, like constitutional limitations or because other legal rules already answer this particular legal question. This restriction is not found in other analyses of analogical argumentation and we consider this to be a newly introduced feature, introduced in this project. The second kind of condition is one that we find in most contemporary works regarding the logical foundation of analogical reasoning. This is what will be called the efficiency requirement or the proportionality-principle. It will be implemented as ways for the challenger to attack the thesis of the defender by providing a counterexample.

The methodology used for analysing analogical argumentation in immanent reasoning is to describe general aspects relevant for arguments by analogy. This comes partially from the comparison of theories in the first part, but we will also argue for including the new aspect called *permission of the analogy*. This aspect is present in the literature from a legal point of view, but absent in the contemporary logical analyses of analogical reasoning. It is the CTT approach to consider both meaning and form in the same language that enables us to also include this in the analysis in a simple way.

STRUCTURE OF BOOK

The book is structured in three main parts. The first part gives a general overview over the notion of analogy and explains different contemporary theories proposed for analysing analogical reasoning. The second part gives an overview over immanent reasoning, which is the logical framework that is used as a basis for the included analysis. Based on the two preceding parts, the third part presents this proposal for formalising analogical reasoning.

Presentation of present theories

The first part of the project describes and compares different theories of analogical reasoning in respect to how they handle different kinds of analogies. It starts by a very brief historical introduction related to the concept of analogy and then goes on by describing some relevant terminological distinctions based on contemporary legal theory that will provide useful for the rest of the work. The different theories of analogy in the second chapter will be categorised in schema-based theories and inference-based theories. The described schema-based theories are the ones by Brewer (1996), Alchourrón (1991) and

Woods (2015). And the described inference-based theories are the ones by Bartha (2010), Prakken and Sartor (1996) and Rahman and Iqbal (2018). The part then finishes with a comparison in respect to how they represent what will be called horizontal and vertical relations and how they handle multiple analogies.

Theoretical background

The second part provides a thorough description of the theoretical framework of immanent reasoning, a very recent interpretation of the constructive type-theoretical framework by Martin-Löf (1984). CTT enables us to describe the interaction between form and meaning in a way that standard logical frameworks are not able to express. The idea was to develop a language where we can reason constructively in the same time with and about mathematics. CTT is then a powerful language that enables the formulation of hypothetical judgments that are not only dependent on objects, but also on categories by its notion of dependent types. Immanent reasoning is presented here in its last version, as given in Rahman, McConaughey, et al. (2018). This framework gives a sophisticated interpretation of both formal and informal reasoning by the means of a dialogical conception of truth. The idea of the dialogical approach is to consider meaning not relevant to some abstract model, but as argumentative moves in a play. By combining this dialogical approach with CTT we get a framework that is able to express the powerful notion of hypothetical judgments from CTT in a comprehensible way, that corresponds well together with the actual utilisation of argumentative moves.

A dialogical interpretation of analogy

The last part of the book describes the implementation of analogical reasoning as presented in the first part, by the framework of immanent reasoning given in the second part. It is this part that constitutes the original development and addition to the contemporary scientific debate particular to this project. This part first provides a description of different particular notions and formalisations in CTT that are essential for the analysis of analogical argumentation. It then goes on by giving a general description of reasoning by analogy, both with characteristics and with heteronomous imperatives. This analysis provides us with a complex formula for analogical reasoning that will need a particular notational practice to be explained. The project continues by describing a way to translate this into a dialogical explanation. It then provides rules for eight different forms of analogical arguments. The permission of the analogical argument will also be described as more refined in the dialogical conception compared to the general CTT approach, as we would allow the permitted analogies to be attached to the relevant particular form of analogical argument. This last part terminates by a discussion of the philosophically relevant aspects of the previously introduced analysis and for the projects choice of a dialogical interpretation of constructive type theory.

INTENTION, MOTIVATION AND GOAL

The role of the logician in a practical context
When attempting to analyse a concept from a domain as a logician we are given a seemingly conflicting role. On one side we should attempt to base the analysis on the actual practice, so that the analysis reflects the use of this concept. On the other side we are also dealing with a domain that seems to have some normative character. The analysis should not simply be an empirical investigation of how the concept is used, but it should also provide some guidelines for distinguishing good from bad practice of this concept. In this sense such project seems to be in conflict. Should our project only describe the actual practice and risk not being useful because of its lack of opinion regarding the practice? Or, should our project only describe the normative foundations for this concept and thereby risk to end up too far away from the concept we originally wanted to analyse?

These questions do not seem to be particular to logic, but rather as attached to something more general regarding the practice of doing philosophy. Philosophical concepts should ideally not be too far away from what we normally understand by these concepts, while at the same time they should make us able to explain a correct use. *Truth* is an obvious example of this problem. A proper philosophical definition of truth should in the same time be able to accommodate our intuitions about what truth is and give us guidelines for a correct usage of such concept. This might be reduced to a question about the relationship between normativity and reality, though it is a problem that one would need to overcome in order to provide the kind of analysis that is intended in this projected. Legal theory does not seem to be any exception.

The role of logic in legal theory seems indeed to be affected by these mentioned problems. Logic is on one hand expected to show the actual practice, while on the other hand also expected to have some effect on the practice. It is not sure that there is one specific way to solve this problem. The best one can do is, as a good legal practitioner, to show discretion. By showing discretion, one can hopefully arrive at an analysis that is neither too far away nor too close to actual practice so that our analysis will be based on reality, without losing the normativity that characterises philosophical and logical concepts.

Why immanent reasoning?

There are multiple reasons for choosing precisely immanent reasoning to represent analogies and a thorough explanation of these reasons is given in chapter 9.

The most important reason is the framework's particular way of explaining meaning. In most classical frameworks there is a clear distinction between the syntax and the semantics, or the form and the meaning. When an expression is assigned a meaning, it is assumed that this expressions is well-formed. CTT has a different approach to this. Here, the form of an expression is not simply assumed to be made in a correct way, but the explanation of this form is also included in the object-language by means of formation rules. Together with the constructive aspect, this enables the framework to provide a clear distinction between the Aristotelean concepts of *meaning*, *actuality* and *potentiality*. CTT is then able to express a very sophisticated notion of conditional that includes dependent types, which will show to be essential for the present formalisations of juridical concepts. It is this notion of dependent types that enables the implementation of *initial conditions* for analogical reasoning.

The introduced analysis is based on a formalisation of a special kind of conditional, called *conditional right* or *moral conditional*. Leibniz analysed these conditionals by imposing some particular requirements that would distinguish them from other conditionals. CTT has proven to be a powerful tool for precisely capturing many important aspects of Leibniz's analysis. The present project utilises this CTT formalisation of moral conditionals as a foundation for its analysis of analogical reasoning. One result of this project is to show that by embedding the expression of one moral conditional inside another, we can achieve a formalisation of the procedure for analogical reasoning. An argument by analogy might therefore be said to be a special and complex form of moral conditional.

The third reason for utilising immanent reasoning is related to the meaning explanations provided by CTT, and particularly by its dialogical interpretation. By means of the hypothetical judgment, CTT enables us to capture not only corresponding truth conditions as for the classical material conditional, but also the precise *dependency* that the consequent has on its antecedent. This is what makes CTT so expressive regarding the formalisation of juridical and moral claims. We can then show how a decision is dependent on its reason and how the deontic qualification is dependent on the performance of the action in very precise ways. Its dialogical interpretation provides a natural and comprehensible framework for meaning explanations that is closely linked to actual legal practice and that unites logical inferences and argumentation theory in one single framework.

Academic context

The project positions itself in a contemporary debate regarding the logical analysis of analogies and analogical reasoning. The goal of the project is twofold. It first intends to present and compare contemporary theories for reasoning by analogy. Second, it intends to provide an independent analysis of such reasoning based on the framework of immanent reasoning. This is based on the comparison of the different theories as it attempts to include important aspects introduced in the contemporary debate, while at the same time provide a more refined analysis accounted for by the particular dependency found in analogical reasoning.

The dialogical approach to logic and argumentation can be traced back to antiquity, by the works of Aristotle and Plato. Logic was then considered to be an activity that was performed as a dialogue regarding some proposition. In the modern approach introduced by Frege, the view on the role of logic changed to become a question about abstract manipulation of formulas. The contemporary dialogical approach was introduced by Lorenzen (1961) who brought back the antique idea to again consider logic as dialectical by utilising a game-theoretical approach to meaning. This modern dialogical approach has been further refined and developed into a framework where a great variety of logical systems have been interpreted and compared, creating multiple branches of dialogical logics. One of these branches is what is now called immanent reasoning. It is the result of describing an intimate connection between dialogues, constructivism and intuitionism, particularly related to the research done in the University of Lille. The goal of this project is to enter into this tradition and show how the framework can be applied also in the context of analogical reasoning in law.

The project introduces a new analysis of analogies in immanent reasoning. The particularities of this framework enables us to provide a formalisation of analogical reasoning in a precise way in line with corresponding contemporary analyses in other frameworks. Furthermore, this project utilises the concept of dependent types to introduce a condition of initial permission for the use of analogies, not introduced in any previously given logical analysis. This condition is indicated by different theorists, particularly from legal scholars, though from the logical perspective this seems to be the first time that this condition is included in the explicit logical representation. It enables the analysis to not only account for the use of analogy, but also to explain the introduction of the analogical argument in the first place.

Part I

What is analogy?

Chapter 1

Preliminary remarks for the notion of analogy

An analogy can be considered as two things that are similar in some aspects. Analogical reasoning is reasoning based upon an analogy. An analogical argument is an explicit representation of analogical reasoning, with premises and a conclusion, where the conclusion depends on an analogy. Here, there will not be made a clear distinction between analogical reasoning and analogical arguments. These terms will be used interchangeably. Furthermore, there is great variance between different theorists regarding terminology in respect to these things. It can be called *parallel reasoning* or *exemplary reasoning*, and some authors make distinctions between their terminology and *analogy*. Based on the previously given definitions, this work understands the word *analogy* in very broad way so that the notion of analogy is not only the strict legal definition, but a notion that covers all similarities in this sense.

Etymologically, the word *analogy* can be traced back to the Latin word *analogia* and the ancient Greek word αναλογια. However, despite the etymological similarities between the Greek and the Latin word, their meanings were slightly different. αναλογια was usually translated to *proportio* or *proportionalitas* and it was understood as a comparison between two proportions. The Latin term, *analogia*, was used as saying that a scripture was not conflicting with another scripture. Today, we then see that it is actually the notion of *proportio* that corresponds best together with the kind of argument that we nowadays call argument by analogy. This is also the kind of argument that is based on Aristotle's notion of *proportionality*, which can be considered to provide a conceptual foundation, not only for legal analogies, but for a large variety of practices.

One of these practices is the applicability in legal argumentation. Today, the world is largely dominated, or at least largely influenced, by two legal traditions, the Civil Law and the Common Law. In Langenbucher (1998), we are provided with a comparison of analogical arguments in the common law tradition and analogical arguments in the civil law tradition. The paper does not provide a theory of analogical argumentation in itself, but contains a comparison of the use of analogies in two legal traditions, including what will be identified as their initial conditions. The analogical arguments can be distinguished into two different kinds, *rule-based* analogies and *principle-based* analogies. This distinction is based upon Dworkin's understanding that we have two different forms of norms, namely rules and principles. A principle is a norm that is value maximising. A case decision can be more or less conforming to a principle. A rule on the other hand is either covering a situation or it is not. It can therefore be applied in a 'all-or-nothing fashion'. (Langenbucher 1998, pp. 502-503)

The rule-based analogy can be used when a set of rules has seemingly omitted a special class of cases. The analogical argument therefore intends to extend the set of rules so that they would also include this class of cases. The goal of the argument is here to extend the applicability of a set of rules. For a principle-based analogy, the goal of the argument is to apply a general principle to a particular case. A rule-based analogical argument is then transferring some rules to another domain, while principle-based analogical arguments is about the interpretation of a general principle to particular cases. Both of these forms of analogical arguments are present in both civil law systems and common law systems, though they do not play the exact same role in the two traditions. The terminological descriptions in this following sections are based on Langenbucher's (1998) paper.

1.1 Civil Law

Analogical arguments in Civil Law can be described as coming in two different forms, a standard case and an exception case. When one refers to analogy in a civil law context, one usually speaks about the standard case. Though even if the exception case might occasionally not be identified as containing an analogy, we can see that they to a great extent share a similar structure and is indeed based on a similarity between two domains.

Standard case
The standard case analogy in the civil law system is intended to fill a gap in the law by extending a rule to cover another legal area. It is therefore identified as a typical rule-based analogy. A normal view on civil law systems is that the code should cover many cases. Though no matter how refined this code is, there might always be situations that do not seem to be covered by it. In order to have a functioning legal system, one might use a rule in the code in a situation that it does not seem to directly cover. This is done by referring to a similarity between the cases that the rule is considered to cover and the cases that we intend the rule to cover. Justification for such reasoning comes from a principle of equal treatment together with the legislative supremacy. If one assume that like cases should be treated alike and that the legislature has decided that one case should be treated in a particular way, a like (or similar) case should also be treated in that way. The argumentation process might be described as a three-step procedure. The first step is to show that

there is a lacuna. The second step is the make sure that there are no constitutional restrictions on the use of analogy. The third step is to establish a similarity relation between the case at hand and the scope of the rule. (Langenbucher 1998, pp. 482-483)

The first step is to establish that there is a lacuna in the code. This part might be described as the *negative-answer question*. In an analogical argument it is necessary, but not considered to be sufficient to only establish that the case at hand is not covered by any rule, that there is a gap in the law. One must also establish that it was not the intention of the legislature to exclude situations like the case at hand from being covered by this or other rules. This means that the purpose of the statute requires a particular solution. (Langenbucher 1998, p. 483)

The second step is to establish that there are no constitutional restrictions that would prohibit the use of analogical reasoning in this particular situation. Such restriction might involve not violating fundamental rights or be further restrictions based on the separation of powers. A widespread principle that restricts the use of analogical reasoning in criminal law is *nulla poena sine lege*, which states that there can be no penalty without a law. This is often considered to restrict the use of analogy for extending a criminal statutory provision to cover the case at hand. The particular formulation of these restrictions might differ between law systems, but there are often restrictions on the use of analogies in criminal law or related to fundamental human rights. Other restrictions might be related to references to decisions of a lower court or have particular areas where rules must be explicitly introduced by the legislation. (Langenbucher 1998, pp. 485-486)

The third step is to develop the actual analogy. This is done by establishing a relevant similarity between one or several cases that are explicitly governed by the rule and the case at hand. In order to establish such relevant similarity, one has to refer to a point of reference, *tertium comparationis*, that one can use to pick out the similarities that are relevant from those that are not. In the standard

1.1. Civil Law

civil-law case this is done by referring to the *ratio legis* of the rule, which will work as standard of comparison when establishing a single relevant similarity. The ratio legis is the purpose of the law, the *ratio* of the statutory rule. The case at hand is therefore relevantly similar in this sense to the case explicitly governed by the rule if the purpose of the rule also encompasses the situation in the case at hand. When this relevant similarity has been established, we can perform the analogical reasoning and also apply the rule to the case at hand. (Langenbucher 1998, pp. 487-489)

Exception case
In Langenbucher (1998, pp. 495-497), we also find a description of an exception case of analogical reasoning in the civil law tradition. Though normally, this is not called analogy by legal theorists or legal reasoners in the civil law tradition. The term *analogy* is restricted to an analogical application of a written statute. This might therefore be called case-based reasoning and is sometimes considered to be a method to establish an interpretation, a variant of the principle-based analogy. This way of reasoning is usually motivated from a need of clarification of statutes. It is sometimes described as a method of establishing the precise meaning of a vague norm. However, this notion of vagueness should not be understood as in the contemporary metaphysical debate, where it is connected to unsolvable borderline cases. In this context, we are speaking about norms that cannot be directly applied to a particular case without further interpretation, independent of whether this is caused by generality, ambiguity, vagueness or something else that prevents us from deciding the applicability of the norm. In order to avoid any confusion with the notion of vagueness, we will speak about legally uncertain norms, which should be understood as norms whose application to particular cases is disputable. This kind of reasoning in civil law systems is then a way of reasoning that can be used to

apply a norm by giving it a precise meaning in a particular case. However, this part of the process will often also depend on other aspects than precedents, like fundamental rights, intention of the law or pragmatic considerations. (Langenbucher 1998, pp. 495-496)

In this case-based reasoning in Civil Law, one tries to establish a certain interpretation that has been made in a previously decided case. When there has been a particular interpretation of a legally uncertain norm in a previously decided case, the legal reasoner might refer to this case in order for the same interpretation to hold in the case at hand, or as a basis in order to provide a further interpretation that might hold in the case at hand. We will take the example *everyone has the right freely to impart his opinion orally, in writing and in images* from the German Basic Law (the German constitution), Art. 5 para. 1 sent. 2. In order for this to be applicable to particular cases one would have to make a certain interpretation, particularly related to the notion of *opinion*. The expression is considered to capture the right of free speech. In order to apply this right to particular cases, the German Court has to settle the scope, contents and limits for this right. This is usually happening stepwise, so that we will have a gradually increasing degree of precision. First *opinion* was interpreted as the combination of facts, personal views and ideas. It was then understood to include merely facts that were independent of opinion. Further interpretation provided an inclusion of facts that precondition the making of an opinion. Afterwards it was also understood to include questions. This shows the general structure of a case-based reasoning regarding interpretation, as every following interpretation would depend on the earlier interpretations as a foundation. The actual further interpretation is not solely based on this case-based reasoning, as there are many other aspects to account for when performing an interpretation. Case-based reasoning occurs in this sense when a legal reasoner depends on an interpretation to either decide the applicability of that norm in this particular case or when providing a further interpretation. That a legal reasoner depends on a previous interpretation in order to decide its applicability would seem to be very common at all levels of the law, also when applying the law outside the context of the court, and does indeed seem crucial in order for case-based interpretations to have any influence beyond the actual case. This kind of case-based reasoning would therefore seem to be present not only when a judge decides a case in court, but also in for example issuing legal documents, practical police work or in general perform an implementation of the law. (Langenbucher 1998, pp. 496-497)

1.2 COMMON LAW

Standard case
The standard case analogy in common law traditions is the application of a *ratio decidendi* of a precedent to new set of facts, which gives us a typical example of principle-based analogies. Common Law systems usually include the principle of *stare decisis*, the doctrine that precedent decisions are binding. The reasoning will be based upon finding a previously decided case or a line of cases that includes a *ratio decidendi* which covers also the case at hand. In some cases it might be unclear that this process actually is reasoning by analogy, but this is clearly illustrated by an example. In the case *Donoghue v. Stevenson*, A.C. 562 (1932), it was decided that a Scottish manufacturer of ginger beer had a responsibility towards their customers when they had accidentally let snails go into their product. The ratio decidendi of this case can then be formulated in different ways. It can have a general form: *manufacturers of products owe a duty to care to the consumer to ensure that no fault in the preparation or putting up of the product, resulting in an injury to the consumer's life or property, will occur.* This will clearly cover any other situation where a manufacturer sells poisoned ice cream or the case *Grant v. The Australian Knitting Mills*, A.C. 85 (1936) where a manufacturer omits the removal of chemicals in clothes so that wearing them result in skin infections. However, if the

ratio decidendi is formulated less general: *Scottish manufacturers of ginger-beer in opaque bottles owe a duty of care not to allow dead snails to get into the product*, neither of the mentioned cases seem to be covered by this ratio decidendi. In the Grant v. The Australian Knitting Mills case, the counsel referred to the Donoghue v. Stevenson case arguing for understanding the ratio decidendi in the following way: *manufacturers of articles of food and drink owe a duty of care not to allow any noxious physical foreign body to get into the product*. The ratio decidendi would then seem to hold for the ice cream case, while in order for it to hold also for the Grant v. The Australian Knitting Mills case, an argument by analogy has to be made. The standard case for analogical arguments in Common Law might be described in two steps. (Langenbucher 1998, pp. 490-491)

The first step to use an analogical argument is to establish that there is no law (normally precedents) in the area that would motivate a conclusion contrary to the one that intends to be established by the analogical argument. This might be called a variant of the negative-answer question. If there are one or several precedents that would seem to prevent the use of the analogical argument that the judge considers, they can be set aside in two ways. The judge might either distinguish or overrule. Distinguishing is the process of rejecting the relevancy of the precedents to the case at hand. This can be done by considering the ratio decidendi of a case to be so narrow that it does not include the case at hand. To suppose that *Scottish manufacturers of ginger-beer in opaque bottles owe a duty of care not to allow dead snails to get into the product* is the ratio decidendi for the Donoghue v. Stevenson case is an example of that. In such interpretation, the ratio decidendi is applicable in very few cases. However, in many situations the generality of the ratio decidendi might be thoroughly established and therefore prevent such narrow interpretation. Another way to deal with this is to add a further condition to the ratio decidendi. This might be done by claiming that the ratio decidendi holds, but only within a certain

1.2. Common Law

context or as long as some other relevant condition is not satisfied. This further condition should then be satisfied in the case at hand while not in the precedent that was intended to be distinguished. The last alternative is to overrule the precedent. This means to ignore the ratio decidendi in the precedent or line of precedents and in order to do this, one usually has to show that the precedent was wrongly decided. (Langenbucher 1998, pp. 491-493)

The second step is the development of the analogy, which can be done after determining the negative-answer question. This step involves creating the relevant similarity between the precedent and the case at hand. Many theories regarding analogical reasoning in Common Law, focuses on determining what this relevant similarity consists of. In order to have a reasonable notion of similarity, one has to include a point of reference. In the standard analogical argument in civil law systems this point of reference was the *ratio*, while in Common Law, this is the principle that underlines decision in a precedent or a line of precedents. This principle is sometimes called the *ratio* or the rationale. The case at hand is then similar to a precedent or a line of precedent if the ratio that underlines the decision also holds for the case at hand. (Langenbucher 1998, pp. 493-494)

Exception case

The exception case analogy in Common Law is the application of a *ratio decidendi* to a new situation that would not initially seem to be covered by it, namely a variant of the rule-based analogy. Among the different variants of analogies, this would seem to be the most controversial and disputed. The analogy intends to extend an established rule to cover another area that lies outside of the original scope of the rule, and does so by referring to the purpose or policy underlying a relevant statutory norm. The essence of the discussion is whether purpose and policy of a statute can be justifiably used in grounding a legal decision. The controversy lies partly in the use of statutes in the first place, as this will depend on some inclusion of statutory law into the body of law. Such inclusion might happen as a result of political agreements or innate to the legal system itself, as some common law systems might have aspects of statutory law, while still be a part of the common law tradition. The exception case of analogy in Common Law, therefore seems to be closely related to the standard case of analogy in Civil Law, as it is including a typical aspect of Civil Law into Common Law, and the procedures for utilising this would follow principles from the traditions of Civil Law. (Langenbucher 1998, pp. 497-499)

1.3 Analogical arguments of two forms

Based on the description in Langenbucher (1998), we can distinguish between rule-based analogies and principle-based analogies. The two forms share the same inner structure, though they differ in how and why they are used. Rule-based analogies intend to extend the application of a rule, while principle-based analogies intend to clarify the application of a principle. We could say that a rule-based analogy makes the rule cover a case that was originally not covered by that rule, and thereby extends the rule. A principle-based analogy clarifies the boundaries for that principle by making the principle more precise. We might think of rule-based analogies as extending the legal norm, while principle-based analogies as interpreting the legal norm. We seem to find both kinds of analogies in both common law and civil law systems, though they have a slightly different status.

1.3. Analogical arguments of two forms

In all forms of analogical arguments, Langenbucher (1998) argues that there might be restrictions regarding the use of analogies in the first place. In the standard case of Civil Law this is means to establish that there is a lacuna in the law (a *negative-answer question*) and that there are no constitutional restrictions on the use of analogy. For the exception case of Civil Law we are restricted as there must be uncertain legal norms. In the both cases of Common Law, we have a similar requirement for there not to be any law that would motivate a conclusion contrary what one intends to establish by the analogy. This can take the form of another precedent or by some other legally binding document. This is another variant of the *negative-answer question*. For the exception case of Common Law, the restrictions have a very similar form as we find in the standard case of Civil Law.

Chapter 2

THEORIES OF ANALOGY

2.1 CATEGORISING THEORIES

When speaking about theories of analogical reasoning, we might distinguish between *schema-based* theories and *inference-based* theories. We might say that a schema-based theory of analogical reasoning tries to capture the notion of analogy by a description of a schema. This schema is then usually added to make the inference based on an analogy deductively valid. Whether the analogical argument is acceptable, usually stands or falls on the justification of this added premise, the schema. In these approaches, analogical reasoning is often reduced to a deductive argument with the addition of a premise. The schema-based theories that will be presented here are the AWR-model by Brewer (1996), the a fortiori and a pari argumentation of Alchourrón (1991) and the GS-model by Woods (2015). An inference-based theory of analogical reasoning does not intend to reduce an analogical argument to a deductive one, but considers an analogical argument as an inference on its own. Inference-based theories therefore intend to describe what should be required of analogical argumentation. The inference-based theories that will be presented here are the articulation model by Bartha (2010), the dialogical model of legal reasoning by Prakken and Sartor (1998) and the dialogical Islamic theory by Rahman and Iqbal

(2018). Common for the inference-based theories (and contrary to the schema-based theories) is that they heavily depend on modifying or extending a particular formal framework. In order to capture the meaning of their analyses, we will also have to briefly present the formal framework each theory is based upon. This means that the presentation of the inference-based theories will take more space than of the schema-based ones. In this chapter we do not claim any original contribution to the literature. All definitions, descriptions and examples are, unless specified otherwise, based on the papers and books where the respective theories are introduced.

2.2 Schema-based approaches to analogical reasoning

Brewer's notion of analogical reasoning

Overview over Brewer's model

The basic idea of Brewer (1996) in his paper is that analogical reasoning is essentially a three-step process where each step is necessary and together they form sufficient conditions for reasoning by analogy. According to Brewer it is a combination of abduction, induction and deduction.

The first step is called abduction in a context of doubt. A context of doubt occurs if a judge or a lawyer cannot clearly take some standpoint in a case. It can be uncertainty whether to apply a certain concept or not. The abduction arises when the lawyer or the judge have some examples and establishes a rule to sort these examples. Brewer calls this kind of rule an *analogy-warranting rule*. (Brewer 1996, p. 962)

The second step is the sorting of the examples. It means to apply the potential analogy-warranting rule to some examples and see if it gives the desired, or at least an acceptable, result. The application is done on some separate set of propositions. This

2.2. Schema-based approaches

set of propositions is distinguished by what Brewer calls *analogy-warranting rationales*. If the potential analogy-warranting rule does not yield an acceptable result by the application on the items given by the analogy-warranting rationales, it should be discharged and a new potential analogy-warranting rule should be made according to the first step. If it yields an acceptable result, it can be used in the third step. (Brewer 1996, p. 962)

The third step is simply to apply the analogy-warranting rule found in the first step, and confirmed in the second step, to the example that was the motivation for the reasoning in the first place. (Brewer 1996, p. 963)

Intuitively, each step corresponds to a different reasoning process. The first step is based on abductive reasoning, by finding an appropriate explanation. The second step is based on some kind of inductive reasoning, justifying the rule from the first step by several similar examples. The third step is based on deductive reasoning, by the application of a general rule to a specific case. The theory that is presented by Brewer (1996) will be called the *AWR-model*.

Step one: making a potential analogy-warranting rule

The first step is an abductive step where one should make a potential analogy-warranting rule. Analogy-warranting rules are abbreviated AWR in Brewer (1996). We will also use this abbreviation.

In an analogical argument, the source is the basis of the analogy. It is what we build our analogy from. The target is what is known to have some shared characteristics with the source and where we do not have knowledge about the characteristic in question. An AWR is a rule that states the logical relation between the different characteristics in one domain.

In fig. 2.1, the horizontal arrows represent similarities between characteristics of the source and the target. The vertical arrows represent the AWR. (Brewer 1996, p. 965)

$$
\begin{array}{ccc}
\textbf{Source} & & \textbf{Target} \\
A & \longleftrightarrow & A' \\
\updownarrow & & \updownarrow \\
B & \longleftrightarrow & (B')
\end{array}
$$

Figure 2.1: Similarities and AWR

These vertical relations in the source and target are things that have to be discovered. (Brewer 1996, p. 978) This is why the first step can be seen as some kind of abduction. The relation, the AWR, is not there already, but it has to be discovered or created outside of the framework. This is the background for using abduction, namely to find the best possible explanation of the specific relation.

The abduction of an AWR should occur in a *context of doubt*. Brewer argues that there are several ways to have a context of doubt. One of them is vagueness in norms. This occurs when the norm cannot be deductively applied to the case, that we do not know whether it is possible to apply a predicate to a particular case. A term that has the possibility of being vague is called an open-textured term. An open-textured term might not be vague in a specific setting, but if the setting changes, it might become a vague term. Another kind of vagueness may occur if a group of users disagree about the meaning of some term. It is not necessarily a term that is vague in itself as the individual users may look at the term as deductively applicable to the case, but because of disagreements between individuals, we do not know what interpretation to choose. Brewer therefore distinguishes vagueness related to an open-textured term and vagueness related to disagreements about meaning. (Brewer 1996, pp. 993-994)

The context of doubt where the potential AWR may be made is then explained as vagueness of some term. The creation of potential AWRs is not a mechanical process. It is in some sense an area where logic cannot help you. A relation between characteristics

2.2. Schema-based approaches

may have many different explanations and logic itself does not seem to help you in sorting the good from the bad ones. One may therefore create a very high number of potential AWRs that may have different effects on the outcome of the analogical argument. The procedure for creating relevant or good AWRs is then first to refer to a requirement of entailment, together with some ideals or virtues of abduced explanations. The entailment requirement is the requirement that the AWR has to make the argument deductively valid. The AWR needs to be broad enough to make the premises entail the conclusion. It also needs to be precise enough to be applicable in the specific argument. The entailment requirement makes us able to look at juridical arguments as deductive. (Brewer 1996, pp. 993, 997, 999)

Even after imposing the entailment requirement, there may still be many potential AWRs that fulfil the entailment requirement without being very "good". Another restriction on the AWRs is that they should strive some values or ideals, like predictability, notice and governmental accountability. Even if we admit that the AWRs may not completely fulfil these ideals, we may still look at them as idealised goals that we try to achieve. The exact values may be discussed, but Brewer (1996, p. 1003) mentions three values (clarity, notice and accountability) that can be considered important in this aspect. The process of creating an AWR stays fundamentally dependent on non-logical aspects, even though it may have some grounds in legal theory. The potential AWR should also be supplied with a proper justification, some analogy-warranting rationals, AWRas. AWRas provide the background or the explanation of the potential AWR and should be independent of the AWR itself. (Brewer 1996, pp. 991-993, 1021)

Step two: confirmation the potential analogy-warranting rule

The next step, after the creation of a potential AWR, is a control mechanism that checks whether the potential AWR is a good one, restricted under some requirements. If the potential AWR passes these requirements, it lets the potential AWR become the actual AWR that will be used in the argument.

The first requirement is that the potential AWR can yield an acceptable sorting of items that are assumed by the reasoner to be relevant. An item in this sense can be seen as a case, factual or hypothetical. It should give a positive answer to the items that are presupposed to have a positive answer and a negative answer to the items that are presupposed to have a negative answer. (Brewer 1996, p. 1021)

The second requirement relates to coherence with the analogy-warranting rationals. The AWRas of a reasoner can be more abstract principles that the reasoner holds. They are often too vague to be directly applicable to specific cases, and will often not satisfy the requirement of entailment. However, they should still be able to provide some justification. They may also underdetermine the choice between different AWRs, in the sense that they do work as justification for not only a single one. (Brewer 1996, p. 1022)

The second step consists of checking the coherence of the AWRs, both to more abstract principles, the AWRas, and to the result of the sorting of items that the AWR does.

If the potential AWR fails some of requirements in this step, there are two alternatives. If the potential AWR yields a result that we refuse to reject, we reject the potential AWR, go back to step one and find a new potential AWR. If the potential AWR is an AWR that we refuse to reject and it is inconsistent with a proposed result, we may reject the AWRas that are incompatible, accept the

2.2. Schema-based approaches

potential AWR and continue to step three. This is a procedure that shows how the reasoner may adapt the background knowledge in order to fit a proposed AWR. The AWRs and the AWRas might then be revised in several combinations. (Brewer 1996, pp. 1023-2024)

Step three: application of the analogy-warranting rule
After the abduction of a potential AWR and the check of coherence of this AWR, the third step is a very simple deductive step. It involves applying the accepted AWR to the item at question and deduce the inferred property. Because of the entailment requirement of the AWRs, there should be no challenge to perform this deductive procedure.

Brewer (1996, pp. 1003-1016) argues that there are two kinds of arguments, analogical arguments and disanalogical arguments. The first is the standard form of the analogical argument. It is an argument based on similar aspects of the source and the target. The second is in some sense the inverted analogical argument. It is an argument based on different aspects of the source and the target.

The analogical argument is explained in the following way, where AWR is the rule that is accepted under the restrictions mentioned, y is the target and x is the source:

1. y has characteristics $F_1, ..., F_n$ (target premise)

2. x has characteristics $F_1, ..., F_n$ (source premise)

3. x has characteristics $H_1, ..., H_n$ (source premise)

4. AWR

5. Therefore, y has characteristics $H_1, ..., H_n$ (conclusion)

The first step shows some characteristics of the target. The second step shows that the source shares the same characteristics (or at least similar characteristics) as mentioned for the target case in the first step. The third step shows that the source has some further characteristics that are not explicitly known to be the shared with the target. The fourth step shows the AWR. The fifth step is the conclusion that states that also the target has the characteristics that were found in the source at the third step. The argument is deductively valid because of the entailment requirement of the AWR. It ensures that the AWR, together with the source premises and the target premise, entails the conclusion. (Brewer 1996, p. 1005)

We can construct a similar pattern for disanalogical arguments. DWR is a *disanalogy-warranting rule*.[1] DWRs behaves in a similar way and are created in the same way, under the same restrictions as analogy-warranting rules. In the same way, we have disanalogy-warranting rationales, DWRas, that explain the DWRs. For disanalogical arguments, the model is slightly modified in the following way:

1. y has characteristics $F_1, ..., F_n$ (target premise)

2. x has characteristics $F_1, ..., F_n$ (source premise)

3. x has characteristics $G_1, ..., G_n$ (source premise)

4. y has characteristics $\neg G_1, ..., \neg G_n$ (target premise)

5. x has characteristics $H_1, ..., H_n$ (source premise)

6. DWR

7. Therefore, that x has characteristics $F_1, ..., F_n$ and $H_1, ..., H_n$ is not sufficient to infer that y has characteristics $H_1, ..., H_n$ (conclusion)

The first step shows some characteristics of the target. The second step shows that the source shares the same characteristics (or at least similar characteristics) as is mentioned for the target in the first step. The third step shows that the source has some further characteristics. The fourth step shows that these characteristics of

---

[1] We assume that there is a mistake in Brewer (1996, p. 1008), calling the DWR a disanalogy-warranting rationale.

2.2. Schema-based approaches

the target are not shared by the source. The fifth step shows that the source has some further characteristics that are not explicitly known to be the shared with the target. The sixth step shows the DWR. The seventh step is the conclusion that states that the characteristics of the source do not provide sufficient basis to infer the hypothetical characteristics of the target. This argument should as well be deductively valid because of the entailment requirement of the DWR. (Brewer 1996, pp. 1007-1012)

We may have two or more competing analogies, analogies that would seem to give incompatible results of the analogical argument. According to Brewer, there are two ways to handle such a problem. The first is to formulate an AWR that manages to explain why one analogy fulfils the requirement, while the other does not. The second is to give an analogical argument that both of the competing analogies fulfil, and then make a disanalogical argument that provides the DWR that distinguishes the cases. The first alternative is constructed simply as an analogical argument, while the second is constructed as first an analogical argument, and then as a disanalogical argument. (Brewer 1996, pp. 1015-1016)

We can see that the logical process in this situation is very simple and more or less straightforward. The real challenge lies in formulating the AWR, or the DWR, and their rationals.

Example of an argument by analogy for Brewer

Brewer (1996) provides plenty of examples throughout his text. We will briefly present one of them here, namely the case of *Adams v. New Jersey Steamboat Co.*, 151 N.Y. 163 (1896), which will also be used as an example for the introduced analysis in section 7.3 and section 8.3. (Brewer 1996, pp. 1003-1006, 1013–1016)

The example is a case about whether or not a certain steamboat owner is liable for a theft from a customer. Adams had rented a cabin in a steamboat owned by New Jersey Steamboat Co. and some of his valuables were stolen. The question was whether the steamboat company was strictly liable towards Adams. There were two references to older cases, one where an innkeeper had been held strictly liable for the thefts of valuables of a customer, and one where a railway company was not held strictly liable for the theft of valuables from an open-berth sleeping car. The question was therefore whether the steamboat was like a railroad or like an inn from a legal viewpoint. The judge decides that the steamboat was similar to an inn, and that the steamboat company therefore was strictly liable for the theft of valuables from its customer. The judge claimed that the relevant similarities were that the client paid for a room for some specified reasons and that the company had tempting opportunity for fraud and plunder of the client. The previous case with an inn was similar in both of these aspects, while the railroad case was not similar in either. (Brewer 1996, pp. 1003–1005, 1013–1015)

It is clear that the judge is in a context of doubt. They do not know whether the case at hand is analogous to the railroad case or the inn case. The first task for the judge is to perform an abduction of a potential AWR, namely: *When someone has a client that procures a room for some specified reasons (privacy etc.) and has a tempting opportunity for fraud and plunder also is strictly liable for thefts of their customers, then everyone that have a client that procures a room for some specified reasons (privacy etc.) and have a tempting opportunity for fraud and plunder also are strictly liable for thefts of their customers.* The judge sees that the AWR fulfils the entailment requirement.

The judge continues to step two. The AWR yields an acceptable sorting of items and it coheres well with the rationales. They manage to give a good explanation for why the AWR is an acceptable rule. A customer that procures a room for the reasons mentioned would expect the avoidance of intrusion into the room and a company that has a tempting opportunity for fraud and plunder should have a

2.2. Schema-based approaches

special responsibility towards their customers, in order to furnish such temptation. These reasons can be considered as the analogy-warranting rationales in this case. The judge therefore accepts the AWR and continues to step three.

In step three, the judge simply applies the accepted AWR to the case at hand and infers the conclusion from the premises together with the AWR. This can then be represented in the following way:

Definitions

Individuals

- a = the steamboat owner (target);
- b = the innkeeper (primary source);
- c = the owner of the railroad sleeping car (secondary source);

Characteristics

- F = has a client who procures a room for specified reasons R (potentially shared characteristic);
- G = has tempting opportunity for fraud and plunder (potentially shared characteristic);
- H = is strictly liable (inferred characteristic).

Argument

1. a has characteristics F and G. (target premise)
2. b has characteristics F and G. (source premise)
3. b has characteristics H. (source premise)
4. AWR: If something that has F and G also has H, then everything that has F and G also has H.

---

5. Therefore, a has characteristics H. (conclusion)

It is not a proof, but the argument should be deductively valid. We may symbolise to the argument in a semiformal manner in the following way:

Formalised argument

1. Fa and Ga. (target premise)
2. Fb and Gb. (source premise)
3. Hb. (source premise)
4. $\exists x((Fx \wedge Gx) \wedge Hx) \to \forall y((Fy \wedge Gy) \to Hy)$. (AWR)
5. Therefore, Ha. (conclusion)

We end up with the conclusion that the steamboat owner is strictly liable. If we try to construct an argument inferring the owner of the railroad sleeping car to be strictly liable, Hc, we can see that we would not manage to derive that conclusion. We could add a premise for the owner of the railroad sleeping car, but since it does not share any of the relevant characteristics, we cannot infer Hc from

$\neg Fc$ and $\neg Gc$.

We had two competing analogies, but they were distinguished by the introduction of the AWR. It corresponds therefore to the second alternative of solving competing analogies. If the judge were to use the first solution to competing analogies, they would have to make a different AWR, one that would make both the railroad case and the inn case analogous to the steamboat case. Then they would have to introduce another disanalogy argument that restricts the analogy of the first analogical argument. (Brewer 1996, pp. 1014-1015)

Beyond Brewer's model

In the light of Brewer's (1996) influential paper, an important debate regarding the status of analogical rules arises. This section goes beyond Brewer's initial model as it describes the legal discussion that came afterwards. For the comparison of different theories, it might be considered as a sidenote, though this discussion is important for the development and features of the analysis introduced in chapter 7 and chapter 8, where we will also use the Steamboat example to illustrate the framework.

2.2. Schema-based approaches

In 2005, Weinreb publishes a book, *Legal reason: The use of analogy in legal argument*, where he argues against the formulation of any rule, policy or purpose for deciding cases by analogy. The argument for this is that no rule or purpose can fully describe the sorting of similarities and dissimilarities in a satisfiable way. Furthermore, he points out that such rule seems absent in the practical performance of analogical reasoning. (Weinreb 2005, pp. 111-112) This point is not only directed to Brewer, but he also explicitly rejects the similar views by for example Westen (1981) and Posner (2003). Despite his reluctance towards rules and purposes, Weinreb (2005, pp. 1-13) establishes the importance of analogies very clearly. Contrary to the other mentioned theorists, he claims that analogical reasoning must be based on similarities, both to accommodate the way he claims we actually do use analogical reasoning and to avoid the mentioned problem with creating acceptable rules.

As a direct reaction, Posner (2006) published a book review (of the very same book), bringing up multiple problems with Weinreb's approach. The core of his objection is however based on the impossibility of even describing such similarities without in the same time providing some reason or general understanding. According to Posner similarities cannot be considered as relevant similarities unless there is some general understanding or reason for claiming their relevancy, and such understanding is in a legal case based on rules, principles, doctrines and policies. In addition, he points out that it seems to be Weinreb that does not understand the practical use of analogies, by not distinguishing between legal rhetoric and legal thought. Such reasons are, according to Posner, often not explicitly articulated, though this does not mean that they do not occur as justification in the substance of the law. So therefore, for an analogy to be guiding for any decision, there must be reasons to determine whether the similarities should be considered grounding for action. (Posner 2006, pp. 765, 768)

At first sight, one might consider the two authors to explore different aspects of legal arguments. From this point of view, Weinreb speaks about analogy from the perspective of arguments legal scholars *give*, while Posner speaks about arguments legal scholars *use*. It seems therefore to be no conflict, as they simply speak about different things, which furthermore seems to give Posner at least partially right when categorising Weinreb's points in the area of legal rhetoric. However, such clear distinction between the two seems potentially problematic. The arguments legal scholars give must clearly be somehow connected with the arguments they actually use. Legal rhetoric surely cannot be entirely independent of the substance of the law. Intuitively, there seems to be two ways of solving this tension. One might consider rhetoric and substance to be the very same or that the substance reflects the rhetoric (as seems to be Posner's view). Or, that rhetoric reflect the substance (the view of Weinreb). This point seems closely connected to the debate about whether we consider law as created or discovered.[2]

What both approaches have in common, and what they also share with Brewer, is their search for *relevant similarity*. The disagreement can be reduced to a question of the precise content of this concept. All approaches describe a logical requirement that should be imposed on legal analogical reasoning. This can be called an *acceptable sorting* (for Brewer) or *consistency and coherence* (for Weinreb). The disagreement lies in their understanding of *relevance*. Posner (2006, p. 773) defends Brewer in stating that the relevance should be viewed as a rule or policy, while Weinreb (2005, p. 126) argues for understanding relevancy in a psychological or epistemological manner. With the proposed analysis for analogical reasoning in chapter 8, we will argue that we can consider both such psychological approach and the rule- or policy-based approach in a unified way by considering analogies in a dialogical framework of rational rhetorics and argumentation. We will then be able to

---

[2]Though here we do not intend to provide any standpoint in this regard as our analysis in chapter 7 and chapter 8 seems compatible with both approaches.

2.2. Schema-based approaches

consider both the psychological state in terms of rational behaviour of an agent and how rules or policies might affect the judgment of relevant similarity, including the effect it has on the behaviour of the agent. This does not mean that the dialogical approach takes any particular standpoint in this discussion, but rather that the dialogical approach can show how the conflict between the two standpoints seems less pressing and thereby reconcile the two positions to a certain extent.

Alchourrón's arguments a fortiori and a pari

In the paper *Los argumentos jurídicos a fortiori y a pari* by Alchourrón (1991), we are provided with a description of two kinds of legal arguments, arguments *a fortiori* and arguments *a pari*. Both can be considered to be closely related to analogies. In short we can say that arguments a fortiori are based on an implicit assumption of a *relation* that links the target case to the source case, while arguments a pari are based on an assumption of *similarity* between the source and the target.

Arguments a fortiori

In Alchourrón's paper, the schemas for arguments a fortiori are introduced as arguments, based on the transitivity of a relation between the source and the target. The idea is that there is a transitive relation that enables us to provide justification for the inference. Alchourrón traces this view back to the Aristotle's work, Topics, where he speaks about argument *a maiori ad minus*, as an inference *from greater to smaller*, which by the scholastics has been named argument *a fortiori*. An example is that if A has more money than B and B has more money than C, we can infer that A has more money than C. This provides a valid argument because the relation 'x has more money than y' is a transitive relation. For us to speak about an argument a fortiori, the relation must also be asymmetric, because if the relation is symmetric, we are not anymore speaking about two things where one is greater than the other, but rather a situation where they are equal. (Alchourrón 1991, pp. 7-9) The mentioned example can be explained by the following inference:

Premise:	*Loans with 12% annual interest are permitted.*
Conclusion:	*Loans with 8% annual interest are permitted.*

If we take Px to represent *'action x is permitted'*, we can formalise the inference in the following way:

Premise:	Px
Conclusion:	Py.

This is clearly not a valid argument as it stands, but in a similar way as the previous example, we can consider it acceptable because of the the transitive relation between action x and action y. A loan with 8% annual interest is less onerous than a loan with 12% annual interest. The relation, regarding loans, *'x is less onerous than y'* is a transitive relation, since if a loan A is less onerous than a loan B and B is less onerous than a loan C, A is also less onerous than C. It is also asymmetric, since if a loan A is less onerous than a loan B, B is not less onerous than A. This provides us with a transitive and asymmetric relation that works as an implicit premise in the argument, which can be made explicit in the following way:

Premise:	*Loans with 12% annual interest are permitted.*
Implicit premise:	*Loans with 8% annual interest are less onerous than loans with 12% annual interest.*
Conclusion:	*Loans with 8% annual interest are permitted.*

2.2. Schema-based approaches

By taking the relation xRy to represent 'loan x is less onerous than loan y', we can also include the relation in the formalisation in the following way:

Premise:	Px
Implicit premise:	xRy
Conclusion:	$Py.$

Alchourrón points out that this does not provide a logically valid argument, as the premises might be true without the conclusion being true. This is because we might doubt whether this particular relation is relevant for comparison. (Alchourrón 1991, pp. 10-12)

The next step is to introduce a notion of inheritance, or paternity. This should be understood as linking the relation R and the predicate P. When it is the case that if Px and xRy, then Py for any x and y, we say that P inherits with respect to R. This inheritance can be represented as $Inh.(P, R)$. That P inherits in respect to a relation R means that R provides the foundation for P. For the loan-example, the permission of a loan is inherited from the relation 'loan x is less onerous than loan y' if the relation holds only when the loan is permitted, which means that all loans that are less onerous should be permitted. (Alchourrón 1991, pp. 11-12) The example can be formulated in the following way:

Premise:	*Loans with 12% annual interest are permitted.*
Implicit premise 1:	*Loans with 8% annual interest are less onerous than loans with 12% annual interest.*
Implicit premise 2:	*Loans that are less onerous than other permitted loans should be themselves permitted.*
Conclusion:	*Loans with 8% annual interest are permitted.*

This should then be introduced in the formalisation for arguments a fortiori in the following way:

Premise:	Px
Implicit premise:	xRy
Inheritance:	$Inh.(P, R)$
Conclusion:	$Py.$

In a similar manner, Alchourrón introduces a second kind of argument a fortiori. Contrary to the previous, it formulates an argument *a minori ad maius*, which is an argument from smaller to greater. In order to introduce this second kind of argument, Alchourrón (1991, pp. 12, 14–15) includes a notion of conversed relation. This is represented as $Inh.(P, Conv.R)$. In the cases of arguments from smaller to greater, we can introduce this inheritance to explain the validity of the argument. An example can be given in the following form:

Premise:	It is allowed to give 25% of the income to the state.
Implicit premise 1:	To give 30% is greater than to give 25%.
Implicit premise 2:	Giving more is allowed when giving less is allowed.
Conclusion:	It is allowed to give 30% of the income to the state.

The formalisation can then be introduced in the following way:

Premise:	Px
Implicit premise:	xRy
Inheritance:	$Inh.(P, Conv.R)$
Conclusion:	$Py.$

2.2. Schema-based approaches

Alchourrón goes on by explaining that arguments of a similar structure can be used to express normative modalities, such as permitted, prohibited, obligatory and facultative. They can be introduced by changing the initial premise and the inheritance relation correspondingly. To represent arguments of these forms, we replace the variable P by the variable V. The inheritance relation holds in an opposite way for arguments with such normative modalities, so that $Inh.(P, R)$ is logically equivalent with $Inh.(V, Conv.R)$ and $Inh.(P, conv.R)$ is logically equivalent with $Inh.(V, R)$. (Alchourrón 1991, pp. 15-17)

Arguments a pari

Arguments a fortiori are based on a relation that is either from the greater to the smaller or from the smaller to the greater. R is then an asymmetric and transitive relation. Arguments a pari are based on a similarity relation. For these arguments S is an equality relation, namely a transitive, symmetric and reflexive relation. (Alchourrón 1991, pp. 19-20)

Both R and S can describe how *comparative concepts* are used in arguments. A comparative concept is one that satisfies the following three conditions:

1. R is transitive and asymmetric.

2. S is transitive, symmetric and reflexive.

3. Given x and y are relational entities, one and only one of the following propositions are true:

    - xSy
    - xRy
    - yRx.

It is comparative concepts of this kind that can form the basis of the juridical arguments by analogy. In a similar manner as with arguments a fortiori, also arguments a pari can be formed with the basis of different normative modalities. The difference lies in what kind of relation that is present in the comparison. For arguments a pari, the comparison will have the form of the equality relation, S. (Alchourrón 1991, p. 20)

In the cases of arguments from equality, we can introduce this inheritance notion to explain the validity of the argument. An example can be given in the following form:

Premise:	*Loans with 12% annual interest are permitted.*
Implicit premise 1:	*A loan with 12% annual interest is as onerous as a loan with 1% monthly interest.*
Implicit premise 2:	*Loans that are as onerous as other permitted loans should be themselves permitted.*
Conclusion:	*Loans with 1% monthly interest are permitted.*

The formalisation can then be introduced in the following way:

Premise:	Px
Implicit premise:	xSy
Inheritance:	$Inh.(P, S)$
Conclusion:	$Py.$

By excluding the logically equivalent notions, Alchourrón ends up with three distinct kinds of inheritance that are possible within his framework, namely:

A $Inh.(P, R)$;

B $Inh.(P, Conv.R)$;

2.2. Schema-based approaches

C $Inh.(P,S)$.

These formulas provide three distinct forms of inheritance relation that can function as basis for an analogical argument. Based on these three kinds, the following results should also hold:

1. If A and B are true, C is also true;

2. If A and B are true, all acts that constitute the determinative comparative concept for R and S have the same normative value;

3. If A and C are true, x and y are two acts that refer to the determinative comparative concept for R and S where x is permitted and y prohibited, the proposition yRx is true;

4. If B and C are true, x and y are two acts that refer to the determinative comparative concept for R and S where x is permitted and y prohibited, the proposition xRy is true.

These results will only hold as long as the included norms are mutually coherent. In the case that they are not, any logical proposition can be inferred from them (by the principle of explosion). (Alchourrón 1991, pp. 21-23)

Generally one can, according to Alchourrón, conclude that analogical arguments are not logically valid, that the necessary conditions introduced in analogical arguments are not logical. Though, where the introduction of formal logic can help is to identify the implicit presumptions present in these arguments. (Alchourrón 1991, p. 24)

John Woods' notion of a GS

In *Is Legal Reasoning Irrational? An Introduction to the Epistemology of Law* by Woods (2015, pp. 271-279), we are presented with an epistemological framework for arguments by parallel reasoning or analogical arguments for handling precedents. The main motivation in the book by Woods is to examine the logical and epistemological foundations that lie as a background in legal reasoning, and particularly so for criminal law in the Canadian legal system. The book goes through many notions used in legal reasoning that seem to depend on an (implicit) epistemological or logical description. Amongst these, we have the notion of argumentation by analogy and the notion of precedent. (Woods 2015, pp. 57-82, 271–279)

The general idea of argumentation by analogy and the role of a precedent here is that they can be described by a schema. This schema is introduced in order to implement the requirement found in analogical reasoning of *sufficient relevant similarity*. Woods (2015, p. 276) introduces what he calls a *generalization schema* (GS). The idea behind this GS is that it should be a general description where the analogue (source) is an instance, so that the analogised (target) also is an instance of this general description.

Stare decisis and applying precedents

Stare decisis is a legal feature, typically found in Common Law. It is the principle for the legal bindingness of a previous legal decision or precedent. It is used to embody the principle of *like cases should be treated alike*. If stare decisis is an accepted principle, a judge may not choose to treat a case differently from a previously decided case when both cases are similar.

Woods (2015, pp. 57-58) identifies six features for the principle of stare decisis:

1. *The decisions of a higher court are binding on all courts below. These are called vertical precedents.*

2. *Courts at all levels must not disoblige their own prior decisions. These precedents are called horizontal.*

3. *Lower court decisions from other common law jurisdiction can have "persuasive authority" for sister courts domestically.*

4. *Binding decisions are precedent-setting.*

2.2. Schema-based approaches

5. Non-binding decisions can be treated, and frequently are, as having "persuasive authority".

6. A decision is binding when it rests upon something with a capable judge would be able without unnatural effort to construe as a "general legal principle" or "rule of law".

There is a distinction between binding and non-binding precedents in the features listed. That a decision is binding means that the reasons for decision provides a rule of law that one cannot disoblige. A decision might be non-binding in the situation that the reasons given for the decision are not coherent, that they cannot be seen as a general principle of law. If a precedent is given several reasons for a decision, these reasons might be in conflict with each other and it would therefore not be possible to take out some general rule to be used in a later decision. Woods uses an example of a decision in Canadian law, *R. v. Morgentaler*, 1988. 1 S.C.R. 30, that considered section 251 in the Criminal Code related to the illegality of abortion as unconstitutional. This decision was provided with three opinions or reasons for the decision, where no individual opinion had a majority in the jury of five members. Even though none of the reasons received a majority in the jury, the decision received a majority based on these three different opinions:

- *the unfairness of procedures,*
- *autonomy of the woman and*
- *unjustness in the security of the person.*

These three reasons were not compatible, and neither did receive a majority in the jury, and could therefore not be used to create a rule of law and therefore a binding decision. In spite of the non-bindingness of this decision, it was decisive, so section 251 is decided to be unconstitutional. (Woods 2015, pp. 58-59)

A precedent that is legally binding is covered by the principle of stare decisis. This means that it stands in all cases of sufficient relevant similarity. A court that will treat a similar case cannot ignore the decision of the precedent. In the case of a binding precedent, the decision is therefore not only a solution to the actual case at hand, but also a *finding for the ages*. (Woods 2015, p. 59)

According to Woods, judges might decide a case 'stupidly' or 'wisely', and in both situations, the case might serve as a precedent for later decisions. If a case is decided 'wisely', the later application should not encounter an immediate problem. However, in the case that we are speaking about a 'stupid' or 'unwelcome' precedent, the future judges still have to apply this precedent, though stay aware that the precedent was 'stupid'. This motivates the following rules of thumb:

1. *The more unwelcome the precedent, the more narrowly it should be interpreted;*

2. *The more welcome the precedent, the more widely it should be interpreted.*

The principle of stare decisis is found mainly in common law systems. It binds the future judges on the ratio decidendi from previous decisions. According to this principle, a ratio, when it is internally consistent and coherent, can and must be taken account of when deciding a similar case at a later stage. We might then say that the ratio embodies a rule of law. (Woods 2015, pp. 60-61)

Describing generalization schemas
In order to describe arguments based on generalization schemas, Woods (2015, pp. 274-277) uses an example by Judith Jarvis Thomson, called "the Violinist Argument", which is a philosophical argument for the permissibility of abortion. The example is described in the following way in *A Defence of Abortion* by Thomson (1971, pp. 48-49):

2.2. Schema-based approaches

But now let me ask you to imagine this. You wake up in the morning and find yourself back to back in bed with an unconscious violinist. A famous unconscious violinist. He has been found to have a fatal kidney ailment, and the Society of Music Lovers has canvassed all the available medical records and found that you alone have the right blood type to help. They have therefore kidnapped you, and last night the violinist's circulatory system was plugged into yours, so that your kidneys can be used to extract poisons from his blood as well as your own. The director of the hospital now tells you, "Look, we're sorry the Society of Music Lovers did this to you–we would never have permitted it if we had known. But still, they did it, and the violinist is now plugged into you. To unplug you would be to kill him. But never mind, it's only for nine months. By then he will have recovered from his ailment, and can safely be unplugged from you." Is it morally incumbent on you to accede to this situation? No doubt it would be very nice of you if you did, a great kindness. But do you have to accede to it? What if it were not nine months, but nine years? Or longer still? What if the director of the hospital says. "Tough luck. I agree. but now you've got to stay in bed, with the violinist plugged into you, for the rest of your life. Because remember this. All persons have a right to life, and violinists are persons. Granted you have a right to decide what happens in and to your body, but a person's right to life outweighs your right to decide what happens in and to your body. So you cannot ever be unplugged from him." I imagine you would regard this as outrageous, which suggests that something really is wrong with that plausible-sounding argument I mentioned a moment ago.

Thomson (1971, pp. 48-49)

In Thomson's article, it is made explicit that she supposes that the fetus is a human person, not because she believes this to be the case continuously from the moment of conception, but for the sake of the argument. The point is then that even in the case that we consider the fetus as a person, it does not have an unrestricted right to life.

Woods (2015, p. 275) claims that the argument is only used as a defence of abortion in cases where the pregnancy is a result of rape,[3] and furthermore supposes that Thomson *takes it as given*

---

[3]This is shown by the following statement, and is also referred to later in the same chapter:

> Contrary to what her title indicates, Thomson's not a defence of abortion in the general case, but is limited to terminations of pregnancies induced by rape.

> Woods (2015, p. 275)

This does not seem to correspond with what is found in Thomson's original work. In the paragraph immediately following the mentioned example of the violinist, she explicitly refuses that the example is restricted to abortion in pregnancies as a result of rape,

> In this case, of course, you were kidnapped, you didn't volunteer for the operation that plugged the violinist into your kidneys. Can those who oppose abortion on the ground I mentioned make an exception for a pregnancy due to rape? Certainly. They can say that persons have a right to life only if they didn't come into existence because of rape; or they can say that all persons have a right to life, but that some have less of a right to life than others, in particular, that those who came into existence because of rape have less. But these statements have a rather unpleasant sound. Surely the question of whether you have a right to life at all, or how much of it you have, shouldn't turn on the question of whether or not you are a product of a rape. And in fact the people who oppose abortion on the ground I mentioned do not make this distinction, and hence do not make an exception in case of rape.

> Thomson (1971, p. 49)

2.2. Schema-based approaches

that any 'fair-minded person' would disagree with the argument of the director in the example.[4]

Despite some differences between Thomson's original description of the argument and Woods' reconstruction of it, the latter seem to contain a weaker conclusion, that would be accepted by the original argument as well. If abortion is generally permissible in a pregnancy, it should also be permissible when the pregnancy is due to rape. However, we should keep in mind that Woods' reconstruction of the argument, and therefore also his analysis, does not seem to capture Thomson's original argument, which seems to be more complex and contain a stronger conclusion.

Woods argues that the essence of this argument is that a 'fair-minded person' would not agree with the argument of the director, that there is no moral justification for this inference. The argument connects to abortion in rape-induced pregnancies by parity of reasoning or parallel reasoning. The analysis of the argument is done by redescribing it by a generalization schema. This connects the particular facts of the example to the particular facts of the analogue by means of general facts, where the particular facts are instances. If we let X, Y and Z be three different human beings, we might analyse this argument by the following schema:

1. Without Y's consent, X has placed Z in a state of vital dependency on Y.

2. The period of dependency is indeterminate (perhaps nine months, perhaps nine years, or the rest of Y's life).

Thomson article should not be considered restricted to a defence of the permissibility of abortion in pregnancies due to rape. It should rather be considered to defend a more general, however still lightly restricted, permissibility in cases where the fetus cannot survive outside the mother's body.

[4]Throughout large parts of her article, Thomson argues precisely for this point, namely why the argument of the director does not hold. See page 55-57 for a discussion of rights and page 63-64 for a discussion on legal requirements related to the example.

3. The dependency is a grievous impediment of locomotion and stationary mobility.

4. The dependency represents a grievous invasion of privacy.

5. It is an invitation to social disaster for Y (and in some cases for Z as well). It gravely constraints employment and most other forms of social engagement.

6. It is also a source of great embarrassment for Y, and sometimes for Z too.

7. Therefore, it would be morally permissible for Y to terminate Z's vital dependency on Y.

If we accept the structure of this generalization schema, that the conclusion actually follows from its premises, any situation where the premises hold, the conclusion also holds. For any set of particular facts that makes instances of this schema, we also have a conclusion that is supported by the premises and that is an instance of the general conclusion in the schema. In the case of the violinist abortion argument, both the example with the sick violinist and a situation of rape-induced pregnancies should be instances of this generalization schema, and when this is the case together with the validity of the schema, we can speak about a good, or possibly sound, analogical argument. (Woods 2015, pp. 276-277)

The generalization schema is used as a reference for the adequacy of the argument. Both the example (source) and the analogue (target) should satisfy it. Woods then links this procedure with the use of ratio decidendi in legal reasoning. The idea is that the ratio decidendi instantiates a generalization schema. When the ratio embodies a rule of law, we might speak about the case being a precedent for later cases. The generalization schema that is instantiated by the ratio decidendi is then the reference of adequacy for when the case is used as a precedent for some later decisions. Woods points out that the judges do not usually provide the generalization schema they use explicitly and that this might indicate that the use of precedents cannot be fully captured by these schemas. A difference according to Woods between generalization schemas and the use of precedents is that while generalization schemas have a rather strict structure, a precedent can be interpreted either narrowly or loosely. A narrow interpretation of a precedent makes it harder to apply widely, while a loose interpretation makes it easier to apply it widely. (Woods 2015, pp. 277-278)

Woods claims that the generalization schemas are always 'tightly constructed entities'. By this he means that its structure is what decides its acceptability, independent of what predicates that are structured. A result of this is that when a target argument is more general than another one, that the second implies the first, and the second is a good argument, also the first one is a good argument. Since it is only the structure of the generalization schema that decides whether we are speaking about a good argument, the more general argument is implied by the special one. This is because all properties in the special implies counterparts in the general. In the legal context of case law this does not seem to hold, since case law is more loosely constructed. It therefore stays a rather open question whether generalization schemas can provide an analysis of the use of case law in actual legal practice. (Woods 2015, p. 278)

2.3 INFERENCE-BASED APPROACHES TO ANALOGICAL REASONING

Bartha's notion of analogical reasoning

Bartha's (2010) project is to make a general, normative theory of analogical arguments. It means to explain them from a logical point of view. The theory is based on what he calls horizontal and vertical relations. According to Bartha, the vertical relations have been neglected in the literature in favour of the horizontal relations. By introducing the articulation model, he intends to reintroduce the vertical relations to the field of analogical arguments. (Bartha 2010, p. 93)

Frames for Bartha's articulation model
In his book, *By Parallel Reasoning: The Construction and Evaluation of Analogical Arguments*, Bartha (2010) introduces what he calls the articulation model. It is a framework that he claims can represent analogical arguments in a satisfactory way, in addition to have the ability to distinguish good from bad analogical arguments. The book focuses on analogical arguments in scientific disciplines, but his theory would seem to be applicable more generally to other kinds of analogical arguments. We will only introduce the kinds of analogies that seem relevant for legal reasoning, which here means to exclude the so-called deductive forms.

We use P to symbolise a factor that is found in the source domain and $P*$ to symbolise a factor that is found the target domain. Q symbolises a factor that is found in the source domain, that is being used as background for the hypothetical analogy. $Q*$ symbolises the factor that is analogised in the target domain, it is the factor that is not observed. The horizontal relations are relations between factors of the two different domains. The vertical relations are relations between the factors internal in one domain. The relations are described by fig. 2.2 (Bartha 2010, p. 24)

Explanation and definitions in the articulation model
The following describes a general and formal explanation of the articulation model. Plausibility is based on what Bartha calls potentially relevant factors. These factors are symbolised $\phi_1, \phi_2, \ldots$ and they may be variables, assumptions or conditions. Bartha uses

2.3. Inference-based approaches

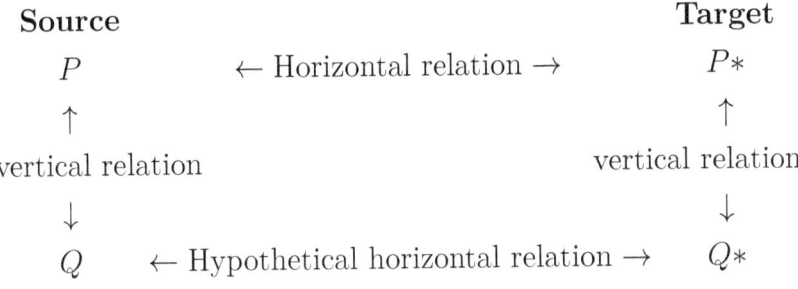

Figure 2.2: Horizontal and vertical relations

the notation $\bar{\phi}$ to symbolise the absence of ϕ in a domain. ϕ is used to symbolise factors in the source domain while $\phi*$ is use to symbolise factors in the target domain. The following definitions are taken from Bartha (2010, pp. 98-102).

The set of potentially relevant factors is defined in the following way:

Definition (Potentially Relevant Factors).
The union of the following sets, gives the set $\mathcal{F}$ of potentially relevant factors for an analogical argument:

- The set φ of all factors (except for the conclusion) that appear explicitly in the argument;

- All sets Ψ of factors (except for the conclusion) that appear in other salient analogical arguments advanced in favour of the same or rival conclusions;

- A set β of unstated background factors (background context).

The prior association creates a relation between the elements of $\mathcal{F}$, which is the aspect that Bartha claims is important with his model as it provides the vertical relations.

Definition (Prior Association).

The prior association is a relation,

$$R(\phi_1, ..., \phi_m, \overline{\pi}_1, ..., \overline{\pi}_n, Q),$$

where each ϕ_1 and π belongs to φ.

The similarity partition is the distinction of the horizontal relations in the model. It distinguishes where we have similar factors in the source and the target domain, where we have different factors in the source and the target domain and where we do not know whether we have the factor from one domain in the other domain.

Definition (Similarity Partition).

$$\varphi = P \cup N \cup O$$

where:

- P is a positive analogy, consisting of all members ϕ in φ represented as belonging to both the source and target domains;

- N is a negative analogy, consisting of all members ϕ in φ represented as belonging to one domain with $\overline{\phi}$ in the other;

- O is a neutral analogy, consisting of all members ϕ in φ represented as belonging to one domain with no information about whether $\phi*$ belongs to the other domain.

The relevance partition offers distinctions, first between relevant factors and irrelevant factors, and second between the relevant factors, whether they are critically relevant or secondary relevant factors. The critical factors are those that have an essential part in the circumstances. Other relevant factors are secondary factors.

Definition (Relevance Partition).

$$\varphi = \varphi^C \cup \varphi^S \cup \varphi^I$$

where:

2.3. Inference-based approaches

- φ^C is the set of critical factors,
- φ^S is the set of secondary factors,
- φ^I is the set of irrelevant factors, members of φ that does not occur in the prior association.

The valence of a factor ϕ is positive ϕ^+ if it is a contributing cause for Q. The valence of a factor ϕ is negative ϕ^- if it is a counteracting cause for Q. The valence of a factor ϕ is neutral if it is neither a contributing nor a counteracting cause for Q. A prima facie plausibility is understood as a modal notion that should make us consider the argument seriously. The first condition is that there is some relevant and contributing factor common in the source and the target domain, namely some relevant factor in a positive analogy. The second condition is that there is no critical factor that is different in the source and the target domain, namely no critical factor in the negative analogy.

Condition (Prima facie Plausibility).

Let $\varnothing$ be the empty set. An analogical argument meets the requirements for prima facie plausibility if the following conditions are met:

1. Overlap,
$$\varphi^+ \cap \neq \varnothing;$$

2. No-critical-difference,
$$\varphi^C \cap N = \varnothing.$$

We can consider the prima facie plausibility as the first test that an argument is put through. If it passes this test, we can use the qualitative plausibility as a second test to establish how good the argument is.

Condition (Qualitative Plausibility).

The qualitative plausibility of an analogical argument is based on the following criteria:

1. Strength of prior association, the argument becomes stronger when the prior association is stronger;

2. Extent of the positive analogy, an analogical argument becomes stronger when critical factors are shifted from neutral to positive analogy, and secondary factors are shifted either from negative to neutral or from neutral to positive analogy;

3. Multiple analogies, favourable analogies support the conclusion and competing analogies undermine it.

Different kinds of analogical arguments

In the articulation model there are four kinds of analogical arguments and two of the kinds can be distinguished into two different modes, deductive and inductive. The different kinds of analogies differ in what association they have between the positive analogy P and the hypothetical analogy Q, explained by Table 2.1 (Bartha 2010, p. 98)

	Predictive $P \to Q$	**Explanatory** $Q \to P$	**Functional** $P \leftrightarrow Q$	**Correlative** $P \downarrow Q$
Deductive	Mathematical	Abductive	-	-
Inductive	Probabilistic	Probabilistic	Functional	Correlative

Table 2.1: Kinds of analogies

From this table we can see that all kinds of analogical arguments may be inductive, while the predictive arguments and the explanatory arguments may also be deductive. That an analogy is deductive means that the relation between P and Q is a logical entailment. That an analogy is inductive means that the relation between P and Q is not a logical entailment, but represents some other relation.

2.3. Inference-based approaches

We will present the alternative inductive analogies that are explained by Bartha by giving their individual definitions for prior association, relevant factors, conditions of prima facie plausibility and eventual individual conditions for each kind of argument. All definitions and descriptions are taken from Bartha (2010, pp. 107-146).

Predictive analogies
The first kind is called predictive analogies. The direction of the predictive analogies is from the positive analogy to the hypothetical analogy, $P \to Q$. We can distinguish the predictive analogies in mathematical analogies and probabilistic predictive analogies. The mathematical analogies have a logical entailment from P to Q. The probabilistic predictive analogies have some relation from P to Q that is not deductive. We will only present the second one, as the mathematical analogies do not seem immediately relevant for legal reasoning. (Bartha 2010, p. 96)

Probabilistic predictive analogies
We have a probabilistic predictive analogy when the relation between the positive analogy and the projected analogy is a causal explanation. in the following way:

- Q is the projected proposition;
- φ^+ is the set of relevant contributing causal factors;
- φ^- is the set of relevant counteracting causal factors;
- $\Pi = \{\pi_1, \pi_2, ...\}$ is a set of defeating factors;
- $\overline{\varphi} = \overline{\{\phi_1, \phi_2, ...\}}$ is a set of factors that are absent from the source.

The prior association for probabilistic predictive analogies is given in the following canonical form:

Definition (Prior Association for Probabilistic Predictive Analogies).

Q because φ^+ and $\overline{\Pi}$, despite φ^-.

For probabilistic predictive analogies, Bartha also introduces a completeness condition. It requires that any contributing cause may not have a known defeating condition. We cannot use a factor as a contributing factor if we know that it is defeated by some other knowledge we have.

Condition (Completeness Condition for Probabilistic Predictive Analogy).

No defeating condition for any contributing cause in the explanation of Q may be known to hold in the source domain.

For probabilistic predictive analogies, all contributing causal factors are critical factors. A salient defeating condition is a defeating condition that belongs to the negative or neutral analogies. The absence of all salient defeating conditions for the contributing causal factors are critical. All counteracting causal factors and non-salient defeating conditions are secondary. (Bartha 2010, pp. 114-118)

Definition (Relevant factors for Probabilistic Predictive Analogies).

The set of critically relevant factors φ^C is the union of the following:

1. All contributing causal factor,

    φ^+;

2. The absence of all salient defeating conditions for the contributing causal factors,

    $\overline{\Pi \cap (\varphi^N \cup \varphi^O)}$;

2.3. Inference-based approaches

The set of secondary relevant factors φ^S is the union of the following:

1. All counteracting causal factors,

   φ^-;

2. All nonsalient defeating conditions,

   $\overline{\Pi} \cap \varphi^P$;

For probabilistic predictive analogies the following condition is imposed for prima facie plausibility:

Condition (Prima facie Plausibility for Probabilistic Predictive Analogies).

1. Overlap, some contributing causal factor must belong to the positive analogy,

   $\varphi^+ \cap P \neq \emptyset$;

2. No-critical-difference,

   - each identified contributing causal factor must not be known to be absent in the target,

     $\varphi^+ \cap N = \emptyset$;

   - each salient defeater must not be known to be present in the target,

     $\overline{\Pi} \cap N = \emptyset$.

Explanatory analogies

The second kind is called explanatory analogies. The direction of the explanatory analogies is from the hypothetical analogy to the positive analogy, $Q \to P$. We can distinguish the explanatory analogies in abductive explanatory analogies from the abductive probabilistic explanatory analogies. The abductive explanatory analogies mathematically describe the positive analogy P by the hypothetical analogy Q. The abductive probabilistic explanatory analogies explain the positive analogy P by the hypothetical analogy Q in only a probabilistic, or at least non-deductive way. We will only present the second one. (Bartha 2010, p. 96)

Abductive probabilistic explanatory analogies

We have an abductive probabilistic explanatory analogy when a cause is partly playing a role in a causal explanation of some result and a similar cause $Q*$ can partly play a role in a causal explanation of some similar result $E*$ in the following way:

- Q is the projected cause;
- E is some observable result;
- C is the set of additional assumptions;
- B is the set of background assumptions;
- $\vdash$ is used as an acceptable mathematical proof;
- φ^+ is the set of relevant contributing causal factors;
- φ^- is the set of relevant counteracting causal factors;
- $\Pi = \{\pi_1, \pi_2, ...\}$ is a set of defeating factors;
- $\overline{\varphi} = \overline{\{\phi_1, \phi_2, ...\}}$ is a set of factors that are absent from the source;

2.3. Inference-based approaches

- $scope(Q)$ is probable consequences of Q together with the additional assumptions in the prior association.

The prior association for probabilistic predictive analogies is given in the following canonical form:

Definition (Prior Association for Abductive Probabilistic Explanatory Analogies).

E because φ^+ and C and $\overline{\Pi}$, despite φ^-, where $Q \subseteq \varphi^+$.

There are some conditions for the explanation of E from C to Q. It states that the explanation should have no defeating condition for the contributing causes in the source domain and that the assumptions C should be justified, as we want the derivation to be sound.

Condition (Pre-conditions for Abductive Probabilistic Explanatory Analogies).

1. No defeating condition for any contributing cause in the explanation may be known to hold in the source domain;

2. The additional assumptions C must be justified.

The potentially relevant factors for abductive probabilistic explanatory analogies are the probable consequences of the projected cause, absence of defeating factors and the assumptions, even if they are often neutral analogies. (Bartha 2010, pp. 129-132)

Definition (Relevant factors for Abductive Explanatory Analogies).

The set of critically relevant factors is the union of the following:

1. Effects of the projected cause,

    $scope(Q)$;

2. The absence of salient defeating conditions,

$$\overline{\Pi};$$

3. The auxiliary assumptions and other contributing causes,

$$C;$$

4. The contributing causes,

$$\varphi^+.$$

For abductive probabilistic explanatory analogies the following conditions should be imposed for prima facie plausibility:

Condition (Prima facie Plausibility for Abductive Probabilistic Explanatory Analogies).

1. Overlap, there must be some overlap between the observable result and the positive analogy,

$$E \cap P \neq \emptyset;$$

2. No-critical-difference,

   a) Observable effects of the projected cause must not belong to the negative analogy,

   $$scope(Q) \cap N = \emptyset;$$

   b) No defeating conditions may be known to hold in the target domain,

   $$\overline{\Pi} \cap N = \emptyset;$$

   c) The additional critical factors C and the contributing causal factors φ^+ must not belong to the negative analogy,

   $$(C \cup \varphi^+) \cap N = \emptyset.$$

2.3. Inference-based approaches

Functional analogies

The third kind is called functional analogies. The directions of the functional analogies are both from the positive analogy P to the hypothetical analogy Q and the other way around. It only exists in an inductive mode as for a deductive bi-directional association, only one direction would be relevant for the argument. It would therefore seem to be reducible to one of the previous kinds. (Bartha 2010, pp. 96-97) The functional analogies have a strong similarity with ethnographic analogies, as it is a structure widely used in archaeology.

We have a functional analogy when a function Q is required by some selection criteria G and a similar function $Q*$ is required by some selection of other similar criteria $G*$, so that:

- ϕ is the set of aspects of physical form;
- Q is the function that objects of type ϕ may have;
- C is the set of environmental conditions;
- G is the set of selection criteria;
- φ^+ is the set of relevant contributing factors;
- φ^- is the set of relevant counteracting factors;
- $\Pi = \{\pi_1, \pi_2, ...\}$ is a set of defeating factors;
- $\overline{\varphi} = \overline{\{\phi_1, \phi_2, ...\}}$ is a set of factors that are absent from the source;
- $scope(Q)$ is the salient observable consequences of Q.

The prior association for functional analogies is given in the following form:

Definition (Prior Association for functional Analogies).

1. Objects of ϕ can have the function Q, given C;

2. The function Q is required by selection criteria G;

3. Objects of ϕ are there because of Q and C.

There are also conditions for the function Q from the selection criteria G, (Bartha 2010, pp. 133-137)

Condition (Pre-conditions for Functional Analogies).

1. No defeating condition for any criteria in the prior association may be known to hold in the source domain;

2. The additional assumptions C must be justified;

3. That Q is required by G should be justified as a uniformity.

The potentially relevant factors for functional analogies are provided as:

Definition (Relevant factors for Functional Analogies).
The set of critically relevant factors φ^C is the union of the following:

1. Aspects of physical form,

    ϕ;

2. Selection criteria,

    G;

3. Environmental conditions,

    C;

4. The absence of salient defeating conditions for the explanation,

    $\overline{\Pi}$;

2.3. Inference-based approaches

5. Salient observable consequences of the function and the environmental conditions,

$$scope(Q).$$

For abductive explanatory analogies the following conditions should be imposed for prima facie plausibility:

Condition (Prima facie Plausibility for Functional Analogies).

1. Overlap, some critically relevant factors belong to the positive analogy,

$$\varphi^C \cap P \neq \emptyset;$$

2. No-critical-difference, none of the critically relevant factors belong to the negative analogy,

$$\varphi^C \cap N = \emptyset.$$

Correlative analogies

The fourth kind is called correlative analogies. There is no direction for the correlative analogies. The positive analogy P does not explain or cause the hypothetical analogy Q, nor the other way around. The relation between P and Q is a statistical correlation. It does not require there not to be any direction between P and Q, as long as we do not have knowledge or information about such relation. (Bartha 2010, p. 97)

We have a correlative analogy when there is a statistical correlation between a set of attributes to the projected phenomenon in the source domain and we find similar attributes in the target domain and projects the similar phenomenon in target domain, so that:

- Q is the projected phenomenon;

- C is a reference class;

- ϕ is a set of attributes;
- $Pr()$ is the objective probability.

The prior association for correlative analogies is that the attributes have a positive relevance to the phenomenon, and it is given in the following form:

Definition (Prior Association for Abductive Probabilistic Explanatory Analogies).

$$Pr(Q/\phi \cdot C) > Pr(Q/C).$$

By a correlative analogy, we want to achieve a similar probability distribution in the target domain as in the source domain,

$$Pr(Q*/\phi* \cdot C*) > Pr(Q*/C*).$$

There are also general conditions for the correlation relation,

Condition (Pre-conditions for Correlative Analogies).

1. The correlation should be statistically significant,
2. Prior to testing, C should be homogeneous with respect to factors known to be causally relevant to Q.

The potentially relevant factors for correlative analogies are the relevance class and the relevant attributes. (Bartha 2010, pp. 138-139) This is given by the following definition:

Definition (Relevant factors for Correlative Analogies).
The set of critically relevant factors φ^C is the union of the following:

1. The reference class,

$$C;$$

2.3. Inference-based approaches

2. The attributes,

$$\phi.$$

For correlative analogies the following conditions should be imposed for prima facie plausibility:

Condition (Prima facie Plausibility for Correlative Analogies).

1. Overlap, some factor in the set of attributes must belong to the positive analogy,

$$\phi \cap P \neq \emptyset;$$

2. No-critical-difference, attributes corresponding to the reference class and the set of attributes must not be known to be absent in the target reference class,

$$(C \cup \phi) \cap N = \emptyset.$$

Multiple Analogies

In order for the articulation model to be an adequate model of analogical arguments, it would need to handle multiple source domains, or multiple analogies. We will very often end up with not only one analogy, but several, and we would want a theory that could handle such multiplicity. The first task for extending the theory to multiple analogies is to explain how the prima facie plausibility for each argument is affected by multiple analogies and second how the general plausibility of the projected hypotheses is affected. (Bartha 2010, pp. 141-146) Assume that:

- $\mathcal{A}$ is an analogical argument;
- $\Gamma = \mathcal{A}_1, ..., \mathcal{A}_n$ is a set of analogical arguments;
- Q is a supported hypothesis;
- S is a source domain for an analogical argument $\mathcal{A}$;

- T is the target domain;
- φ_Γ^C is a critical factor relative to Γ.

The prima facie plausibility is individual for each argument and should be the same as the original definition of prima facie plausibility.

Condition (Prima Facie Plausibility in Multiple Analogies, the Independence Condition).

A provisional assessment of prima facie plausibility is made independently for each individual analogy under consideration. This assessment remains unchanged for optimal analogical arguments, but is defeated if there is a more highly ranked analogical argument that supports an incompatible conclusion.

The first step for formulating a concept of relevant factors for multiple analogies is to give a partial ordering on the different analogies in Γ, so that:

Definition (Ranking on Γ).

A ranking $\prec$ on Γ is a partial ordering on the arguments in Γ,

$\mathcal{A} \prec \mathcal{A}'$ if $\mathcal{A}'$ is superior to $\mathcal{A}$.

The second step is to use the ranking and define the critically relevant factors in the following way:

Definition (Critical Factors Relative to Γ and $\prec$).

For each i, the set of critically relevant factors $\varphi_{\Gamma,i}^C$ is the union of:

1. the critically relevant factors of argument i,

   φ_i^C;

2. the critically relevant factors of every argument superior to argument i,

   every φ_j^C where $\mathcal{A}_i \prec \mathcal{A}_j$.

2.3. Inference-based approaches

The ranking of analogies can be dependent on the area that it is applied in, but Bartha also offers a standardised, general ranking for analogies in the following way:

Definition (Standard Ranking).
Suppose $\mathcal{A}_1$ and $\mathcal{A}_2$ are arguments in Γ, and φ_1^C and φ_2^C represent the respective critical factors. Then $\mathcal{A}_1 \prec \mathcal{A}_2$ if:

1. $\varphi_1^C \cap P \subseteq \varphi_2^C \cap P$;
2. $\varphi_1^C \cap N \subseteq \varphi_2^C \cap N$.

Procedure for analogical arguments

The articulation model depends on the notion of similarity between two domains. It is needed for the theory to work. If we do not have a notion of similarity, it is not possible to use the articulation model to evaluate analogical arguments. Bartha (2010, pp. 195-237) introduces different kinds of horizontal relations for analogical arguments. The horizontal relations are the similarity relations between the objects in the source domain and the objects in the target domain.

Excluding the mathematical similarity relations, Bartha claims that we can distinguish the different horizontal relations in at least three different variants:

Feature matching: Two features match when they have a high degree of resemblance;

Formal similarity: Two features are formally similar when they have corresponding positions in two formal analogous theories;

Parametric similarity: Two features are parametrically similar when they can be appropriately described by a variable or a set of variables or if they are linked by a range of intermediate features corresponding to intermediate variable values.

These are only some ways that we can have a horizontal relation. The relevant aspect here is that we have a theory of similarity that can cover the examples we find in the source domain and the target domain. It would not seem to be the case that the articulation model is depending on a specific theory of similarity to work. However, a very strict theory of similarity will restrict our ability to create analogical arguments. The procedure for the articulation model can be distinguished in three different steps. (Bartha 2010, pp. 195-196)

Step 1, Prior association
The first step in the articulation model is to establish that the prior association of the analogical argument holds. The requirement of a prior association is described both generally and individually for each argument type in the formal presentation. They are individually described for each kind of analogy as it is the vertical relation in the domains and will therefore be of wide variety, depending on the application. (Bartha 2010, p. 103)

Step 2, Relevance
The second step is to find the relevant features of the source and the target domains. This includes to distinguish critical from secondary relevant features.

This step is intended to include all features that are known and thought to be relevant for the source and the target domains, while excluding all features that are not relevant or not known. What counts as relevant, critically relevant or secondary relevant features is described individually for each kind of analogy. We do not have any guarantee that we include all relevant features, nor that we have excluded all irrelevant features. This may be considered problematic, but we do not seem to be able to make a general rule for it, and it is therefore in some sense the best we can hope for when it comes to analogical arguments. (Bartha 2010, pp. 103-104)

Step 3, Generalisation
The third step is to verify that the argument satisfies the prima facie plausibility and in what degree it may have a qualitative plausibility.

The first part of the third step is to see if the analogy satisfies a minimal requirement for generalisation, the prima facie plausibility. This is defined generally for all analogical arguments, but a precision is included in the description of each kind. The second part of the third step is to asses the quality of the analogical argument, the qualitative plausibility. The qualitative plausibility consists of three criteria and a measurement of each criteria is needed. This notion of generalisation should be seen as a potential for generalisation, rather than the actual generalisation itself as it is not sure that we are able to make a generalisation for all analogical arguments. (Bartha 2010, pp. 104-105)

Advocate and Critic
Bartha (2010) introduces the notions of an advocate and a critic in order to explain the articulation model. It will be mentioned here, as it seems to be closely related to the dialogical theory of meaning. It does not seem to be the case that Bartha (2010) introduces these concepts in order to create a theory of meaning for analogical arguments, but he refers to this notion as a rhetorical device. However, the introduction of this rhetorical device seems to open up the possibility for a dialogical interpretation.

The rhetorical device of an advocate and a critic is made to introduce challenges and advantages with an analogical argument. The advocate presents the argument and tries as good as possible to convince the critic to an acceptance of the argument. The critic tries as good as possible to find faults and problems with the argument presented by the advocate. It is essentially one agent that argues for the argument and one that argues against the argument. The discussion should be held only within rational and reasonable frames and both the advocate and the critic should accept a reasonable claim of the other. What is important in this view is not whether one of them claims the truth, but whether they can agree. (Bartha 2010, p. 5)

Prakken and Sartor's model of legal reasoning

Prakken and Sartor (1996, 1998, 2016) provide in several articles a dialogical model of general legal reasoning. They claim that cases have a dialectical structure, which means that they contain arguments supporting the decision together with arguments attacking the decision, and arguments attacking and defending arguments. The paper distinguishes four moves that might be described when reasoning with precedents, *Following a precedent*, *Analogising a precedent*, *Distinguishing a precedent* and *Overruling a precedent*. (Prakken and Sartor 1998, pp. 12-16) We will briefly present this theory on handling precedents in this text and the descriptions and definitions are based on Prakken and Sartor's (1998) work. It will be presented as a theory of legal reasoning, rather than as a theory of analogical reasoning because, even though it also has a notion of analogy, the theory is mainly intended to be a general framework to represent legal reasoning and not a theory for handling only analogies.

The first part will present the notion of case and show how this can be formalised and considered from a logical point of view. The second part will present different moves one can do with a precedent. The third part will describe how the theory handles conflicting precedents.

Judicial rationales and the representation of cases

Prakken and Sartor (1998) points out that *case* seems to be an ambiguous notion. It can either refer to whole proceedings of lawsuit or a single decision of a judge together with some support for this decision. It is the second variant that can be used as an authority for

2.3. Inference-based approaches

future decisions and will therefore be the notion that is interesting to represent here. According to Prakken and Sartor, a case has a dialectical structure. This means that they contain not only the decision and arguments supporting the decision, but also arguments attacking the arguments supporting the decision and arguments counterattacking these arguments, explaining why the attacking arguments do not succeed. The dialectical structure is important in order to preserve the context and limits for the supporting argument and the possible complexity of the argumentation itself. A case should, at least potentially, be represented as a multi-step argument with a decision as a conclusion. A case does not have to include several steps, but that should rather be considered as a particularity rather than the general rule. Even if we interpret cases as being dialectical, it does not mean that they have to contain several arguments, rather that they have this possibility. (Prakken and Sartor 1998, pp. 7-8)

Dialectical multi-argument structures

Prakken and Sartor describe the inadequacy of the deductive view of justification of legal decisions. This view states that in order to justify a legal decision, we have to produce a consistent set of legally valid and factually true premises so that they deductively imply the decision. The deductive view on legal justification does not depend on any particular source for these premises, as they might come from precedents, natural law, law texts, definitions and so on. However, the deductive view is often understood as requiring the explicit statement of these premises that are used to derive the conclusion. Prakken and Sartor (1998) argue that this variant of the deductive view is inadequate because of the disputational, or dialectical, nature of legal arguments. A legal decision cannot always be justified by a single argument, but will often have to explain how the winning argument prevails over the arguments for the other side. This is not something that can be done only by a consistent set of arguments for the conclusion. A judge must reply to arguments of the parties, and this reply is the nature of the dialectical aspect of legal justification, which is not something that can be captured in the deductive view of legal justification as such. If a judge does not reply to an argument, particularly arguments that were brought forward by the loosing party, it could be considered lacking justification, even though the judge might have provided a consistent set of premises that logically implied the decision. (Prakken and Sartor 1998, pp. 8-10)

Multi-step structures
Judicial reasoning consists of several linked inference steps. The conclusion of one inference might be used as premises in later inference steps. This means that legal decisions are not a result of a single argument, but rather of several connected arguments that are used together to provide justification for the final conclusion. The use of a precedent in a case is considered in an inference of a step to reach the final conclusion. By considering judicial reasoning as multi-step structures, we might consider the precedents as autonomous case-law rules. (Prakken and Sartor 1998, pp. 10-11)

Multi-level structures
Prakken and Sartor claim that there are in general two ways to consider conflicting arguments. The first is to claim that it is solved by an unreasoned decision of the judge, that it simply pertains to the judge's free evaluation. The second way is to demand some kind of higher-order argument that can provide justification for preferring one argument over another. There are also two aspects of such higher-order decisions, to either produce an argument that back one of the conflicting arguments or to produce an argument that adjudicate the conflict. Prakken and Sartor focus on the second aspect, that the judge has to produce a preference of the arguments, but ground this preference in a reason. If there is a conflict between arguments, the judge should produce an argument for preferring one of the conflicting arguments. (Prakken and Sartor 1998, pp. 11–12)

2.3. Inference-based approaches

Moves for handling precedents in legal reasoning

There might be several ways that a precedent might affect future decision-making. These ways are represented as four different moves that can be done with a precedent, *following, analogising, distinguishing* and *overruling*. We might argue that only the three first moves are really moves that concern the way that a precedent effects future decision-making, since the fourth one is a kind of rejection of its effect. However, it is a situation where a precedent is explicitly mentioned in a later case and it seems reasonable to consider it a move in this sense.

Prakken and Sartor (1998, p. 12) identify three kinds of problems that should be addressed in order to make a theory of precedents,

1. How to provide the structure of a dialectical argument move with precedents;

2. How to handle conflicting precedents;

3. How to understand the dynamics in play when using precedents.

A case is inherently a dialectical process and a precedent is only a previous case that is used in an argument in a later case. A precedent will also have an internal dialectical structure. The moves that might be performed on precedents are therefore in some sense deciding what role the precedent might play in the argument of the later case. When using a precedent, we might depend on only some relevant parts of the precedents in a given situation. This means that we do not have to reconstruct the whole precedent case in order to refer to it, but rather refer to some more particular aspect of its dialectics. The moves that we might perform on the precedent should then be considered the role that the precedent plays in this present situation, not something that is attached to the precedent case in itself. The different moves therefore provide different kinds of links between the case at hand and the precedent case. (Prakken and Sartor 1998, pp. 12-13)

Following a precedent
The first move one can do with a precedent is to follow it. This can be done when a rule that is established in the precedent can be directly used in the new case. (Prakken and Sartor 1998, p. 14)

Analogising a precedent
The second move is the analogising of a precedent, namely to use a decision in a precedent as support for the same decision in the case at hand, even though the new case cannot directly apply the rules in the precedent. This might be done by creating a new rule that covers both the precedent and the case at hand. This rule might be a result of a broadening of a rule in the precedent or an abstraction of a factor. The theory of Prakken and Sartor only covers the broadening of a rule, namely to remove some of the conditions found in the precedent rule. (Prakken and Sartor 1998, pp. 14-15)

Distinguishing a precedent
The third move is the distinguishing of a precedent, to claim that the case at hand is different than the precedent and should therefore have a different result. In some sense we might consider distinguishing of a precedent as opposite to analogising. We also differ between non-restrictive distinguishing and restrictive distinguishing. (Prakken and Sartor 1998, p. 15)

We speak about a non-restrictive distinguishing when the use of an analogy is contested. It points at a problem with the analogy, for example that the broadening cannot be performed since the condition that is proposed to be removed is essential for the justification of the argument. Non-restrictive distinguishing might have different forms, but it has to be related to some proposed analogy and would provide reason for not accepting that particular analogy. (Prakken and Sartor 1998, p. 15)

2.3. Inference-based approaches

Restrictive distinguishing is to contest the use of the rule that would normally be applicable to the situation at hand. This kind of distinguishing would point at some additional feature that is present in the case at hand and that should prevent the application of the rule. Restrictive distinguishing might happen based on a rule from either the analogising of a precedent or from following a precedent. Instead of attacking the analogy, it attacks the lack of precision in the formulation of the rule in the precedent. (Prakken and Sartor 1998, p. 15)

Overruling a precedent

The last move is the overruling of a precedent. Overruling is understood as accepting that a precedent would cover the case at hand, but still reject the application in this particular case despite not being able to distinguish the precedent. It does not say that the precedent was wrong, but simply states that there seems to be some difference between the precedent and the case at hand. However, it is difficult to point at exactly what it is. In many civil law systems, the court is not bound by the precedents and might depart from an earlier decision in a similar way, without pointing to a particular difference between the precedent and the case at hand. This would also correspond to some kind of overruling. (Prakken and Sartor 1998, p. 16)

Conflicting precedents

We may end up with a situation where we have two precedents that would seem to be applicable in the case at hand, but where they have conflicting decisions. This poses a problem because we have an inconsistency. There seems to be several approaches to solving this inconsistency, but they might generally either take the form of ruling one of them out, to claim that one precedent is not really relevant in this situation or giving priority to one of the precedents, while still admitting that they are inconsistent.

Prakken and Sartor describe several criteria that might be used when dealing with conflicting precedents. Two alternatives are already described here, as it is possible to distinguish or overrule a precedent if there is some conflict. These approaches would correspond to the first alternative, to rule out a precedent in a conflict. Though, there are alternatives for prioritising one precedent, while still maintaining that they are both seemingly applicable to the situation and incompatible. The most common is the degree of similarity, which means that if one precedent is more "on-point", that it shares more properties with the case at hand than another precedent, we should prefer the first one. We might prefer a precedent over another precedent on the basis of it being decided by a higher court or being more recent. Other considerations might be their justification in the substantive policy or serving more general justice to the case. These approaches often depend on informal notions that would need to be settled upon before such decision is made. If we try to solve a conflict by these means, it is also important to have some way to compare the different considerations, for example if a case is decided by a higher court, but where another conflicting precedent is more recent. (Prakken and Sartor 1998, pp. 16-17)

Logical system and preliminaries
Logical operators
The logical system is based on an extended programming language that contains two kinds of negation. There is a classical, called strong, negation $\neg$ and there is negation as failure $\sim$. A formula in the language will also contain a name. A rule can be either strict $\rightarrow$ or they can be defeasible $\Rightarrow$. If a rule is strict, the rule is beyond debate and if a rule is defeasible, it can be contested. A fact a (that is beyond debate) is represented as a strict rule with

2.3. Inference-based approaches

an empty antecedent $\to a$. The input of the system is a collection of strict and defeasible rules. This collection works as premises. The defeasible rules should also be ordered, so it makes an ordered theory. (Prakken and Sartor 1998, pp. 27-28)

A notion of priority is also introduced in the logical theory. To say that y is preferred over x is written $x \prec y$. This should be understood as a notion of rule priority for defeasible rules. This is used to give an ordering on these rules so that we are able to represent the preference of one rule over another rule. Such preference, for example that r_1 is decided by a higher court than r_2 that should therefore have some (defeasible) preference, is written $\Rightarrow r_2 \prec r_1$.

Based on this, we might introduce a notion of *defeat*. An argument Arg_1 might defeat another argument Arg_2 and if Arg_2 does not defeat Arg_1, Arg_1 strictly defeats Arg_2. Arg_2 might defeat Arg_1 in three different ways:

Undercutting: Arg_2 undercuts Arg_1 if Arg_1 has $\sim L$ in its body, while Arg_2 has L in its conclusion;

Excluding: Arg_2 excludes Arg_1 if Arg_1 contains some rule r that is concluded not-applicable by Arg_2, $\neg appl(r)$;

Rebutting: Arg_2 rebuts Arg_1 if Arg_1 contains a rule r_1 that is in direct conflict with a rule r_2 in Arg_2 and r_2 does not have lower priority than r_1.

It is important to note that defeat and the priority relations are defined as rules in the system and should be developed and justified in a similar way as other rules in the legal context. In this sense, they do not have a special status with regard to justification. Based on taking all potential interactions on arguments into account, an argument might be distinguished into three different classes, based on a dialogical understanding:

Justified: An argument is justified if a dispute on that argument can be won;

Overruled: An argument is overruled if a dispute on that argument should be lost, namely that it cannot always be won;

Defensible: An argument is defensible if a dispute on that argument should be left undecided.

These different classes of arguments are related to their justification and it depends on a dialogical interpretation of the logical theory. (Prakken and Sartor 1998, pp. 27-28)

Representing cases

A precedent is represented as a collection of arguments. According to the theory of Prakken and Sartor, these arguments have a dialectical structure, which means that it is not only the arguments supporting the conclusion that should be included in the precedent, but also competing arguments against the conclusion and the interaction of these arguments. The arguments are not explicitly present in the representation of precedents. It only contains the rules that can be used to construct the arguments. This means that only the arguments that are relevant for the purpose of bringing up the precedent would be constructed. A rule where a factor gives some support for a conclusion, a tendency, is represented as:

$r : f \Rightarrow d.$

This reads that f is a reason pro d. In general, it is usually this kind of rules that will be relevant when using a precedent. The facts will have to be established individually for every case and will not normally be transferable from a case to another. It is usually the defeasible rules, including the priority relations that might have a relevance for later decisions. The rules in the precedent will usually contain variables rather than constants for the same reason. The precedent itself will act as an argument and can therefore, together with another argument be a part of a priority relation. We can see based on this that the priority relation can be used on several different grounds, like general legal principles or particular aspects that are case-directed. (Prakken and Sartor 1998, pp. 28-30)

2.3. Inference-based approaches

Dialectical understanding of cases

The dialectical interpretation can be considered the semantics of the logical theory. The dialogical interpretation is based on the inherent dialectic of judicial argumentation. We might also consider it a proof theory since it provides a way to not only represent judicial reasoning, but also contains a normative aspect of judging the justification of judicial arguments. This takes the form of a dialogue game. We might therefore distinguish between the dialogical semantics and the dialectical proof theory.

A dialogue game intends to determine whether a given formula is justifiable in a certain theory based on some premises. It is a game of defeasible argumentation, and the conclusion will therefore not be proven logically. The conclusion will be justified rather than a logically derived.

Prakken and Sartor describe the game as normative dialectics where there is a dialectical asymmetry between the players. A proof in the theory that justifies a formula has the form of a dialogue tree. The root is the formula in question while each branch is a dialogue. A move in a dialogue is an argument that attacks the last stated move of the other player. Asymmetry is found in the requirement of the attack for the different players. The Proponent's attack must be strictly defeating since he wants to provide justification for the formula. The Opponent's attack needs only to be defeating, since he does not intend to provide justification for some formula, only to defeat the proposed justification of the Proponent. (Prakken and Sartor 1998, p. 30) A dialogue game can be defined in the following way:

Definition (Dialogue).
A *dialogue* is a finite nonempty sequence of moves $move_i = (Player_i, Arg_i)(i > 0)$, such that

1. $Player_i = P$ iff i is odd; and $Player_i = O$ iff i is even;
2. If $Player_i = Player_j = P$ and $i \neq j$, then $Arg_i \neq Arg_j$;

3. If $Player_i = P$, then Arg_i is a minimal argument such that:

   a) Arg_i strictly Arg_i-defeats Arg_{i-1}; or
   b) Arg_{i-1} does not Arg_i-defeat Arg_{i-2};

4. If $Player_i = O$, then Arg_i $\emptyset$-defeats Arg_{i-1};

A *dialogue* bases on a set of rules ? iff all rules of Arg_i are in ?.

The first part states that a dialogue consists of numbered moves under four conditions. The first condition states that the players take turns in their moves and the Proponent starts. The second condition states that the Proponent cannot repeat a move. The third condition consists of two kinds of moves. The first kind is an attack on the previous move of O that also provides a priority argument that makes the argument succeed. The second kind is a priority argument that neutralises the force of the last move of O. The fourth condition states that O can ignore priorities. (Prakken and Sartor 1998, pp. 30-31) The next definition is of a dialogue tree:

Definition (Dialogue tree).
    A *dialogue tree* based on an ordered theory ? is a tree of moves, such that:

1. Each branch is a dialogue based on ?;

2. If $Player_i = P$, then the children of $move_i$ are all defeaters of Arg_i based on ?.

The first condition states that every branch is a dialogue. The second condition states that the tree should include all possible ways for O to defeat P. This corresponds to the notion of proof and will be relative to an ordered theory. (Prakken and Sartor 1998, p. 32) The last definition relates to when a player wins.

2.3. Inference-based approaches

Definition (Winning).

- A player *wins a dialogue* based on ? iff the other player does not have any possible moves;
- *P wins a dialogue tree* based on ? iff P wins every branch;
- *O wins a dialogue tree* if O wins one of the branches;
- An argument A is *justified* on the basis of ? iff there exists a dialogue tree based on ? with A as its root and the dialogue tree is won by P;
- An argument A is *overruled* on the basis of ? iff it is defeated by a justified argument;
- An argument A is *defensible* on the basis of ? iff it is neither justified nor overruled;
- A claim C is a *justified conclusion* on the basis of ? iff there is a justified argument for C based on ?.

The most important aspect is the difference between the winning conditions (for dialogue trees) for the Proponent and the Opponent. The Proponent has to win all branches in order to win the dialogue tree. If the Opponent wins at least one, it will be the Opponent winning that dialogue tree. The system will have a "weakest-link" principle, which means that an argument can only be justified if its subarguments are also justified. (Prakken and Sartor 1998, pp. 32-34)

Representing precedents

We have now described the general framework for representing judicial reasoning by dialogue games according to Prakken and Sartor (1998). Now we will describe how it is possible to represent precedents in this framework. This will provide a background for describing the different moves, namely how precedents might be used in a dialogue.

A precedent is defined in the following way:

Definition (Precedent).
A *precedent case* is a pair $(CaseFacts, CaseRules)$, where

- $CaseFacts$ is a set of strict rules;
- $CaseRules$ is a set of rules.

If $Cases$ is a set of precedents, then *Rules-of-Cases* is the union of the sets $CaseRules$ of all precedents in $Cases$.

A precedent can be considered either to consist of facts and rules or to consist of arguments. The arguments in a precedent are those that can be built from the ordered theory,

$$Case = (CaseFacts, CaseRules).$$

These arguments can therefore be justified, defensible or overruled on the basis of ?. This might also be used to distinguish between ratio decidendi and obiter dictum. Ratio decidendi can be found in the rules in a justified argument, while obiter dictum can be found in the rules in a non-justified argument. (Prakken and Sartor 1998, pp. 34-35)

The next definition is for the background information of a precedent. The background information can be defined in the following way:

Definition (Background Information).
A *background information theory (BI)* is a triple

$$(Cases, CFS, CFRules),$$

where

- $Cases$ is a set of precedents;
- CFS is a set of strict rules, the current fact situation;

2.3. Inference-based approaches

- *CSRules* is a set of rules, the 'common sense' knowledge.

In order to actually use precedents in a dialogue game, it must be introduced rules for handling information that is received from precedents. One way to implement information from a precedent is to state that a move should only consist of rules from *Rules-of-Cases*, *CFS* or *CSRules*. In addition to this, there must also be rules for analogising and distinguishing precedents. Prakken and Sartor also provides two different kinds of rules that might describe these operations. One kind is broadening that keeps the consequent of a rule, but omits one or more of the antecedents. The other kind is distinction stating that we need some other antecedent for the justification of the consequent. (Prakken and Sartor 1998, pp. 34-36)

In order to introduce these new rules, some new notation is required. For any rule r, $AntLits(r)$ denotes the set of literals that occurs in its antecedent. The antecedent is denoted $ANT(r)$ and the consequent is denoted $CONS(r)$. For any set $R = \{r_1, ..., r_n\}$ of rules, $AntLits(R) = AntLits(r_1) \cup ... \cup AntLits(r_n)$, and similarly for $ANT(R)$ and $CONS(R)$. Broadening is defined in the following way:

Definition (Broadening a rule).
A defeasible rule r *broadens* a defeasible rule r' iff

1. the first argument of r's name is r'; and

2. r and r' have the same consequent; and

3. $AntLits(r) \subseteq AntLits(r')$.

There is also a further distinction between strong distinguishing and weak distinguishing. Weak distinguishing claims the inapplicability of the rule while strong distinguishing claims the opposite conclusion. A rule might also be distinguished, and similarly there are two kinds of distinguishing of rules. A weakly distinguished rule concludes the broadening rule to be inapplicable. A strongly distinguished rule concludes that if the omitted literals cannot be proven, the opposite conclusion of the broadened rule holds. A distinguishing rule d is concerned with a broadening rule b. The antecedent in d consists of the weakly negated literals that have been omitted in b while the consequent contains the complement of the consequent of b in the case of strong distinguishing and $\neg appl(r)$ in the case of weak distinguishing. The definition of distinguishing is given as follows:

Definition (Distinguishing a rule).
A defeasible rule r *strongly distinguishes* a defeasible rule r' iff

1. r and r' have contradictory consequents and

2. there exists a defeasible rule r'' broadened by r' and there exist literals $L_1, ..., L_n$ such that

    a) $L_1, ..., L_n$ are included in $ANT(r'')$, but not in $ANT(r')$;
    b) $ANT(r) = \sim L_1 \wedge ... \wedge \sim L_n (n > 0)$;

A defeasible rule r *weakly distinguishes* a rule r' iff

1. the consequent of r is $\neg appl(r')$ and

2. condition (2) of strong distinguishing holds.

The second condition of distinguishing takes the literals that were omitted in the broadening of r'', $L_1, ..., L_n$ and uses them as a conjunction of the negated literals, $\sim L_1 \wedge ... \wedge \sim L_n$, in the antecedent of the distinguishing r'. (Prakken and Sartor 1998, pp. 35-37)

The theory of Prakken and Sartor (1998) is intended to not only work as a proof theory, but also as a representation of actual dialogues. This means that the theory should include a way to introduce arguments during the dispute. For the triple $BI = (Cases, CFS, CSRules)$, the set of broadenings of a rule in *Rules-of-Cases* is denoted $Broadenings_{BI}$ and the set of all distinguishing of any rules in $Broadening_{BI}$ is denoted $Distinctions_{BI}$. The definition of introducible rules is the following:

2.3. Inference-based approaches

Definition (Introducible rules).

$$Introducibles_{BI} \supseteq Broadenings_{BI} \cup Distinctions_{BI}$$

This definition states that broadenings and distinctions are two kinds of rules that might be introduced during the dialogue. The definition states that they together form a subset of the introducible rules, not that these are the only introducible rules that are possible. (Prakken and Sartor 1998, p. 38)

The difference that is made between a dialogue game and an actual dialogue is that an actual dialogue opens the possibility for introducing rules during the play. The notion of an actual dialogue is therefore build upon the notion of a dialogue game, but where also introducible rules are included. Similarly, we also have a notion of actual dialogue trees based on the actual dialogue games. The notion of actual dialogues provide the content of the ordered theory ? that the dialogue game is defined relative to. An actual dialogue can be defined as follows: (Prakken and Sartor 1998, p. 39)

Definition (Actual dialogues).
For any BI,

- An *actual dialogue* based on BI is a dialogue D and based on $CFS \cup CSRules \cup Introducibles_{BI}$.

- An *Actual dialogue tree* based on BI is a tree of actual dialogues based on BI.

An actual dialogue tree does not need to contain all possible moves, like for a dialogue tree. The making of an actual dialogue tree will depend on a protocol, but the theory of Prakken and Sartor does not describe any particular variant of this. The most relevant feature here is that the model opens up for changing both the leaves and the earlier nodes. (Prakken and Sartor 1998, p. 39)

An actual dialogue tree should be described by an actual winning. Based on a certain $move_i$, it should be possible to construct (based on some protocol) an actual dialogue tree T_i. The notion of winning in this sense is relative to an ordered theory ?. ? is considered as set and might be described in at least two different ways. If we assume that CFS and $CSRules$ are fixed, that they are not constructed dynamically, we might have the following definition of ?:

$$? = CFS \cup CSRules \cup Introducibles_{BI}.$$

This states that we have the two sets of rules together with the introducibles. ? might also be defined with only the rules that have been introduced in the dispute. $Rules_T$ is the set of all rules occurring in any tree T. The second definition is the following:

$$? = CFS \cup CSRules \cup \textit{Rules-of-Cases} \cup$$
$$(Introducibles_{BI} \cap Rules_{T_i}).$$

The first definition describes the situation when all possible distinctions and broadenings are included and that the parties can analogise and distinguish the best possible way. The second one restricts this significantly, as only disputes relevant for the analogies and the distinctions are introduced in T, until a certain stage. Prakken and Sartor claim that there is no need to choose between the two definitions, but that they can be relevant and used in different situations. Based on some (undecided) definition of ?, it is possible to define the notion of actually winning a dialogue tree in the following way:

Definition (Actually winning).
For any actual dialogue tree T_i:

1. P wins T_i if there is a dialogue tree on the basis of $?_i$ with the same root as T_i won by P, and containing only arguments of T_i;

2. O wins T_i if there is no dialogue tree on the basis of $?_i$ with the same root as T_i, won by P;

3. otherwise, T_i is undetermined.

2.3. Inference-based approaches

If P uses a broadening rule, O always has the possibility to distinguish the broadening. If the Opponent always does the right move, the Proponent can win only if he does not use analogies. The Opponent's use of distinction (also other rules for both parties) will be object for the procedural level of judicial reasoning, where the judge has the power to evaluate the introduced arguments. This dialogical model therefore leaves the final evaluation of arguments to a procedural level that is not subject for the study of the model. Prakken and Sartor admit that a full model of legal reasoning should address also the procedural level. These definitions provide the formal background for the dialogical theory for judicial reasoning by Prakken and Sartor (1998, pp. 93-41).

Using the system to represent precedents
The dialogical system has for now only been described by definitions and it is not yet clear exactly how this system can represent the process of reasoning with precedents. The intention here is therefore to explain how the rules that have been introduced can be used to represent reasoning with precedents in the way that is described previously.

On-pointness
The first aspect is the on-pointness of ordering between cases. A case that is more 'on-point' than another case should be preferred. This corresponds to choosing the case that is more similar to the case at hand. A case is similar to the case at hand if they share some characteristic. If a second case shares the same characteristics with the case at hand and in addition it also shares some further characteristic that is not shared by the first case, the second case is more on-point to the case at hand than the first case. If A's overlap with the case at hand is a superset of B's overlap with the case at hand, A is more on-point than B. (Prakken and Sartor 1998, p. 42)

The dialogical theory does complicate matters slightly for the implementation of on-pointness. This theory allows for referring to only a portion of a precedent, meaning that you do not have to include all rules in a precedent when using it in a later case. This makes it more complicate to compare two precedents with regard to their on-pointness. The challenge occurs because some case might be more on-point than another case when considering all rules in the cases, but because both precedents are cited partially, we cannot decide the on-pointness based on this partial citation. (Prakken and Sartor 1998, pp. 43-44)

The implementation of on-pointness is done as an assessment of the parties. This means that it has the form of a rule that is implemented as any other rule. The notion of on-pointness can therefore be implemented as a defeasible rule of the form:

$$\Rightarrow (\neg) More\text{-}on\text{-}point(Prec_1, r_1, Prec_2, r_2).$$

This should be understood as that the part r_1 of the precedent $Prec_1$ is more on-point than the r_2 of $Prec_2$ with respect to the issue dealt with r_1. We might also represent the priority relation that is given by such on-pointness as the following defeasible rule: (Prakken and Sartor 1998, p. 46)

$$mop : More\text{-}on\text{-}point(Prec_1, r_1, Prec_2, r_2) \Rightarrow r_2 \prec r_1.$$

Distinguishing precedents

A portion of a precedent might also be distinguished. A weak distinguishing of a portion of a precedent will be in respect to a factor by providing a rule that attacks the intermediate conclusion based on the factor or attacks the final conclusion based on the intermediate conclusion. (Prakken and Sartor 1998, pp. 46-47)

2.3. Inference-based approaches

Interacting factors

Some computational theories of precedents like HYPO provide a system where deleting a factor con a decision and adding a factor pro a decision makes the support for the conclusion stronger. This is a controversial and possibly unwanted feature of a theory for legal reasoning. Even if both rain and heat can be individual reasons not to go running, a combination of both heat and rain can be a good reason to actually go running. If we have two reasons against a decision, a combination of them might support the decision. They might be considered to cancel each other out. (Prakken and Sartor 1998, p. 47)

Having two reasons in support of a conclusion d, $f_1 \Rightarrow d$ and $f_2 \Rightarrow d$, does not imply that their conjunction supports the conclusion, $f_1 \wedge f_2 \Rightarrow d$. To claim the conjunction, we have to add it as a separate rule. We might also introduce a defeasible rule that gives this by default in the system. r^+ means any rule that is obtained by adding zero or more literals pro the conclusion, to r's antecedent. r^- means any broadening of r. The following (defeasible) rule may then be added to $CSRules$ to have this feature in the system: (Prakken and Sartor 1998, p. 47)

$$r : r_1 \prec r_2 \Rightarrow r_1^- \prec r_2^+.$$

Relevant notions in the dialogical theory of Prakken and Sartor

Approaches to precedent

The dialogical theory of Prakken and Sartor distinguishes four kinds of approaches one might have towards a precedent in a case. It is possible to follow the precedent, analogise the precedent, distinguish the precedent or overrule a precedent.

To follow the precedent means to take a rule that was established in a precedent and use it in the case at hand. Analogising a precedent is to create a rule that governs both the precedent and the case at hand. Distinguishing a precedent is to claim that the case at hand is somehow different from the precedent and should not be governed by it. Overruling a precedent is to say that the case at hand should be distinguished from the precedent in some way, but we do not manage to spell out the difference.

Requirements for precedent-based reasoning

We might distinguish requirements of analogies into the horizontal relations and vertical relations. In Prakken and Sartor (1998), the horizontal relations should be considered as some kind of similarity requirement between the rules in the precedent and the rules in the case at hand. Prakken and Sartor have several approaches to precedents, not just as analogies. The notion of horizontal relations does therefore hold not only for analogies, but also for the other approaches. When following a precedent, we say that there is some similarity between the precedent and the case at hand so that we can take a rule from the precedent and directly apply it in the case at hand. When analogising a precedent, the horizontal relations correspond to the similarity that is there when introducing the new rule that governs both the precedent and the case at hand. It is what enables one rule to be applied in both cases. When distinguishing a precedent, the similarity is found in the attempted analogy or the following of a precedent. However, by distinguishing we claim that the similarity relation is not sufficient. The cases are not similar, and we point at this difference. It rejects the similarity relation. Overruling of a precedent is the same as distinguishing except that it does not point at any difference, but rejects the similarity relation nevertheless.

Handling conflicting precedents

The theory of Prakken and Sartor provides an explicit way to represent some preference of one precedent or rule over another. This representation does not take place in an explicit higher-order formulation of the theory, but rather as a rule in the argumentation of the case. That x is preferred over y is written $x \prec y$. However, this

2.3. Inference-based approaches

shows that even though this rule is included in the same way as any other rule, it is indeed of higher-order. This resembles the approach that Bartha (2010) has taken in his theory of analogy, namely to include a special priority operator on domains. A difference is that Bartha introduces an operator on domains, while Prakken and Sartor introduce an operator on rules. It seems to be crucial here to avoid the generalised forms of the preference operator, like rules of that and that kind, is preferred over some other rules of some other kind. When using the preference operator, they always include particular rules and not any general kind of rule. This might be done in order to avoid falling into a variant of Russel's paradox, with a 'rule of rules'. However, Prakken and Sartor (1998, p. 29) mention that these priorities might reflect general legal principles, but because of the point mentioned earlier, they will have to be individually included as applied particulars, rather than general rules.

The handling of conflicting precedents can be done in several ways. One way is to distinguish one of the conflicting precedents. This will in some way remove the inconsistency by claiming the inapplicability of one precedent. An overruling can be used in the same way, except that while distinguishing points at a particular difference, overruling simply states the inapplicability without pointing to any difference. Distinguishing might often be considered the preferred way of handling conflicting precedents as it actually resolves the conflict. If distinguishing is not possible, a conflict of precedents might also be solved by including a priority of one rule over another. The exact formulation of such a priority will depend on what the conflict consists of. However, the introduction of a priority of rules will not solve the conflict as such as it is indeed of higher-order. The conflict will still be there, it only explains that one rule is preferred over another rule without stating that the other rule is wrong or inapplicable.

Rahman and Iqbal's theory of co-relational inference

Overview and motivations for the theory

This dialogical theory by Rahman and Iqbal is an analysis of co-relational inferences, found in Islamic jurisprudence. It was introduced in the paper «Unfolding Parallel Reasoning in Islamic Jurisprudence (I) epistemic and dialectical meaning in Abu Ishaq al-Shirazi's system of co-relational inferences of the occasioning factor» and provides a notion of fine-grained analogical reasoning by the notion of qiyas.

The reasoning is performed in two different steps. The first step consists of finding a case that is covered by the same ruling as the ruling in question for the newer case. The case that is referred to is called the root-case and the newer case is called the branch-case. The second step consists of either looking at the grounds for the ruling for the root-case and see if it applies also for the branch-case, or to find a way to relate the branch-case to the root-case in some other way. The work of Rahman and Iqbal only examines the first alternative in a systematic way. All the following definitions are taken from Rahman and Iqbal (2018, pp. 79-91).

Structure of the dialogical approach

The first step consists of bringing forward a root-case that is proposed to be relevant for the branch-case. This step involves processes that require a background knowledge of the earlier judgments that have been made. It requires the agent to know these judgments and to be able to find one or several that can be used in the next step.

A relevant root-case in this aspect is one where we can make a generalisation that includes both the root-case and the branch-case in question. We have the following terminological remarks:

- $\mathcal{H}(x)$ is the juridical ruling;

- $\mathcal{P}$ is a property;

2.3. Inference-based approaches

- 'illa^P is the occasioning factor, the application of the method to a particular case;
- tard is the condition of co-extensiveness;
- 'aks is the condition of co-exclusiveness;
- ta'thir is the condition of efficiency.

The constructive type-theoretical framework contains hypothetical judgments in the following way:

$B(x) : prop(x : A)$.

This should be understood as a judgment that $B(x)$ is a proposition under the assumption that x is contained in the set A. The judgment presupposes that A is a set, $A : set$. We can understand the proposition $B(x)$ in this expression as the juridical ruling that is performed for objects in A. A is then understood as a certain set of cases. The introduced example is about violating privacy,

$x :$ Privacy-Violation.

It is presupposed that Privacy-Violation is a set, Privacy-Violation : set. On this set, it is possible to introduce the juridical ruling $\mathcal{H}(x)$ in the following way:

$\mathcal{H}(x) : prop(x :$ Privacy-Violation$)$.

This is the structure that is used for a certain juridical ruling that is an instance of a general set.(Rahman and Iqbal 2018, pp. 79-80)

There are some restrictions on the property for the generalisation. This property is what the ruling or generalisation is based upon. It will be called the *occasioning factor*. If we have a root-case that we claim to be relevant for the branch-case, we have to show that we make a generalisation by the occasioning factor and that it is present in the branch-case. The occasioning factor is the link found in the ruling between the property and the result. The following restrictions can be imposed on the occasioning factor:

Condition (Restrictions on the occasioning factor).

- *Co-extensiveness*: whenever a factor is present, we also have the judgment present,

$$\text{tard}(x) : \mathcal{H}(x)(x : \mathcal{P}).$$

- *Co-exclusiveness*: whenever a factor is absent, we also have the judgment absent,

$$\text{'aks}(x) : \neg\mathcal{H}(x)(x : \neg\mathcal{P}).$$

- *Efficiency*: a factor is efficient if it satisfies co-extensiveness and co-exclusiveness,

$$\text{ta'thir} : (\forall x : \mathcal{P})\mathcal{H}(x) \wedge (\forall x : \neg\mathcal{P})\neg\mathcal{H}(x).$$

Co-extensiveness is a condition stating that the occasioning factor should give a positive judgment for all cases where it is present. Co-exclusiveness is a condition that there should be a positive judgment (based on the occasioning factor), only when the occasioning factor is present. Together these two conditions form the condition of efficiency.

The efficiency of a property is a pair of tard and 'aks in the following way:

Definition (Efficiency of a property $\mathcal{P}$).

$$\text{ta'thir}^{\mathcal{P}} =_{def} < \text{tard}^{\mathcal{P}}, \text{'aks}^{\mathcal{P}} > : (\forall x : \mathcal{P})\mathcal{H}(x) \wedge (\forall x : \neg\mathcal{P})\neg\mathcal{H}(x).$$

Given $a : \mathcal{P}$ and $a* : \neg\mathcal{P}$, the efficiency is a pair of applications where the left part of the expression is evidence for the co-extensiveness of the factor,

$$\text{'illa}^{\mathcal{P}+}.a : \mathcal{H}(a).$$

2.3. Inference-based approaches

The right part of the expression is evidence for the co-exclusiveness of the factor,

$$\text{'illa}^{P-}.a* : \neg\mathcal{H}(a).$$

Cases of $\mathcal{P}$ occasion the interdiction $\mathcal{H}$ (given the efficiency of $\mathcal{P}$ in relation to $\mathcal{H}$). That $\mathcal{P}$ is efficient in relation to $\mathcal{H}(x)$ means that there is a method to apply $\mathcal{H}(x)$ to every instance of $\mathcal{P}$ and applying $\neg\mathcal{H}(x)$ to every instance of $\neg\mathcal{P}$. (Rahman and Iqbal 2018, pp. 80-81) The occasioning factor is the application of the method from the generalising property to the particular juridical ruling,

Definition (Occasioning factor).
 'illa^{P} in the relation to $\mathcal{H}(x)$, defined over $\mathcal{P}$ is the application of the function from all instances of $\mathcal{P}$ into the set of instances of $\mathcal{H}(x)$.

The last step is to apply the decided ruling to the branch-case in question,

Condition (Applying ruling to a branch-case).

1. Recognising that the root-case is an application of the function that takes us from every instance of $\mathcal{P}$ to a suitable instance of $\mathcal{H}(x)$;

2. Recognising that this general norm also applies to the branch-case.

In some situations, there might be an established property relevant for the ruling in the source case. This is indicated by the $\mathcal{S}$ in 'illa,

$$\text{'illa}^{S-P}.a : \mathcal{H}(a).$$

We may also end up with a situation where we have not established the relevance of the property, but where it is only assumed to be relevant for the source and target case,

$$\text{'illa}^{P}.a : \mathcal{H}(a).$$

In the second situation the property needs to satisfy the criteria of efficiency, co-exclusiveness and co-extensiveness. We then have to make explicit the reasons for choosing exactly that property and not another one. (Rahman and Iqbal 2018, pp. 79-82)

Notion of dialogues
The theory considers analogical reasoning in a game-theoretical approach. This means to look at reasoning as a game with two players, one Proponent and one Opponent, where the player that has the last word wins. If it is the Proponent that has a winning strategy, the reasoning holds and if it is the Opponent, the reasoning does not hold. The Proponent tries to argue in favour of the thesis, while the Opponent tries to argue against the thesis. The goal of the Proponent in this dialogical framework is to make the Opponent concede that the branch-case instantiates the property in question. This may also include some informal justification for certain propositions. (Rahman and Iqbal 2018, pp. 84-87)

Formal rule
A very important notion in the dialogical framework is the formal rule. It states that the Proponent may use every move that has been forwarded by the Opponent in the defence of the thesis. In some interpretations for the constructive type-theoretical framework, the notion of epistemic assumption can be considered problematic as the proof has not yet been demonstrated. This problem may be considered less pressing in the dialogical framework, where an epistemic assumption means that the Opponent has taken responsibility for its content, not that there has been an actual demonstration of its proof. This what is captured in the formal rule. (Rahman and Iqbal 2018, p. 88).

In the context of Islamic legal reasoning, the formal rule is provided with some refinement. The theory distinguishes between different degrees of force. The maximal force is in play if a player refers directly to the *sources*. Another alternative is that the Pro-

2.3. Inference-based approaches

ponent refers to a previous move by the Opponent and the force of such reference is *logical*. The last alternative is a reference to *similarities* which has the weakest kind of force. (Rahman and Iqbal 2018, p. 15)

Termination
A dialogue may terminate in two different ways, that the Proponent wins or that the Opponent wins. A victory for the Proponent can be seen as bringing the Opponent to silence, namely that the Opponent is forced to accept the thesis. A victory for the Opponent can be seen as the Proponent accepting the objections of the Opponent and therefore giving up the thesis. (Rahman and Iqbal 2018, pp. 87-88)

The relevant notion for the victory of a player is the existence of a winning strategy. In the traditional dialogical framework the existence of a winning strategy corresponds to the notion of validity, though here it rather corresponds to legitimacy. In developing such a winning strategy, it is only the successful moves that are kept. We can consider it to be based on a collective effort in pursuing the truth. (Rahman and Iqbal 2018, p. 88)

Criticism
The dialogical model distinguishes two different kinds of criticism. The first kind is a constructive criticism. This involves that the Opponent disagrees with the Proponent's choice of property for the occasioning factor. The Opponent does that by showing that there is a case contradicting the choice of property and then proposing a new property that could constitute the occasioning factor. The Opponent does not disagree with the thesis as such, but rather the reasons that the Proponent forwarded to defend the thesis. (Rahman and Iqbal 2018, p. 92)

The second kind is destructive criticism. This kind of criticism can be distinguished in two different subkinds. The first subkind is a destruction of the thesis, which means that the Opponent disagrees with the thesis as it is proposed by the Proponent. This can be done in three different ways, bringing forward a root-case where we find the exact opposite ruling, bringing forward a root-case that has a different and incompatible ruling even though they may share the same occasioning property or bringing forward a root-case that has a different ruling and that the property unifies cases where the ruling differs. The main structure is that the Opponent forces the Proponent to admit that the counterexample is incompatible with the claimed ruling in the branch-case. The second subkind is a destruction of the 'illa, claiming that it does not satisfy the condition of efficiency. This involves the Opponent either bringing forward a root-case where the occasioning property has given a different ruling than the one claimed by the Proponent or a root-case where the claimed ruling is applied in the absence of the claimed occasioning factor. The criticism then requires the Opponent to find a counterexample to the thesis forwarded by the Proponent. This can be done in several ways, but in general this process seems to correspond to the creation of a negative analogical argument. (Rahman and Iqbal 2018, pp. 93-95)

Conclusion

The dialogical theory of analogical argumentation is based on the Islamic framework for parallel reasoning. It uses the constructive type-theoretical framework to formalise analogies as hypothetical judgments where the context corresponds to the ruling that governs the older case. The criticism seems to correspond to an argument by negative analogy or counterexample as the Opponent is asked to bring forward a case that is intended to destroy the thesis of the Proponent.

Chapter 3

Comparison of contemporary theories

3.1 Horizontal relations

Though the term is taken from Bartha (2010), a very important aspect for all theories of analogy would seem to be the notion of horizontal relations. The horizontal relations provide the connection between the source domain and the target domain. Because of this, the horizontal relations are also important in all the theories explained here. However, the theories do not seem to shed very much light on this aspect, as they consider the horizontal relations to a great degree to already be given in the context.

Schema-based theories
In the AWR-model, the notion of horizontal relations stays implicit. It does not seem to present any explicit requirement regarding the horizontal relations, but simply assumes that characteristics can be shared by different domains. Based on the usage of shared characteristics, it would seem like Brewer (1996, pp. 966-967) considers a characteristic of a domain to be an instance of a general characteristic. The horizontal relations can then be explained as being two

instances of the same general property. A target domain shares a characteristic with the source domain when the characteristic found in the source domain is an instance of the same general characteristic as the characteristic in the target domain instantiates.

In Alchourrón's (1991) description of arguments a pari and a fortiori, we can identify the horizontal relations by the notion of *comparative concepts*. Contrary to Brewer, Alchourrón introduces this relation in an explicit way and imposes particular restrictions on this relation. For arguments a fortiori, this relation should be transitive and asymmetric, while for arguments a pari the relation should be transitive, symmetric and reflexive. This is also clear in the formalisations, where the comparative concepts are introduced as one of two implicit premises in the argument.

Woods (2015) introduces the concept of a *generalization schema* in order to explain analogical reasoning. The idea is that this schema should be general in the way that it covers both the source case and the target case. So to speak, it is this that provides Woods' notion of horizontal relations by its ability to explain *sufficient relevant similarities* (Woods 2015, p. 276). A generalisation schema should consist of general facts that explain the similarities between the particular facts of the source and the particular facts of the target.

Inference-based theories
The articulation model claims that the horizontal relations are similarities. The articulation model does not depend on any specific notion of similarity, but can according to the author, be easily adapted to different theories of similarity. It would seem to be the case that the articulation model opens up for similarities that are depending on the setting that the analogical argument occurs in. However, Bartha distinguishes three different kinds of similarity (excluding mathematical similarities) that he thinks are important for the development of analogical arguments. The first one is feature matching, that two features have high degree of resemblance. The

3.1. Horizontal relations

second one is formal similarity, that two features have corresponding positions in two formal analogous theories. The third one is parametric similarity, that two features can be described by the same variable. (Bartha 2010, p. 197)

Prakken and Sartor (1998) do not include a particular notion of horizontal relations or similarity in their dialogical approach to analogical reasoning, though it is assumed that rules and facts from one case can be directly transferred to another case. This seem to indicate that the notion of horizontal relations in this approach is based upon a notion of identity.

The theory by Rahman and Iqbal (2018) does not seem to depend on any particular notion of similarity. The relevant horizontal relations in this theory is the relation that two instances of a general ruling has to each other. It does not depend on any similarity between the two cases, except that they would both need to fall under the same ruling. The horizontal relations are therefore found between the ruling in question and the result of applying this ruling. As with the two other inference-based theories, this approach seem to either be open in regard to the notion of similarity or reduce it to a question of identity.

Similarity

The schema-based theories and the inference-based theories seem to explain the notion of horizontal relations in two very different ways. Generally, the inference-based theories reduce the question of horizontal relations to be a question of identity. An exception here is the articulation model by Bartha, that mentions explicitly that there might be several kinds of similarity in play. Formal similarity and parametric similarity seem to be reducible to identity and feature matching might be considered to be some kind *overall* similarity.

The schema-based theories on the other side all introduce explicit formal structures to represent horizontal relations. In the AWR-model this is given by the notion of *general characteristics*, while Alchourrón introduces an explicit notion of *comparative concepts*. Woods operates with the notion of a *generalization schema*.

That the schema-based theories all introduce such notions is very likely to be related to the way that they intend to explain analogical reasoning. The background for the schema-based approaches is that they intend to reduce analogical arguments to a question about *implicit premises*. Since these horizontal relations form an essential part of an analogical argument, it therefore seems comprehensible that the schema-based theories also include it in an explicit way in their formal structure. The inference-based theories on the other side explain analogical reasoning as a particular kind of inferential structure. In some sense, we might say that these approaches attempt to explain analogical reasoning in logical terms. These theories therefore seem less dependent on the introduction of an explicit structure that explains these horizontal relations, as the already existing notion of identity (and eventually other theories of similarity) is considered to be sufficient to explain the direct relation between two cases.

3.2 Vertical relations

Restrictions on the vertical relations are found in all six theories. The vertical relations provide the connection that the elements inside a domain may have to each other. We might identify these relations in terms of *relevancy*. Contrary to the horizontal relations that explain the relations between the source and the target, the vertical relations explain the relations between what is known and what is inferred. In some theories, such as the one by Brewer (1996), we also see that there is a distinction between the vertical relations and the justification of these vertical relations.

3.2. Vertical relations

Schema-based theories

For Brewer, the vertical relations are explained by one or several *analogy-warranting rules*. A good analogy-warranting rule should explain the relation the known characteristics have to the inferred characteristics. The AWRs are made under an entailment requirement. This means that they together with the other premises, need to logically entail the inferred characteristic in the target. The AWRs are also depending on some informal virtues, but more importantly needs to yield an acceptable sorting in the second step of the theory. An acceptable sorting in this sense means that it explains the inferred characteristic in all domains where this characteristic occurs and that it does explain the non-existence of the characteristic in all domains where it does not occur. (Brewer 1996, pp. 997, 1021–1022)

The vertical relations for Alchourrón are explained in terms of *inheritance relations*. These relations work as a second implicit premise in the analyses of arguments a fortiori and a pari. The inheritance relations connect the original premise with the other implicit premise (for the horizontal relations) so that the premises together entail the conclusion. It shows how the horizontal relation provides the foundation for the target. Though without developing further, Alchourrón (1991, p. 23) also includes a restriction that the norms in these arguments must be mutually coherent.

For Woods, the notion of *generalization schema* does not seem to cover only the horizontal relations, but does also seem to include aspects that should be understood in terms of vertical relations. The generalization schema does not only explain in what way the source and the target are similar, but also how this can affect the conclusion in the argument, namely how they are *relevantly* similar. In order to determine these relevant similarities, Woods (2015, pp. 276-277) describes a generalization schema in terms of *adequacy*. An adequate argument in this sense is one that satisfies both the example (the source) and the analogue (the target).

Inference-based theories

In the articulation model, the vertical relations are described by the *prior association* which defines what kind of analogy we speak about. The prior association is a relation on the existing and non-existing factors in a domain. This relation is defined specifically for each kind of analogical argument and does not have any particular restriction in its general formulation. (Bartha 2010, p. 100) It would seem like analogies in legal reasoning would in general fall under the first kind of argument, where we have a vertical relation from the positive analogy to the hypothetical analogy. A legal argument by analogy would typically be of the kind where a previous case (or a hypothetical case) would be used to argue for or explain a certain result of the case in question. The kind of analogy therefore seems to be of a predictive or explanatory kind in this theory. It does not exclude the other kinds to be applied in a legal setting. Bartha also introduces a notion of *relevance* and *generalization*. Together, they form the a condition imposed for deciding the overall strength of the analogical argument.

In Prakken and Sartor (1998), the vertical relations can be identified in their definition of *rules*. In their dialogical model, a rule is defined as some reason (or factor) in support for some conclusion. This means that the vertical relations are described by the definition of a rule. A rule in this sense is then not only the ruling, it also includes the reason one gives for this ruling. The strength of an analogical argument will depend on the strength that is found between the ruling and its reason. There are here several ways to formally represent the weakening of this relation, such as distinguishing and on-pointness.

In the Islamic model, the vertical relations are seen as a *hypothetical judgment* in constructive type theory. This means that the ruling works as an assumption for the older case, and the analogical argument claims that this ruling also can work as an assumption for the newer case. The relation in question may be said to be a logical relation. It means that the ruling provides a method for yielding a

3.2. Vertical relations

result for the case. There should also be an occasioning factor that is the application of the ruling under a certain property that provides the justification for the decision of the case. The occasioning factor is an application of efficiency that consists of a pair of applications, namely co-extensiveness, that the property must be present when the ruling present, and co-exclusiveness, that the property is absent when the ruling is absent. (Rahman and Iqbal 2018, pp. 79-80)

Relevancy
The different theories has widely different terminology for explaining the vertical relations. Despite such differences, we can see that the schema-based approaches differ slightly from the inference-based approaches. In the different schema-based theories, the vertical relations are generally introduced as an explicit premise that is usually considered tacit in the legal discourse. While in the inference-based theories, these relations are described in terms of a particular logical structure.

The idea in the schema-based approaches is precisely to formulate these tacit assumptions that are made when performing arguments by analogy. The vertical relations are then introduced either as an explicit and distinct assumption or premise (as for Brewer and Alchourrón) or as a part of a more complex schema (as for Woods). The different theories utilises their own terminology to name this tacit premise. Brewer introduces the notion of *analogy-warranting rules*, Alchourrón introduces *inheritance relations* and Woods introduces *generalization schemas*. They all describe a premise that makes the argument deductively valid, claimed to be usually taken for granted in the actual argumentation process. Woods' *generalization schemas* seem to be slightly more complex than the corresponding notions in the other theories since it does not only intend to capture vertical relations, but also horizontal relations.

In the inference-based theories, the vertical relations are not introduced as a tacit assumption as in the schema-based theories. Here, they are rather to be found in the definition of a case in itself. For Bartha, this is given by the *prior association*, which defines the kind of analogy we are speaking about. For Prakken and Sartor the notion of *rule*, consisting of both a conclusion and its reason, plays this role. In the Islamic model, these relations are given by the notion of a *hypothetical judgment*. Prakken and Sartor and Rahman and Iqbal seem to differ from Bartha in the way that they both consider vertical relations to be a dependency of the ruling on its reason. The articulation model on the other hand considers it to be a relation over some elements given by a model. This difference might be explained by the constructive approach taken in the two other theories compared to the non-constructive approach of Bartha. In all three theories, the strength of the analogy seems reducible to the strength given by this association or hypothetical.

3.3 Multiple analogies

A theory of analogical arguments should be able to handle different analogies. The most important aspect of multiple analogies occurs when they give incompatible results. If we have multiple analogies in support of the same conclusion it does not seem to pose any particular challenge as we may simply consider both arguments to be supportive of a common claim. The difference will be discussed in the light of incompatible arguments.

Schema-based theories
Brewer introduces two ways to handle multiple analogies. The first way is to introduce an *AWR* that can handle the difference in a satisfactory way. We may question whether this really is a situation of multiple analogies or if it simply is a part of controlling the AWR by the proposed procedure. The second way is to create a *DWR* that distinguishes one analogy from the other by claiming that one

3.3. Multiple analogies

holds and the other does not. It would seem to be the case that both of these procedures may be used for multiple analogies and whether to choose one rather than the other one depends more on practical purposes rather than logical. The theory requires of the proposed AWR or DWR to yield an acceptable *sorting*, which means that it should give a positive answer to items (cases) that are presupposed to have a positive answer and a negative answer to items that are presupposed to have a negative answer. This step is by Brewer identified as *inductive*.

Neither Alchourrón nor Woods seem to provide any explicit account for how to deal with multiple competing analogies. Competing analogies would indeed seem like a pressing question that would demand an answer. That neither authors account for this aspect can likely be understood in (at least) two ways:

1. competing analogies can be solved by introducing a new *generalization schema* or *comparative concept* that could be used to distinguish the two or,

2. competing analogies should be solved by other aspects of legal reasoning, such as a competent authority performing discretion.

A combination of the two is of course also an alternative, which seems indicated by both authors in their respective works. In this situation they would indeed seem to be closely in line with Prakken and Sartor and to some extent Bartha.

Inference-based theories
The articulation model by Bartha introduces a special apparatus of *ranking* for handling multiple analogies. This involves to first assert that each analogy satisfies certain requirements of prima facie plausibility in order to exclude the bad analogical arguments. The second step is introducing a partial ordering, a ranking, on the different arguments. If an analogical argument has a higher rank than another competing analogical argument, the first analogical

argument is the one that should be considered. The critical factor of every higher ranked argument is included as a critical factor in the lower ranked ones. This way of handling multiple analogical arguments introduces an operator on the arguments and makes us able to evaluate different analogical arguments against each other, but it does not seem to show how an analogical argument may interact directly with another one as it introduces a higher-order structure to handle the multiplicity of analogies.

The dialogical model by Prakken and Sartor provides several ways to deal with multiple and potentially conflicting analogies. An analogy can have an effect on another on the basis of *on-pointness*, *distinguishing* or *interacting factors*. Rejecting an analogy on the basis of on-pointness means that there is another analogy that describes the present case more precisely than the first. An analogy might also be distinguished by another analogy, which means that we introduce a new rule that holds for one and not the other one. Last, an analogy might counteract another by means of interacting factors. This means that both analogies might hold, but their conjunction does not. All these interactions are explained by a notion of *priority*, that describes how a rule should be preferred over another rule. As for Bartha, the concept of preference is introduced in higher-order terminology.

The Islamic model by Rahman and Iqbal introduces multiple arguments as *criticism*. A competing analogical argument may be introduced by the Opponent as two kinds of criticism of the proposed analogy by the Proponent. In the constructive criticism, the Opponent claims that there is another analogy that is better than the analogy proposed by the Proponent. The other kind is a destructive criticism, where the Opponent suggests some incompatibility in the proposed analogy. This creates a subplay, where the Opponent defends the new analogy, and at the end forces the Proponent to

3.3. Multiple analogies

accept the new analogy instead of the original one (assuming that it satisfies the requirements). This kind of subplay introduces a new analogy which is tested against the previous analogy. In this way, it introduces a way of handling multiple analogical arguments.

Competing analogies

Regarding how the different theories handle multiple analogies, we see considerable differences across the schema-based and the inference-based approaches. Both Alchourrón and Woods seem to indicate that the problem of handling multiple analogies can at best only be partially solved by a formal theory of analogy. From this perspective, other considerations also affect this assessment and these considerations might be difficult or impossible to formalise in a formal framework.

Bartha and Prakken and Sartor both introduce higher-order operators, *ranking* and *priority*, intended to deal with any potential conflicts between analogies. The idea here is that some analogies might be preferred over others and that this formal notion can be used to represent this hierarchy of preference. As mentioned, both approaches do this in a higher-order language. The use of this kind of higher-order notions has challenges in itself (as their interpretation in actual practice), but more particular for analogical reasoning it does seem difficult to explain distinguishing when an analogy is used in the distinguishing process itself. Typically analogies are explained, not in the higher-order language, but in the object language. In order to explain this, the theories would need to implement a notion of analogy also in this higher-order language. For a similar reason, we might even need to introduce the notion of analogy in the higher-order language of the higher-order language, and so on.

The theories of Brewer and Rahman and Iqbal have a very different approach than the previously mentioned. The AWR-model and the dialogical model, consider multiple analogies as something that can motivate the change of the original analogy in some way, but the two analogical arguments may not co-exist. For Brewer, an incompatible analogy can motivate the creation of a new AWR or DWR that makes enables us to distinguish the arguments from each other or motivate the change in the original analogical argument. In the dialogical model, the incompatible analogy is rather a proposal of replacement by means of a concept of *criticism*. These two approaches do not introduce any formal notion of higher-order, but instead considers competing analogies in light of a condition of *efficiency* or that it yields an acceptable *sorting*. These theories are able to explain how multiple analogies may interact without introducing any higher-order notion to provide such comparison. This also means that analogies can be used to explain distinguishing in these theories. An objection however is that neither makes attempts to show how other aspects might affect the interaction between different analogies.

Part II

Formal and informal background

Chapter 4
CONSTRUCTIVE TYPE THEORY

Constructive type theory (CTT) was developed by Martin-Löf in order to have a language to reason constructively both about and with mathematics. The idea is to have a system where you do not distinguish between syntax and semantics in the same way as it is traditionally done. This enables us to keep meaning and form on the same level and therefore also interact with each other in a way that is explicit in the language itself. This introduction is based mainly on Martin-Löf's (1984) original paper.

4.1 JUDGMENTS

In CTT a judgment is a statement inside the language. We distinguish between categorical judgments and hypothetical judgments. A categorical judgment is the most fundamental form of judgment that we find in CTT while a hypothetical judgment is a dependent judgment that consists of at least two judgments.

Categorical judgments

We may distinguish two forms of categorical judgments:

- $a : \mathcal{C}$;

- $a = b : \mathcal{C}$.

The first form should be understood as "a is an object of category $\mathcal{C}$" while the second form should be understood as "a and b are identical objects of the category $\mathcal{C}$". The notion of category is understood as a predicate. In CTT we have a potentially infinite number of categories, but every category occurring in a judgment needs to be associated with a criterion of application and a criterion of identity. The criterion of application should tell what the category is, what criterion an object of that category should satisfy, and this is the condition for the first form of categorical judgment. The criterion of identity should express what it takes for two objects in this category to be identical and this is the condition for the second form of categorical judgment. We can therefore distinguish two principles of CTT from Quine's *no entity without identity*:

- no object without category;
- no category without a criterion of identity.

For us to predicate over a certain object, we first have to state what kind of object we are speaking about, namely determining what category it belongs to. What this category is needs to be explained together with its criterion for identity.

We may distinguish between two different representations of CTT, one higher-order representation and one lower-order representation. The most common is to describe the lower-order representation, as it requires a smaller machinery. It is also the variant that is described in the original paper by Martin-Löf (1984) and the one that is presented here.

Even though we have a potentially infinite number of categories, some of them are more important for logical purposes than others. One example of this is the category *set*. For any *set A*, A is also a category. In this category, we therefore have four different forms of categorical judgments, shown in Table 4.1 (Martin-Löf 1984, p. 5).

4.1. Judgments

$A : set$	A is a set.
$A = B : set$	A and B are equal sets.
$a : A$	a is an element of the set A.
$a = b : A$	a and b are equal elements of the set A.

Table 4.1: Categorical judgments of *set*

When we have a judgment of the first form $A : set$, the criteria of application for the category *set* is defining what a canonical element of A is and the equality between canonical elements of A. The first and the third form can be read in a multiple ways according to the Table 4.2 (Martin-Löf 1984, p. 4).

$A : set$	$a : A$	
A is a set.	a is an element of the set A.	A is non-empty.
A is a proposition.	a is a proof of the proposition A.	A is non-empty.
A is an expectation.	a is a method of realising the expectation A.	A is realisable.
A is a problem.	a is a method of solving the problem A.	A is solvable.

Table 4.2: Readings of $A : set$ and $a : A$

The second and fourth form of categorical judgment requires a criteria of identity. The equal canonical elements of A has a relation that is reflexive, symmetric and transitive and the same goes for any set A. The rules for the category *set* is therefore given in the following way, by being reflexive, symmetric and transitive:

$$\frac{A : set}{A = A : set;} \text{ Reflexivity}$$

$$\frac{A = B : set}{B = A : set;} \; Symmetry$$

$$\frac{A = B : set \quad B = C : set}{A = C : set;} \; Transitivity$$

$$\frac{a : A}{a = a : A;} \; Reflexivity\ of\ equality$$

$$\frac{a = b : A}{b = a : A;} \; Symmetry\ of\ equality$$

$$\frac{a = b : A \quad b = c : A}{a = c : A.} \; Transitivity\ of\ equality$$

Propositions

We have given the criteria of application and identity for the category *set*, which naturally leads us to continue with another very relevant category, namely the category of propositions. The category of propositions, *prop*, is identified with *set*,

$$prop = set.$$

This means that the criteria that we have introduced for the category *set* also holds for the category *prop*. However, we may ask ourselves what it means to be an element of a proposition. An element of a proposition should be considered a proof for that proposition. This comes from the Brouwer-Heyting-Kolmogorov-interpretation of propositions. A proposition that is non-empty is therefore a proposition with a proof and a true proposition. That a proposition A, $A : prop$ is non-empty, $a : A$, means that the proposition is true, A *true*, and that a is its proof. The notion of truth can therefore be introduced as a new form of judgment by a proof,

$$\frac{a : A}{A\ true.}$$

4.1. Judgments

For a proposition A to be true, it must have a proof a as an element. This a should be understood as a method that when executed evaluates a canonical proof of A. If two objects, a and b, evaluate identical canonical proofs of A, a and b are identical objects of A, so that $a = b : A$. In CTT, a is called a proof object for A.

Hypothetical judgments

We also have hypothetical judgments as a way to implement dependencies. For the category of sets, a hypothetical judgment has the form:

$B : set(x : A)$.

Sometimes this is also expressed by a turnstile:

$x : A \vdash B : set$.

Such hypothetical judgment should be understood as "Given that x is an element of A, B is a set". For set, we have four different forms of hypothetical judgments:

$B : set(x : A)$;
$B = C : set(x : A)$;
$b : B(x : A)$;
$b = c : B(x : A)$.

Hypothetical judgments may as well contain more than one assumption. The assumptions in a hypothetical judgment is called a context, Γ. Generally, hypothetical judgments have the form:

$x : A \, (x_1 : A_1, \, x_2 : A_2, \, \ldots, \, x_n : A_n)$, such that

$$A_1 \ type,$$
$$A_2 \ type \ (x_1 : A_1),$$
$$A_n \ type \ (x_1 : A_1, \ x_2 : A_2, \ \ldots, \ x_{n-1} : A_{n-1}),$$
$$\frac{A : type \ (x_1 : A_1, \ x_2 : A_2, \ \ldots, \ x_n : A_n)}{x : A \ (x_1 : A_1, \ x_2 : A_2, \ \ldots, \ x_n : A_n).}$$

By introducing hypothetical judgments of the form:

$$f(x) : B(x : A),$$

we have introduced functions into the framework of CTT. A function from A to B is introduced by this statement. The element of B is explicitly written as a function from the element x of A. (Ranta 1994, p. 21) This statement can be read in several different ways:

$f(x) : B$ for arbitrary $x : A$;
$f(x) : B$ under the hypothesis $x : A$;
$f(x) : B$ provided $x : A$;
$f(x) : B$ given $x : A$;
$f(x) : B$ if $x : A$;
$f(x) : B$ in the context $x : A$.

Functions also occur in the standard four forms of hypothetical judgments. Each form can be understood as a substitution and therefore a function from the assumption. (Rahman, McConaughey, et al. 2018, pp. 26-27) The judgment $B : set(x : A)$ should be understood as the following:

$B[a/x] : set$ given $a : A$;

$B[a/x] = B[a'/x] : set$ given $a = a' : A.$

4.1. Judgments

$B[a/x]$ should be understood as "in B, substitute x with a". This motivates the substitution rules:

$$\frac{\begin{array}{c}(x:A)\\ B:set \quad a:A\end{array}}{B[a/x]:set;} \text{ Substitution of a set}$$

$$\frac{\begin{array}{c}(x:A)\\ B:set \quad a=a':A\end{array}}{B[a/x]=B[a'/x]:set.} \text{ Equality of substitution of sets}$$

The judgment $B = C : set(x : A)$ should be understood as:

$B[a/x] = C[a/x] : set$ given $a : A$.

This motivates the following substitution rule:

$$\frac{\begin{array}{c}(x:A)\\ B=C:set \quad a:A\end{array}}{B[a/x]=C[a/x]:set.} \text{ Substitution in equal sets}$$

The judgment $b : B(x : A)$ should be understood as:

$b[a/x] : B[a/x]$ given $a : A$;

$B[a/x] = b[a'/x] : B[a/x]$ given $a = a' : A$.

This motivates the following substitution rules:

$$\frac{\begin{array}{c}(x:A)\\ b:B \quad a:A\end{array}}{b[a/x]:B[a/x];} \text{ Substitution of an element}$$

$$\frac{\begin{array}{c}(x:A)\\ b:B \quad a=a':A.\end{array}}{b[a/x]=b[a'/x]:B[a/x].} \text{ Equality of substitution of elements}$$

The judgment $b = c : B(x : A)$ should be understood as:

$b[a/x] = c[a/x] : B[a/x]$ given $a : A$.

This motivates the following substitution rule:

$$\frac{(x : A) \\ b = c : B \quad a : A}{b[a/x] = c[a/x] : B[a/x].} \text{ Substitution of equal elements}$$

4.2 Rules in CTT

In CTT, we distinguish between four different kinds of rules:

1. Formation rules;

2. Introduction rules;

3. Elimination rules;

4. Equality and computation rules.

    Introduction and elimination rules are similar to the ones that are developed in the sequent calculus of Gentzen (1935). The introduction rules tell you what you need in order to introduce an operator. The elimination rules tell you when you can eliminate the operator. The notion of formation rules is a particularity of CTT. It tells you what category-declarations that needs to be made in order to introduce a certain judgment with a category. The premises of the formation rules are therefore also implicit premises of the corresponding introduction rules. The equality and computation rules tell you how to perform transformations. (Rahman, McConaughey, et al. 2018, p. 29)

    In this section, we will give the rules for operators forming *sets* and elements of *sets*. We will explain the rules for set-theoretical operators and the identity operator and we will use the set-theoretical operators to define the traditional logical connectives and operators.

4.2. Rules in CTT

The important aspect here is the equality between *prop* and *set*.[1] In accordance with recent notational practice, we will not explicitly write which variables that are replaced as this will be clear from the context. Instead of writing $A[b/x, c/y]$ and $a[b/x, c/y]$, we will simply write $A[b, c]$ and $a[b, c]$. Square brackets stand for substitution, not function application. We also assume in the introduction, elimination and equality rules, that they are correctly formed. This means that the premises and the conclusion of the corresponding formation rules are assumed to be implicit premises in the other rules. (Rahman, McConaughey, et al. 2018, pp. 29-46)

Cartesian product of a family of sets

The first operator is the cartesian product of a family of sets, Π. The first two rules are formation rules for Π. The first rule states that whenever we have a *set* A and a family of *sets* B on A, we can form the product of B over A. It gives us ability to judge that $(\Pi x : A)B$ is a *set*.[2]

$$\frac{A : set \quad B : set \quad (x : A)}{(\Pi x : A)B : set} \;\Pi\text{-}Formation\ 1$$

The second formation rule is a rule for when two sets of the form $(\Pi x : A)B$ can be judged identical.

$$\frac{A = A' : set \quad B = B' : set \quad (x : A)}{(\Pi x : A)B(x) = (\Pi x : A')B' : set} \;\Pi\text{-}Formation\ 2$$

---

[1] For detailed accounts for these rules, see Martin-Löf (1984) and Rahman, McConaughey, et al. (2018, pp. 29-46), where the explanations here are taken from.

[2] We intentionally exclude the use of punctuation marks "." in the description of the CTT-rules in order to avoid any potential ambiguity with the computation of a function.

The justification for Π is provided by two introduction rules.

$$\frac{(x : A) \\ b : B}{\lambda x.b : (\Pi x : A)B} \ \Pi\text{-}Introduction\ 1$$

This first introduction rule for Π states that we may judge $\lambda x.b : (\Pi x : A)B$ whenever we have a proof object for B that depends on A.

$$\frac{(x : A) \\ b = b' : B}{\lambda x.b = \lambda x.b' : (\Pi x : A)B} \ \Pi\text{-}Introduction\ 2$$

The second introduction rule states that we have the canonical element $\lambda x.b$ of $(\Pi x : A)B$ when $b[a] : B[a]$ whenever $a : A$. $\lambda x.b$ and b do not belong to the same category, as $\lambda x.b$ belongs to $(\Pi x : A)B$ and b belongs to $B(x : A)$. We may consider b to be a function from A to the family of B and $\lambda x.b$ may be seen as an individual that codes b.

The elements of Π are described by the two elimination rules.

$$\frac{c : (\Pi x : B) \quad a : A}{Ap(c, a) : B[a]} \ \Pi\text{-}Elimination\ 1$$

The first elimination rule states that $Ap(c, a)$ is an element of *set* $B[a]$. $Ap(c, a)$ is an application consisting of a method for obtaining a canonical element of $B[a]$.

$$\frac{c = c' : (\Pi x : B) \quad a = a' : A}{Ap(c, a) = Ap(c', a') : B[a]} \ \Pi\text{-}Elimination\ 2$$

The second elimination rule states that the applications $Ap(c, a)$ and $Ap(c', a')$ are equal elements of $B[a]$. We are given justification for c being an element of C by showing that it can be computed to a canonical element of C. We give this justification by an equality

4.2. Rules in CTT

rule.

$$\frac{a : A \quad b : B \quad (x : A)}{Ap(\lambda x.b, a) = b[a] : B[a]} \; \Pi\text{-}Equality$$

This rule provides the specification how $Ap(c, a)$ computes where $\lambda x.b$ is the canonical form of c from the assumption $c : (\Pi x : A)$. (Rahman, McConaughey, et al. 2018)

To develop logical interpretations, we will rely on the assumption that $prop = set$. This enables us to consider the definitions of the universal quantifier and the implication by means of the cartesian product of a family of sets in the following way:

$$(\forall x : A)(B) \equiv (\Pi x : A)B : prop \text{ when } A : set \text{ and } B : prop(x : A);$$

$$(A \supset B) \equiv (\Pi x : A)B : prop \text{ when } A : prop \text{ and } B : prop.$$

This provides the definitions for the universal quantifier and the implication in CTT. The logical operators are interpreted as instances of the set-theoretical rules provided. Since propositions are interpreted as sets, propositions will form the basis for the formation rules.[3] (Rahman, McConaughey, et al. 2018, pp. 30-33)(Martin-Löf 1984, pp. 14-18)

The universal quantifier can then be formed on the basis of the Π-formation rule.

$$\frac{A : set \quad B : prop \quad (x : A)}{(\forall x : A)B : prop} \; \forall\text{-}Formation$$

---

[3]Note that also the second formation, introduction and elimination rules regarding identity also holds for the logical connectives and operators, though we leave their specific formulation implicit.

The quantification $(\forall x : A)B$ is a *prop* whenever A is a *set* and B is a *prop* under the assumption that $x : A$. Note that the universal quantifier ranges over a set A. The introduction rule for the universal quantifier is formed on the basis of the Π-introduction rule.

$$\frac{\begin{array}{c}(x:A)\\ B \; true\end{array}}{(\forall x : A)B \; true} \; \forall\text{-}Introduction$$

$(\forall x : A)B$ is true whenever B is true under the assumption $x : A$. The explicit proof b from the Π-introduction rule is suppressed.[4] The elimination rule for the universal quantifier is recovered from the Π-elimination rule.

$$\frac{(\forall x : A)B \; true \quad a : A}{B[a] \; true} \; \forall\text{-}Elimination$$

This reads that by the introduction of a particular proof $a : A$, we can by the truth of $(\forall x : A)B$ infer that $B[a]$ is true.

The implication is also introduced in a similar manner. We get the implication formation rule as an instance of the Π-formation rule.

$$\frac{\begin{array}{c}(A \; true)\\ A : prop \quad B : prop\end{array}}{A \supset B : prop} \; \supset\text{-}Formation$$

$A \supset B$ is a proposition when A is a proposition and B is a proposition that may depend on the assumption that A is true. The implication introduction rule is an instance of the Π-introduction rule.

$$\frac{\begin{array}{c}(A \; true)\\ B \; true\end{array}}{A \supset B \; true} \; \supset\text{-}Introduction$$

---

[4]See Martin-Löf (1984, pp. 17-18) or Rahman, McConaughey, et al. (2018, p. 32) for details regarding suppression and for rules restoring the proof.

4.2. Rules in CTT

$A \supset B$ is true whenever B is true under the assumption that A is true. Also in the case of the introduction and elimination rules, the proofs are suppressed, though they might be recovered. (Rahman, McConaughey, et al. 2018, p. 33) The implication elimination rule is made as an instance of the Π-elimination rule.

$$\frac{A \supset B \; true \quad A \; true}{B \; true} \supset\text{-}Elimination$$

We can infer that B is true whenever A is true and that there is an implication $A \supset B$ that is true.

$\rightarrow$ can also be defined in the same way as $\supset$ so that:

$$(A \supset B) \equiv (A \rightarrow B).$$

In CTT, absurdity $\bot$ is defined as the proposition that does not have an introduction rule. The formation rule assumes that $\bot$ is a proposition.

$$\frac{}{\bot : prop} \bot\text{-}Formation$$

Since $\bot$ is assumed to be a proposition, $\bot : prop$ is always derivable. The elimination rule of absurdity corresponds to *ex falso quodlibet* or *the principle of explosion*.

$$\frac{\bot \; true}{A \; true} \bot\text{-}Elimination$$

From $\bot$ being true, we can infer the truth of any A. Negation is defined as a special form of implication.

$$\neg A \equiv (A \supset \bot)$$

Though they might be derived from this definition, we might also explicitly describe the formation, introduction and elimination rules for negation.

$$\frac{A : prop}{\neg A : prop.} \neg\text{-}Formation$$

The formation rule states that $\neg A$ is a proposition when A is a proposition.

$$\frac{\begin{array}{c}(A\ true)\\ \bot\ true\end{array}}{\neg A\ true}\ \neg\text{-}Introduction$$

The introduction rule states that $\neg A$ is true whenever we can infer that $\bot$ is true from the assumption that A is true.

$$\frac{\neg A\ true \quad A\ true}{\bot\ true}\ \neg\text{-}Elimination$$

The elimination rule states that from both $\neg A$ and A being true, we can infer that $\bot$ is true. (Martin-Löf 1984, pp. 26-38) (Ranta 1994, p. 30)

Disjoint union of a family of sets

The second group of rules is based on the disjoint union of a family of sets. The formation rule for the Σ-operator enables to judge when $(\Sigma x : A)B : set$ is a set.

$$\frac{A : set \quad \begin{array}{c}(x : A)\\ B : set\end{array}}{(\Sigma x : A)B : set}\ \Sigma\text{-}Formation$$

When A is a set and B is a set under the assumption that $x : A$, $(\Sigma x : A)B$ is a set. The introduction rule for Σ provides its justification.

$$\frac{a : A \quad b : B[a]}{\langle a, b\rangle : (\Sigma x : A)B}\ \Sigma\text{-}Introduction$$

4.2. Rules in CTT

By $a : A$ and $b : B[a]$, we are given a pair $\langle a, b \rangle$ that forms the canonical elements of $(\Sigma x : A)B$. The elements of Σ are described by its elimination rule.

$$\frac{c : (\Sigma x : A)B \quad \begin{array}{c}(x : A, y : B)\\ d : C[\langle x, y \rangle]\end{array}}{\mathbf{E}(c, xy.d) : C[c]} \quad \Sigma\text{-}Elimination$$

By assuming that $B : set(A : set, x : A)$, we may form $(\Sigma x : A)B : set$. C is here a family of sets. The operation $\mathbf{E}$ in the conclusion $\mathbf{E}(c, xy.d) : C[c]$ binds x and y in d. We are here given a function defined for all elements of $(\Sigma x : A)B$. The equality rule for Σ describes the computation from the elimination rule.

$$\frac{a : A \quad b : B[a] \quad \begin{array}{c}(x : A, y : B)\\ d(x, y) : C[\langle x, y \rangle]\end{array}}{\mathbf{E}(\langle a, b \rangle, xy.d) = d[a, b] : C\langle a, b \rangle} \quad \Sigma\text{-}Equality$$

When c is in the canonical form, the equality rule of Σ provides us with the way to compute $E(c, xy.d)$ from the elimination rule.

By the disjoint union of a family of sets, we can get definitions of the existential quantifier and the conjunction:

$$(\exists x : A)(B) \equiv (\Sigma x : A)B : prop \text{ when } A : set \text{ and } B : prop(x : A);$$

$$(A \wedge B) \equiv (\Sigma x : A)B : prop \text{ when } A : prop \text{ and } B : prop.$$

This provides the definitions for the existential quantifier and the conjunction in CTT. The logical operators are interpreted as instances of the set-theoretical rules provided.[5] (Martin-Löf 1984, pp. 20-26)(Rahman, McConaughey, et al. 2018, pp. 33-36)

---

[5]Note that, as for previously mentioned group of rules, also the second formation, introduction and elimination rules regarding identity also holds for the logical connectives and operators, though we leave their specific formulation implicit.

The existential quantifier can then be formed on the basis of the Σ-formation rule.

$$\frac{A : set \quad B : prop \quad (x : A)}{(\exists x : A)B : prop} \; \exists\text{-}Formation$$

The quantification $(\exists x : A)B$ is a *prop* whenever A is a *set* and B is a *prop* under the assumption $x : A$. Note that the existential quantifier ranges over a set A. The introduction rule for the existential quantifier is formed on the basis of the Σ-introduction rule.

$$\frac{a : A \quad B[a] \; true}{(\exists x : A)B \; true} \; \exists\text{-}Introduction$$

$(\exists x : A)B$ is true whenever $B[a]$ is true and $a : A$. The explicit proof b from the Π-introduction rule is suppressed.[6] The elimination rule for the existential quantifier is recovered from the Σ-elimination rule.

$$\frac{(\exists x : A)B \; true \quad \begin{array}{c}(x : A, B \; true)\\ C \; true\end{array}}{C \; true} \; \exists\text{-}Elimination$$

This reads that when C is true, under the assumption $x : A, B \; true$, we can by $(\exists x : A)B$ being true infer that C is true.

The conjunction is also introduced in a similar manner. We get the conjunction formation rule as an instance of the Σ-formation rule.

$$\frac{A : prop \quad B : prop}{A \wedge B : prop} \; \wedge\text{-}Formation$$

---

[6] See Rahman, McConaughey, et al. (2018, pp. 32, 36) for details regarding suppression of the proof object in this situation.

4.2. Rules in CTT

$A \wedge B$ is a proposition when A is a proposition and B is a proposition. The conjunction introduction rule is an instance of the Σ-introduction rule.

$$\frac{A\ true \quad B\ true}{A \wedge B\ true}\ \wedge\text{-}Introduction$$

$A \wedge B$ is true when A is true and B is true. The conjunction elimination rule is an instance of the Σ-elimination rule.

$$\frac{A \wedge B\ true \quad \overset{(A\ true,\ B\ true)}{C\ true}}{C\ true}\ \wedge\text{-}Elimination$$

We can infer that C is true whenever $A \wedge B$ is true and that C is true under the assumption $A\ true, B\ true$.[7] By letting C be either A or B, we can get both standard conjunction elimination rules. (Martin-Löf 1984, pp. 39-49)

Disjoint union of two sets

The third group of rules are based on the disjoint union of two sets. The formation rule of the $+$-operator describes when we can form $A + B : set$.

$$\frac{A : set \quad B : set}{A + B : set}\ +\text{-}Formation$$

When A is a set and B is a set, $A+B$ is a set. The first introduction rule for $+$ provides justification for the left part.

$$\frac{a : A}{\mathrm{i}(a) : A + B}\ +\text{-}Introduction\ 1$$

---

[7] See Rahman, McConaughey, et al. (2018, p. 36) for the conjunction introduction and elimination rules with proof objects.

$\mathbf{i}(a)$ is an injection for the left part of $A + B$ that is given by $a : A$. The second introduction rule for $+$ provides justification for the right part.

$$\frac{b : B}{\mathbf{j}(b) : A + B} \ \text{+-Introduction 2}$$

$\mathbf{j}(b)$ is an injection for the right part of $A + B$ that is given by $b : B$. The elimination rule for $+$ describes how to obtain a canonical element.

$$\frac{c : A + B \quad d : C[\mathbf{i}(x)] \quad e : C[\mathbf{j}(y)]}{\mathbf{D}(c, x, d, y, e) : C[c]} \begin{array}{c}(x : A) \quad (y : B)\end{array} \ \text{+-Elimination}$$

$\mathbf{D}(c, x, d, y, e) : C[c]$ stands for execution of c so that it either yields a canonical element $\mathbf{i}(a)$ that we substitute x in d for a, or it yields a canonical element $\mathbf{j}(b)$ that we substitute y in e for b. This gives us an understanding of whether an element is originating in A or B when we have it in $A + B$. The equality rules describe this computation of $\mathbf{D}(c, x, d, y, e) : C[c]$. The first +-equality rule provides the left part of $+$.

$$\frac{a : A \quad d : C[\mathbf{i}(x)] \quad e : C[\mathbf{j}(y)]}{\mathbf{D}(\mathbf{i}(a), x, d, y, e) = d(a) : C[\mathbf{i}(a)]} \begin{array}{c}(x : A) \quad (y : B)\end{array} \ \text{+-Equality 1}$$

The second +-equality rule provides the right part of $+$.

$$\frac{b : B \quad d : C[\mathbf{i}(x)] \quad e : C[\mathbf{j}(y)]}{\mathbf{D}(\mathbf{j}(b), x, d, y, e) = e[b] : C[\mathbf{j}(b)]} \begin{array}{c}(x : A) \quad (y : B)\end{array} \ \text{+-Equality 2}$$

By the disjoint union of a two sets, we can get definitions of the disjunction:

$$(A \vee B) \equiv A + B : prop \text{ when } A : prop \text{ and } B : prop.$$

4.2. Rules in CTT

This provides the definition of the disjunction in CTT.[8] The disjunction can then be formed on the basis of the +-formation rule.

$$\frac{A : prop \quad B : prop}{A \vee B : prop} \; \vee\text{-}Formation$$

$A \vee B$ is a proposition when A is a proposition and B is a proposition. The first disjunction introduction rule is an instance of the first +-introduction rule.

$$\frac{A \; true}{A \vee B \; true} \; \vee\text{-}Introduction\;1$$

Whenever A is true, we can infer that $A \vee B$ is true. The second disjunction introduction rule is an instance of the second +-introduction rule.

$$\frac{B \; true}{A \vee B \; true} \; \vee\text{-}Introduction\;2$$

Whenever B is true, we can infer that $A \vee B$ is true. The disjunction elimination rule is an instance of the +-elimination rule.

$$\frac{A \vee B \quad \overset{(A\;true)}{C\;true} \quad \overset{(B\;true)}{C\;true}}{C\;true} \; \vee\text{-}Elimination$$

We can infer that C is true whenever $A \vee B$ is true and that C is true both under the assumption $A \; true$ and under the assumption $B \; true$. (Rahman, McConaughey, et al. 2018, pp. 33-36)

---

[8] Note that, as for previously mentioned groups of rules, also the second formation, introduction and elimination rules regarding identity also holds for the logical connectives and operators.

4.3 Specification and contexts

Modality

In CTT, we may introduce specifications of a context. This is what corresponds to the notion of modal logic or possible worlds in the classical framework. The main idea is to claim that somethings holds relatively to a certain possible world and this works as a specification of the present context. This is the way to introduce new information. The implementation of these terms in CTT has been done by Ranta (1991) and it is his work that will be used here.

We will see that the relations between specifications in CTT ends up being reflexive and transitive. It corresponds to an S4-system in classical modal logic. The reason for this is the further specification of a context. One may look at the specification of contexts as a never-ending project of adding more and more precise information. Since the notion of *world* is widely used in classical modal logic and that it is what Ranta uses in his paper, we will continue to use this notion. However, it is important to remember that a world is nothing more than any other hypothetical judgment and should not be understood to have any inherent metaphysical aspect. That something is the case in a world should simply be understood as claiming that it depends on some further judgment. The notion of world, w, is therefore just any category in the same way as previously described.

Contexts in possible worlds

The main idea behind specifying contexts is to claim that they hold relative to a world. If we have a judgment $a : A$, we can claim that this only holds relative to a certain world w. What we end up with is a hypothetical judgment. Since we have four forms of judgments in CTT, we also have four forms that may be specified, described by Table 4.3 (Ranta 1991, p. 83).

4.3. Specification and contexts

$A : set$ in w	$A(x) : set(x : w)$
$A = B$ in w	$A(x) = B(x) : set(x : w)$
$a : A$ in w	$a(x) : A(x)(x : w)$
$a = b : A$ in w	$a(x) = b(x)(x : w)$

Table 4.3: Specifications w of set

Whenever a world w_2 is a specification of another world w_1, we say that w_2 is accessible from w_1. Everything that is contained in w_1 is also contained in w_2. If we are in w_1, w_2 is a possible extension. By this we can see that we have also introduced a notion of possibility. The relation between worlds is reflexive as the hypothetical judgment $x : w(x : w)$ is trivial and it is also transitive as everything that is contained in w_1 is also contained in w_3 whenever w_3 is a specification of w_2 that again is a specification of w_1. When w_2 is a specification of w_1, there exists a function from w_2 to w_1,

$$d(y) : w_1(y : w_2).$$

The transitivity of the relation can be shown by the following inference:

$$\frac{d(d(y)) : w_1(d(y) : w_2(y : w_3))}{d(y) : w_1(y : w_3).}$$

Specification of contexts may therefore be seen as a potentially infinite process of further and more precise information. This seems to be closely related to a notion of scientific research as a never-ending project. (Ranta 1991, p. 85)

Specification by context

As mentioned earlier, a world is nothing more than a list of hypotheses or judgments. A world is therefore a context, where Γ is used to denote contexts. When we have a specification by a context, the four forms of judgment are described by Table 4.4 where $\Gamma = x_1 : A_1, \ldots, x_n : A_n(x_1, \ldots, x_{n-1})$.

$A : set$ in Γ		$A(x_1 \ldots, x_n) : set$ $(x_1 : A, \ldots, x_n : A_n(x, \ldots, x_{n-1}))$
$A = B$ in Γ	$A, B : set$ in Γ	$A(x_1 \ldots, x_n) = B(x_1 \ldots, x_n) : set$ $(x_1 : A, \ldots, x_n : A_n(x, \ldots, x_{n-1}))$
$a : A$ in Γ	$A : set$ in Γ	$a(x_1 \ldots, x_n) : A(x_1 \ldots, x_n)$ $(x_1 : A, \ldots, x_n : A_n(x, \ldots, x_{n-1}))$
$a = b : A$ in Γ	$A : set$ in Γ, $a, b : A$ in Γ	$a(x_1 \ldots, x_n) = b(x_1 \ldots, x_n) : A(x_1 \ldots, x_n)$ $(x_1 : A, \ldots, x_n : A_n(x, \ldots, x_{n-1}))$

Table 4.4: Specifications of contexts

For simplicity, we will use vector notation so that

$$J(x_1, \ldots, x_n)(x_1 : A_1, \ldots, x_n : A_n(x_1, \ldots, x_{n-1}))$$

can be written as

$$J(\mathbf{x})(\mathbf{x} : \Gamma).$$

A specification should be understood as a function. A specification of a context Γ to another context Δ can be described by the following function:
Let Γ and Δ be contexts where Δ is a specification of Γ, $\Gamma \leq_{\mathbf{f}} \Delta$. When

$$\Gamma = x_1 : A_1, \ldots, x_n : A_n(x_1, \ldots, x_{n-1}) \text{ and}$$

$$\Delta = y_1 : B_1, \ldots, y_m : B_m(y_1, \ldots, y_{m-1}),$$

4.3. Specification and contexts

the function f from Δ to Γ is a sequence of functions, $\mathbf{f} : \Delta \to \Gamma$ where

$$f_1(y_1, \ldots, y_m) : A_1(y_1 : B_1, \ldots, y_m : B_m(y_1, \ldots, y_{m-1})),$$
$$\ldots,$$
$$f_n(y_1, \ldots, y_m) : A_n(f_1(y_1, \ldots, y_m), \ldots,$$
$$f_{n-1}(y_1, \ldots, y_m))(y_1 : B_1, \ldots, y_m : B_m(y_1, \ldots, y_{m-1})).$$

When $\Gamma \leq_{\mathbf{f}} \Delta$ any set A in Γ is also in Δ, $A(\mathbf{f}(\mathbf{y})) : set(\mathbf{y} : \Delta)$. This holds for all judgments in Γ. (Ranta 1991, pp. 87-88)

Chapter 5

IMMANENT REASONING

5.1 PRELIMINARY NOTIONS OF DIALOGICAL LOGIC

Dialogical logic should not be considered a logical system by itself, but rather a framework where we can interpret different logical systems. It may be considered as a general approach to meaning. We can therefore use it to develop and compare different logical systems. The definitions, rules and descriptions of the dialogical system and the dialogical explanation of CTT, called immanent reasoning in this section is taken from Rahman, McConaughey, et al.'s (2018) book *Immanent reasoning or Equality in Action*.

The idea is to consider meaning as being constituted in the argumentative interaction between two agents. The meaning is developed by showing how it may be used in interaction. We may trace this back to Wittgenstein's idea that meaning is use.

The connection between CTT and dialogical logic does also seem to be strong. We can again refer to Wittgenstein and his remark that one should not go outside language when trying to determine meaning. In CTT, we do not consider syntax and semantics to be distinguished in a similar way as is done in classical logic. For propositions, we have formation rules that explain when they can be formed and they are described by inference rules, not as distinct syntactical rules. In the dialogical approach, meaning and semantics are considered to be their use in interaction. Because of this aspect, we may consider the dialogical approach to be a pragmatical approach to meaning. If we link CTT to the dialogical approach, we do not only consider syntax to be a kind of semantics, but both to actually be part of the pragmatics. What we end up with is a system where we do not distinguish syntax, semantics and pragmatics from each other. The pragmatical aspect found in the dialogical approach is the interaction. Interaction in this sense is in some way an obligation of interaction, which in turn is a moral notion. In this sense, logic is considered to be a result of the moral obligation of interacting. Logic is not something essentially fundamental, but it is rather found in the investigation of ethics.

The dialogical approach is based on a dialogue between two players. These players may be called 'Opponent' and 'Proponent'. The two players argue on a thesis. A thesis is a statement that is subject for the dialogue. The Proponent begins by stating the thesis and the Opponent will try to challenge the thesis. The Proponent will again try to defend the thesis from the Opponents attacks.

Particle rules

Particle rules are rules for logical constants and they are concerned with determining allowed moves in a play. It is easily understood when using the example of chess, the particle rules provide the rules for how the individual pieces may move on the board. They decide how to formulate a proper challenge and defence to constants. A certain constant requires an appropriate attack, and this attack requires an appropriate defence. The particle rules therefore decide how reasons are asked for and given in different kinds of statements. They do therefore also provide the meaning of the statement. The meaning of each logical constant is understood by how it may be challenged and defended in a dialogue. We do therefore not require

5.1. Preliminary notions of dialogical logic

a distinct semantical framework to develop meaning, but instead the meaning of logical constants is provided in the dialogue itself, namely in the way the players interact. (Rahman, McConaughey, et al. 2018, pp. 58-59)

Structural rules

Structural rules decide the course of the dialogue. They provide how the play starts, how it is played and how it ends. In chess, examples of structural rules are how the pieces should be placed in the starting position, who starts and how one wins. The structural rules do not intend to give meaning to logical constants, but rather to explain the limits of the interaction between the players to attain certain logical features. The distinction between particle rules and structural rules enables us to separate between the meaning of what is said and what kind of game it is used in.

A particular structural rule in the dialogical approach of immanent reasoning is the copy-cat rule, called the Socratic rule in the CTT formulation. It restricts the Proponent to only assert elementary judgments that have previously been stated by the Opponent. The particularity is that it only restricts one of the players. It makes the rules for the Opponent and the Proponent being slightly different from each other. The Copy-cat rule explains the analyticity in the dialogue as it ensures that the defence of the thesis does not depend on any element outside of the thesis itself. Since the Proponent cannot bring any elementary statement into the play, except when it has already been conceded by the Opponent and the moves have to follow the particle rules, the statements of the Proponent is only those that can be found in the meaning of the thesis. (Rahman, McConaughey, et al. 2018, pp. 59-60)

General definitions of the dialogical language

The language of standard dialogical logic $\mathcal{L}$ is a first-order language that includes propositional connectives, first-order quantifiers, a finite set of individual variables, a finite set of individual constants and a finite set of predicates. The two players **O** and **P**, utterance ! and question ? are also introduced to $\mathcal{L}$. When it does not matter whether it is **O** or **P**, we will write **X** and **Y** where $\mathbf{X} \neq \mathbf{Y}$. (Rahman, McConaughey, et al. 2018, pp. 76-77)

Move
A move is of the form $\mathbf{X} - e$ where e is either of the form $!\varphi$ for some formula φ in $\mathcal{L}$ or of the forms specified in the particle rules.

Play
A play ς is a sequence of moves σ that respects the particle rules and the structural rules where every move in σ has been assigned a position p_σ.

Challenge and defence
Challenge and defence are certain moves defined by the particle rules that are given based on a posit.

- Let σ denote a sequence of moves. Let the function ρ_σ, starting from 0, assign a position to every move in σ.
- To certain moves $\mathcal{M}$ in σ, the function $\mathcal{F}_\sigma$ assigns a pair $[m, Z]$, where m is a smaller position than $\rho_\sigma(\mathcal{M})$ and Z is either A or D. A stands for 'attack' and D stands for 'defence'.

Dialogical game
A dialogical game $\mathcal{D}(\varphi)$ for a formula φ is the set of all plays with φ as a thesis.

5.2 Standard dialogical logic

Rules of dialogical logic

Particle rules

We can distinguish the rules of the language of standard dialogical logic $\mathcal{L}$ in two categories, particle rules and structural rules. Particle rules relate to what counts as a move at a certain stage, attack or defence for a certain formula. Structural rules explain how the particle rules should be used.

The standard particle rules can be given after introducing utterance ! and question ?. !φ means that a player claims that φ is the case. ?φ means that a player asks the other player whether φ is the case. We use **X** and **Y** for players when it does not matter whether it is the Proponent or the Opponent that has the original posit. **X** can be either the Proponent or the Opponent as long as **Y** is the opposite. We will explain the meaning of the logical constants in the dialogical approach by the particle rules. This means to not define them by their truth-values, but rather by how they can be challenged and defended. We will use the definitions given in Rahman, McConaughey, et al. (2018, pp. 60-62)

Conjunction

Truth-functionally, a conjunction is true when both of its conjuncts are true. Dialogically, the meaning of the conjunction is that the challenger may choose what conjunct of the conjunction to challenge by a request. The defender has to answer with the conjunct that has been challenged by the challenger. The defender does not have a choice. Since the challenger of a conjunction is not bound to any posit by the challenge, the challenge is a request. (Rahman, McConaughey, et al. 2018, p. 60) In a situation when a player posits a conjunction, **X** ! $A \land B$, we can therefore end up with two situations:

- The challenger may challenge the left side of the conjunction, **Y** ? $L^\wedge$, and the defender must then provide the left conjunct as a defence, **X** ! A;

- The challenger may challenge the right side of the conjunction, **Y** ? $R^\wedge$, and the defender must then provide the right conjunct as a defence, **X** ! B.

The particle rules for the conjunction can also be given by the following scheme:

Move	Challenge	Defence
X ! $A \wedge B$	**Y** ? $L^\wedge$ or **Y** ? $R^\wedge$ **Y** has the choice	**X** ! A respectively **X** ! B

Disjunction

Truth-functionally a disjunction is true when one of the disjuncts is true. Dialogically, the meaning of the disjunction is that the defender may choose what disjunct of the disjunction to defend. The challenger has to demand the defender to provide one of the disjuncts, but cannot decide which one. The challenger does not have a choice. Since the challenger of a disjunction is not bound to any posit in the challenge, the challenge is a request. (Rahman, McConaughey, et al. 2018, p. 61) In a situation when a player posits a disjunction, **X** ! $A \vee B$, we can therefore end up with two situations:

- After the challenger has challenged the disjunction, **Y** ?$_\vee$, the defender can provide the left disjunct as a defence, **X** ! A;

- After the challenger has challenged the disjunction, **Y** ?$_\vee$, the defender can provide the right disjunct as a defence, **X** ! B.

5.2. Standard dialogical logic

The particle rules for the disjunction can also be given in the following scheme:

Move	Challenge	Defence
X ! $A \vee B$	**Y** ?$_\vee$	**X** ! A or **X** ! B **X** has the choice

Implication
An implication is true when either the consequent is true or the antecedent is false. Dialogically, the meaning of the implication is that the challenger posits the antecedent and the defender defends it by stating the consequent. In the case of an implication, none of the players has a choice. (Rahman, McConaughey, et al. 2018, p. 61) In a situation when a player posits an implication, **X** ! $A \supset B$, we can therefore end up with one situation:

- A challenger that challenges an implication states the antecedent, **Y** ! A, and the defender has to provide the consequent as a defence, **X** ! B.

The particle rule for the implication can also be given in the following scheme:

Move	Challenge	Defence
X ! $A \supset B$	**Y** ! A	**X** ! B

Negation
A negation is true when the statement that is negated is false. Dialogically, the meaning of the negation is that the challenger states the negated proposition. There is no defence to this challenge. As in the case of an implication, none of the players has a choice.

We use the symbol — to represent that there is no defence. (Rahman, McConaughey, et al. 2018, pp. 61-62) In a situation when a player posits a negation, **X** ! $\neg A$, we can therefore end up with one situation:

- A challenger that challenges a negation states the negated statement, **Y** ! A, and the defender cannot defend it.

The particle rule for the negation can also be given in the following scheme:

Move	Challenge	Defence
X ! $\neg A$	**Y** ! A	—

Universal quantifier

The universal quantifier means that every individual that is an instance of the bound variable satisfies the proceeding statement. Dialogically, the rule for the universal quantifier is similar to the rule for the conjunction. The challenger chooses any individual constant a_i and requests the substitution for every free occurrence of the variable x. The defender then has to replace every free occurrence of x with the chosen constant in the statement. (Rahman, McConaughey, et al. 2018, pp. 78-79) In a situation where a player posits a universal quantifier, **X** ! $\forall x B(x)$, there is one situation for every potential substitution of x:

- A challenger to a universal quantifier requests a substitution of every free occurrence of x with an individual constant a_i, chosen by the challenger, **Y** ? $[x/a_i]$, and the defender must state the requested proposition where every free x has been substituted with a_i, **X** ! $B(x/a_i)$.

5.2. Standard dialogical logic

The particle rules for the universal quantifier can also be given in the following scheme:

Move	Challenge	Defence
$X \: ! \: \forall x B(x)$	$Y \: ? \: [x/a_i]$ Y chooses x	$X \: ! \: B(x/a_i)$

Existential quantifier

The existential quantifier means that at least one individual that is an instance of the bound variable satisfies the proceeding statement. Dialogically, the rules for the existential quantifier are similar to those for the disjunction. The challenger requests the substitution for every free occurrence of the variable x with some constant. The defender then has to replace every free occurrence of x with an individual constant a_i chosen by the defender. (Rahman, McConaughey, et al. 2018, pp. 78-79) In a situation where a player posits an existential quantifier, $X \: ! \: \exists x B(x)$, there is one situation for every potential substitution of x:

- A challenger to an existential quantifier requests a substitution of every free occurrence of x by some individual constant, $Y \: ?_\exists$, and the defender must state the requested proposition where every free x has been substituted with an individual constant a_i chosen by the defender, $X \: ! \: B(x/a_i)$.

The particle rules for the existential quantifier can also be given in the following scheme:

Move	Challenge	Defence
$X \: ! \: \exists x B(x)$	$Y \: ?_\exists$	$X \: ! \: B(x/a_i)$ when $1 \leq i \leq n$ X chooses x

Particle rules for standard dialogical logic

The different particle rules have properties that distinguish them from each other by how they are used in a play. This is shown by Table 5.1. (Rahman, McConaughey, et al. 2018, p. 79)

	Nature of the challenge	Who has the choice	Step to
Conjunction	Request	Challenger	State the requested proposition
Universal quantification	Request	Challenger	State the requested proposition
Disjunction	Request	Defender	State the desired proposition
Existential quantification	Request	Defender	State the desired proposition
Implication	Statement	No choice	State the consequent
Negation	Statement	No choice	None

Table 5.1: Particle rules in play

To sum up, the standard particle rules are given in Table 5.2. (Rahman, McConaughey, et al. 2018, p. 79)

5.2. Standard dialogical logic

Move	Challenge	Defence
X ! $A \wedge B$	**Y** ? $L^\wedge$ or **Y** ? $R^\wedge$ **Y** has the choice	**X** ! A respectively **X** ! B
X ! $A \vee B$	**Y** ?$_\vee$	**X** ! A or **X** ! B **X** has the choice
X ! $A \supset B$	**Y** ! A	**X** ! B
X ! $\neg A$	**Y** ! A	—
X ! $\forall x B(x)$	**Y** ? $[x/a_i]$ **Y** chooses x	**X** ! $B(x/a_i)$
X ! $\exists x B(x)$	**Y** ?$_\exists$	**X** ! $B(x/a_i)$ when $1 \leq i \leq n$ **X** chooses x

Table 5.2: Standard dialogical particle rules

Structural rules

The structural rules provide the global meaning. The structural rules are concerned what we may can call the frames of the dialogue. They specify how to start, what moves that are allowed, the end of the play and the winner of the play. A play is said to be terminal when there are no further moves that are possible to play in accordance with the rules. A play is said to be **X**-terminal if the last move in a terminal play is an **X**-move. (Rahman, McConaughey, et al. 2018, pp. 82)

SR0 (Starting rule)
The first structural rule is the starting rule. The Opponent begins by stating the initial concessions. The Proponent states the thesis in question and this move is labelled move 0. Beginning with the Opponent, the players choose their repetition ranks. They decide how many times the players can attack or defend a single move in the play. After the initial concessions, usually labelled $I, II, III, ...,$ the play starts by the Proponent stating the thesis,

$$p_\varsigma(\mathbf{P}!\varphi) = 0$$
$$p_\varsigma(\mathbf{O}n := i) = 1$$
$$p_\varsigma(\mathbf{P}m := j) = 2.$$

For all $\varsigma \in \mathcal{D}(\varphi)$, i and j are positive integers and φ is a complex sentence in $\mathcal{D}$. For all ς in $\mathcal{D}(\varphi)$, ς starts by **P** positing φ. This happens in move 0. In move 1 the Opponent chooses his repetition rank. In move 2 the Proponent chooses his repetition rank. This is done in order to ensure that every play is finite. (Clerbout and Rahman 2015, pp. 12-13)

SR1c (Classical game-playing rule)
The next rule is the classical game-playing rule. After the choices of repetition rank, each move corresponds to either an attack or a defence in compliance with the particle rules.

- Let $\varsigma \in \mathcal{D}(\varphi)$. For every M in ς with $p_\varsigma(M) < 2$ we have $F_\varsigma(M) = [m', Z]$ with $m' < p_\varsigma(M)$ and $Z \in \{C, D\}$.

- Let r be the repetition rank of player **X** and $\varsigma \in \mathcal{D}(\varphi)$ such that

5.2. Standard dialogical logic

- the last member of ς is a **Y**-move,
- M_0 is a **Y**-move of position m_0 in ς and
- $M_1, ..., M_n$ are **X**-moves in ς such that $F_\varsigma(M_1) = ... = F_\varsigma(M_n) = [m_0, Z]$.

The first part of this rule states that every move after choosing the repetition ranks is a challenge or a defence. The second part of the rule states how the repetition ranks limit the maximum number of times the players can challenge or defend a move by the opposite player. If we are in a classical framework, this rule should be sufficient. If we are in an intuitionistic framework we should add the condition SR1i.

SR1i (Intuitionistic game-playing rule)
If we want to be in an intuitionistic framework, we can simply add a further condition on the SR1c (Classical game-playing rule): A player can only answer to the last non-answered challenge of the other player. This condition is called the condition of Last Duty First and its addition changes the framework from classical to intuitionistic.

SR2 (Copy-cat rule)
The next rule is the Copy-cat rule. The Proponent may not state an elementary statement if the Opponent has not stated it before. In this formulation, a play cannot have an elementary statement as a thesis, since an elementary statement cannot be challenged.

Let ψ be an elementary sentence, N be the move **P** ! ψ and M be the move **O** ! ψ. A sequence ς of moves is a play only if we have: if $N \in \varsigma$, then $M \in \varsigma$ and $p_\varsigma(M) < p_\varsigma(N)$.

This rule states that the Proponent can only play an elementary sentence if the Opponent already played it.

SR3 (Winning rule)
The last rule is the winning rule.

Player **X** wins the play ς only if it is **X**-terminal.

This rule states that the player that has the *last word* is the winner of the play.

Equality and example of a play

In important aspect of the dialogical approach is the symmetry between the players. The particle rules and the meaning of logical constants are player independent. This means that the challenger can be any of the two players, the Opponent or the Proponent. The same goes for the defender. This is important because it is the particle rules that give meaning to the logical constants. If the particle rules were to be different for the two players, we would struggle explaining how they could be speaking about the same thing. When particle rules are the same for both players, we call them symmetric. The symmetry of the particle rules enables the dialogical approach to be immune to connectives such as Prior's 'tonk'. These kinds of trivialising connectives are often not possible to implement in the dialogical approach without breaking the symmetry. If we try to formalise 'tonk' in the dialogical approach, we discover that they require a particle rule that is different for the Proponent and the Opponent. By making the restriction of symmetry on particle rules, we exclude many variants of trivialising connectives. (Rahman, McConaughey, et al. 2018, p. 83)

In the dialogical approach, there is a distinction between symmetry and harmony. Symmetry is player independence for the particle rules, while harmony is an aspect of the structural rules and the strategy level. The structural rules are not exactly the same for both players. In particular there are two rules that are different for the players. The starting rule (SR0) states that the player that begins the play will be the Proponent. The reason for this is simply that there can be only one player starting the play. The other rule is the

5.2. Standard dialogical logic

Copy-cat rule in the classical framework, called the Socratic rule in the CTT framework. This rule states that the Proponent can only state an elementary statement if the same elementary statement has already been stated by the Opponent in an earlier move. It is a restriction on the Proponent's moves. The reason for this is to keep analyticity in the moves of the Proponent. The Proponent has to base his dialogue on only what he can force the Opponent to state by the thesis stated in the beginning. Anything that the Proponent may state will therefore be justified within the dialogue. The justification then arises from the Opponent's statements. (Rahman, McConaughey, et al. 2018, pp. 79-81)

SR2s (Special Copy-cat rule)

In the original formulation of the Copy-cat rule, there cannot be a play with an elementary statement as a thesis since they cannot be challenged. However, we may formulate a special Copy-cat rule where this is possible. The Opponent may in this rule challenge an elementary statement of the Proponent by **O** $?_A$ and the Proponent defend it by stating that the Opponent already stated it at move n, by **P** ! $sic(n)$,

Move	Challenge	Defence
P ! A For elementary A	**O** $?_A$	**P** ! $sic(n)$ **P** indicates that **O** stated A at move n

This rule is a structural rule that is not player independent. We can see that as the Proponent is explicitly stated as the defender while the Opponent is the challenger. It introduces a way to have a play with elementary statements, and the main idea is that the grounds that the Proponent has for stating the proposition is the same that the Opponent had for stating the very same proposition. The justification for the Proponent to state the elementary statement is the fact that the Opponent already said it. (Rahman, McConaughey, et al. 2018, p. 83)

Notation and example of a play

We may illustrate the rules with an example of a play. This is a ς in $\mathcal{D}(p \supset (p \vee q))$:

P ! $A \supset (A \vee B)$
O $n := 1$
P $m := 2$
O ! A
P ! $A \vee B$
O ?$_\vee$
P ! A.

In order to make organise the challenges and defences we write this sequence of moves in the way described by Play 1.

	O			P	
				! $A \supset (A \vee B)$	0
1	$n := 1$			$m := 2$	2
3	! A	0		! $A \vee B$	4
5	?$_\vee$	4		! A	6

Play 1: Example of notation

The first row shows the players. The first and the sixth columns show p_ς, the position of the moves. The first column shows the position of the moves played by the Opponent and the sixth shows the position of the moves played by the Proponent. The third and

5.2. Standard dialogical logic

the fourth columns show $F_ç$, they describe the position of the move that they challenge. The third column is for the challenges posed by the Opponent and the fourth for the Proponent. The defence to a challenge is written on the same line as the challenge. The second and the fifth columns show e, what is being uttered by the player. Together with the first row these columns give M, the moves. The second column is the utterance of the Opponent and the fifth column is the utterance of the Proponent.

In move 0, the Proponent states the thesis, the play is about $\mathcal{D}(A \supset (A \vee B))$. In move 1 and 2, the players choose their repetition ranks r, n for the Opponent and m for the Proponent. In move 3, the Opponent challenges the implication in move 0 by playing the antecedent. In move 4, the Proponent defends the challenge in move 3 with the consequent of the implication in move 0. In move 5, the Opponent challenges the disjunction in move 4, demanding the Proponent to show one the disjuncts from move 4. In move 6, the Proponent defends this challenge by stating the left side of the conjunction, already stated by the Opponent in move 3. After move 6, the Opponent does not have any possible moves left to do and the play is won by the Proponent. The Proponent has the last word.

This is however just one play in $\mathcal{D}(A \supset (A \vee B))$ and in order to ensure that the Proponent actually has a winning strategy and did not win by accident or luck, for example if the Opponent had played a bad move, we have to introduce the extensive form of games. This means to consider all possible plays in $\mathcal{D}(A \supset (A \vee B))$, generally $\mathcal{D}(\varphi)$.

We will also demonstrate another example play, namely the rule of the excluded middle. This is a good example both of the difference between the classical and the intuitionistic game-playing rule and of the importance of the repetition ranks. The classical demonstration of the rule of the excluded middle is given in Play 2.

	O			P	
				$A \vee \neg A$	0
1	$n := 1$			$m := 2$	2
3	$?_\vee$	0		$!\neg A$	4
5	$!A$	4		—	
				$!A$	6

Play 2: Demonstration of the rule of the excluded middle, classical

Move 0 is the statement of the thesis. In move 1 and 2, the players choose their repetition ranks. In move 3, the Opponent challenges the disjunction. In move 4, the Proponent defends the challenge in move 3 by stating the left part of the disjunction, the negated A. In move 5, the Opponent challenges the negation in the move 4. The Proponent cannot answer to this challenge, because there is no defence to a negation. Because the Proponent chose the repetition rank to be 2, he can defend the challenge from move 3 one more time. Now he can also choose A as a defence because the Opponent already stated A in move 5. The Opponent does not have any possible moves left to do and the Proponent wins the play. The corresponding example for intuitionistic logic is given in Play 3.

	O			P	
				$! A \vee \neg A$	0
1	$n := 1$			$m := 2$	2
3	$?_\vee$	0		$! \neg A$	4
5	$! A$	4		—	

Play 3: Demonstration of the rule of the excluded middle, intuitionistic

5.2. Standard dialogical logic

In the intuitionistic demonstration of the third excluded, move 0 to move 5 are the same as in the classical demonstration. The difference is that the Proponent is allowed to defend the challenge at move 3 again at move 6 in the classical variant. The intuitionistic game-playing rule prevents him from this by the condition of Last Duty First. In move 5, the Opponent challenges the negation, that cannot be defended, in move 4 and the last open challenge is therefore the challenge in move 5. In the intuitionistic variant, there are no more legal moves after move 5 and the Opponent wins the play. (Rahman, McConaughey, et al. 2018, pp. 84-85)

Extensive forms and strategies

Extensive forms

The extensive form of a dialogical game is the collection of all possible plays for a given thesis. In the parallel to chess, it is all potential variants that may be played given a certain starting position.

The extensive form of a dialogical game $\mathcal{D}(\varphi)$ is the tree representation. Such tree representation has infinitely many immediate branches after stating the thesis. This is because the players can choose any positive integer they want as repetition rank. This does not however mean that the branches can be infinitely long because the repetition rank needs to be finite. For a $\mathcal{D}(\varphi)$, the extensive form $\mathfrak{E}_\varphi$ is a triple (T, ℓ, S) such that:

- Every node t in T is labelled with a move occurring in $\mathcal{D}(\varphi)$;
- $\ell : T \mapsto \mathbb{N}$;
- $S \subseteq T^2$ when
    - there is a unique t_0 (the root) in T such that $\ell(t_0) = 0$, and t_0 is labelled with the thesis of the game,
    - for every $t \neq t_0$ there is a unique t' such that $t'St$,

- for every t and t' in T, if tSt' then $\ell(t') = \ell(t) + 1$ and
- let $\varsigma \in \mathcal{D}(\varphi)$ such that $p_\varsigma(M') = p_\varsigma(M) + 1$. If t and t' are respectively labelled with M and M', then tSt'.

This is a normal definition of tree representations. The first part states that every node has labelled a move. The second part states that there is a ranking for every node in T that each yields a natural number. The third part states that there is a relation on the nodes in T that is transitive. (Rahman, McConaughey, et al. 2018, p. 90)

Description of strategies

Based on the extensive forms, we may now introduce strategies. A winning strategy is a way for a player to win, no matter what the other player does. The strategy level provides a way to compare different plays with the same thesis. This level is not an aspect of a play, but rather an aspect of the extensive form of a game. A winning strategy is built from the point of view of a specific player, the Opponent or the Proponent. This means that they are perspectives on the possible plays of a thesis and the strategies are not actually played by the players. More particularly, we are usually interested in the **P**-winning strategies, as they are what links a dialogue to logical validity or truth. A **P**-winning strategy is a strategy that describes how the Proponent may win the play, no matter the Opponent's choices. A **P**-winning strategy therefore takes account of every alternative that the Opponent has to develop the play, and makes sure that the Proponent may win in every situation.

The procedure for creating a **P**-winning strategy is first to construct a normal play. Then we start by the last move and go progressively back to the first move, but stop every time there is a choice made by the Opponent. From this choice, the play is branched and we create a play as if the Opponent had chosen differently, but with the same moves earlier in the play. The procedure is then repeated on the new branch and when this have been done, the

5.2. Standard dialogical logic

procedure continues further in the original play. When we have looked at all choices made by the Opponent, we can see if the Proponent has a winning strategy. If the Opponent won any of the plays, the Proponent does not have a winning strategy. Based on the particle rules described in the classical dialogical logic, the Opponent has a choice in the cases of challenging a conjunction or a universal quantification and in defending a disjunction or an existential quantification. (Rahman, McConaughey, et al. 2018, pp. 89-91)

In order to develop a strategy, we have to make some initial assumptions. Since the strategy levels are based upon possible plays, it means that they are aspects not in, but about plays. We will therefore use the notation $\mathcal{P}_1, \mathcal{P}_2, ...$ to represent different plays. In classical logic, the notion of validity is linked to having a **P**-winning strategy. If the Proponent has a winning strategy for a thesis, the thesis is logically valid. That a play is won by the Proponent is understood as a play being **P**-terminal. The following definitions and assumptions are found in Rahman, McConaughey, et al. (2018, pp. 91-96)

Assumptions on repetition ranks
We assume 1 to be the repetition rank for **O**.[1]

The repetition rank for **P** will have to be chosen so that it is sufficient for **P** to win the first play. When making new plays, **P** needs to choose a repetition rank that is sufficient to win that actual play.[2]

---

[1] **O** does not have any restriction from the copy-cat rule. **O** may therefore always choose the move in his interest. If some bad move is made, **O** may change this move in a new play.

[2] The repetition rank does not have to be sufficient to win every possible play, but only to be sufficient to win every individual play. **P** may choose a new repetition rank in the new plays.

Assumption on move preferences for the Opponent

Whenever **O** has to choose an individual constant, **O** will choose a new one.[3]

Whenever **O** can challenge a move where **P** has several defensive moves, **O** will challenge before making any other moves.[4]

O-decisions

We can distinguish five different cases where the Opponent makes a decision in $\mathcal{P}_n$:

1. When **O** *challenges a conjunction or an existential*, **O** must choose whether to ask for the left side or the right side;

2. When **O** *defends a disjunction*, **O** must choose whether to defend the left side or the right side of the disjunction;

3. When **P** has challenged **O** by stating the antecedent of an implication, that **O** *has an implication to defend*, **O** must choose whether to defend this implication by stating its consequent or to counterattack, which means that **O** challenges the antecedent that **P** stated to attack the implication;

4. When **O** *defends an existential*, **O** must choose a new constant to substitute the variable bound by the existential;

5. When **O** *challenges a universal*, **O** must choose a new constant to substitute the variable bound by the universal.

---

[3]It is the best option for **O** to always choose a new constant because **P** is restricted by the Copy-cat rule. The best attempt to block the use of the Copy-cat rule is to choose a new individual constant every time there is a choice.

[4]This is also an assumption that is in the best interest of **O** since it forces **P** to make a choice as early in the play as possible. **O** may therefore try to make **P** make the choice early, so **O** may adapt the later play on this choice.

5.2. Standard dialogical logic

Explaining O-decisions
In the two last cases, 4. *challenging an existential* and 5. *defending a universal*, we already stipulated that **O** will choose a new, unused constant to replace the variable. The procedure for **O**-decisions is therefore relevant to the three first cases, 1. *challenging a conjunction or an existential*, 2. *defending a disjunction* and 3. *having an implication to defend*. This is shown in Table 5.3. (Rahman, McConaughey, et al. 2018, pp. 93-94)

O has a choice and takes a decision when:	
O challenges a ...	**O** defends a ...
Conjunction	Disjunction
Existential	Implication

Table 5.3: Choices for the Opponent

Choices and using up options
A decision has *used up* the available options if and only if this decision chooses an option and the other option has previously been chosen.

A decision has *not used up* the available options if **O** only chooses one of two available options and the other option has not previously been chosen. Because of **O**'s repetition rank being 1, only one option might be chosen. The other option that remains not chosen is *unused*.

Definition of dependent moves
When there is a chain of applications of particle rules leading from move M' to move M, we say that M *depends on* M'.

Left- and right-decisions
- A *left-decision* is when **O** either

- defends the left side of a disjunction,
  - challenges the left side of a conjunction or
  - counterattacks instead of defending an implication.

- A *right-decision* is when **O** either
  - defends the right side of a disjunction,
  - challenges the right side of a conjunction or
  - defends an implication instead of counterattacking.

Last unused decision
Proceeding bottom up in the order of moves in play m, the last decision that is taken by **O** that does *not use up* the available options is called the *last unused decision*.

Labelling decisions for conjunctions and disjunctions
When a decision is taken, the moves are labelled. For conjunction and disjunction, the label is simply placed on the right hand side of the move in the following forms:

- $[\sigma_n, ...]$ is the label when the left option has been chosen and the right option is still unused;

- $[..., \sigma_n]$ is the label when the right option has been chosen and the left option is still unused;

- $[\sigma_n, \sigma_m]$ is the label when both options have been chosen and the decision is used up, where the left has been taken in play m and the left decision has been taken in play n.

Labelling decisions for implications and subplays
Whenever **O**, in play $\mathcal{P}_n$, has a choice that is motivated by an implication, there will be opened two *subplays*, $\mathcal{P}_{n.L}$ and $\mathcal{P}_{n.R}$ such that

5.2. Standard dialogical logic

- $\mathcal{P}_{\mathbf{n.L}}$ indicates a subplay where **O** takes a decision to attack the antecedent, a left decision, and
- $\mathcal{P}_{\mathbf{n.R}}$ indicates a subplay where **O** takes a decision to defend the implication, a right decision.

When both subplays have been opened, the implication has been used up.[5]

Starting a subplay

Every subplay starts with the **O**-move immediately succeeding the **P**-move that challenged the implication that was stated by **O**.[6]

The first move of the play $\mathcal{P}_{n.R}$ is the defence of the implication and graphically, dots are inserted in the upperplay in the space of defence and the subplay in the space of challenge.

---

[5]The reason for dividing the play into two subplays is to avoid **P** to get an unfair advantage as he otherwise would be able to use the information that is developed in one subplay as defence in the other one. The point is therefore for **P** to win using only information that has been developed in the present subplay. The subplays are not full plays, but only a division of a play that is introduced in order to check **P**'s moves. The representation of a play and the division into two subplays should be considered a graphical device that presents both options in the same main play. Such opening of two subplays in a play is also called *branching rule*. The motivation for this rule is found on the strategy level, as it is relevant for developing a demonstration.

[6]An implication that has been challenged in move n in a play $\mathcal{P}_n$, will create two subplays, $\mathcal{P}_{n.L}$ and $\mathcal{P}_{n.R}$, where both will start with move $n+1$.

Moving from subplays to upperplays

P may be allowed to use a move, given by **O** in the subplay, in the upperplay. When this is the case, it will be indexed according to what subplay it stems from.[7]

P- and O-terminal plays

A play $\mathcal{P}_n$ is **P**-terminal if and only if every path starting with the thesis, continuing with $\mathcal{P}_{n.L}$, $\mathcal{P}_{n.R}$, and all further subplays are **P**-terminal.

A play $\mathcal{P}_n$ is **O**-terminal if and only if at least one of the paths is **O**-terminal.[8]

---

[7]For example, if **P** uses a subplay $\mathcal{P}_{n.R}$ in move 12, it will have the index $12[\mathcal{P}_{n.R}]$. We may use the following example to show how subplays are used together with upperplays:

	O			P		
			$!\,((A \supset B) \supset A) \supset A$		0	
1	$n := 1$		$m := 2$		2	
3	$!\,(A \supset B) \supset A$	0	$!\,A$		$6[\mathcal{P}_{1.L}]$	$(\mathcal{P}_1)$
			$!\,A$		$6[\mathcal{P}_{1.R}]$	
	...		3	$!\,A \supset B$		4

5	$!\,A$	4			
	P wins.				$(\mathcal{P}_{1.L})$

5	$!\,A$			...	
	P wins.				$(\mathcal{P}_{1.R})$

[8]These definitions correspond to the previous definition of terminal plays, but makes explicit the role of subplays in the definition.

5.2. Standard dialogical logic

Presentation of the core

The core of a **P**-winning strategy is a collection of plays $\mathcal{P}_1, \mathcal{P}_2, \mathcal{P}_3...$ that is generated from the explained procedure. We assume that we have a play $\mathcal{P}_n$ that is won by **P** with respect to the previously described assumptions. The description of this procedure is taken from Rahman, McConaughey, et al. (2018, pp. 96-99).

Procedure

Step 0: Starting with a P-terminal $\mathcal{P}_1$

We start with a play $\mathcal{P}_1$ that is **P**-terminal when **O**'s repetition rank equals 1. The repetition rank of **P** should be high enough for **P** to win this play. If there is no such repetition rank to be found, we cannot find a winning strategy for **P** and the process should stop.

Step 1: Unused decisions?

If there are remaining unused decisions for **O** in $\mathcal{P}_n$, go to step 2. Otherwise, if there are no remaining unused decisions for **O** in $\mathcal{P}_n$, go to step 4.

Step 2: Using up decisions

By proceeding from the bottom to the top, do the following for **O**'s last unused decision in $\mathcal{P}_n$:

- For a conjunction or a disjunction that has not yet been labelled, label $[\delta_n, ...]$ for left decision and $[..., \delta_n]$ for right decision;

- For a conjunction or an existential that has already been labelled, open a new play by applying substep 2.1. For a disjunction that has already been labelled, open a new play by applying substep 2.2;

- For an implication, open two subplays by applying substep 2.3.

Step 2.1: Decision concerning a challenge of a conjunction or an existential

If the decision δ concerns a conjunction or an existential, a new play $\mathcal{P}_{m=n+1}$ should be opened where the move uses the other decision option, following:

- The repetition rank of **P** might be changed;

- Take the left-decision if $\mathcal{P}_n$ is a right-decision and take the right decision if $\mathcal{P}_n$ is a left-decision. In this way, both sides of the conjunction or existential ends up being challenged by two different plays, $\mathcal{P}_n$ and $\mathcal{P}_m$;

- The decision in $\mathcal{P}_m$ should be labelled $[\delta_m, \delta_n]$ in the case of a left-decision and $[\delta_n, \delta_m]$ in the case of a right-decision. This labelling shows that both available options have been used in the decision;

- The new play continues as if the challenge of the conjunction or existential had not taken place in $\mathcal{P}_n$;

- The moves in $\mathcal{P}_n$ previous to the decision δ_n should be imported in the new play;

- Go to step 3 if the new play is **O**-terminal and if not, go to step 1.

Step 2.2: Decision concerning a defence of a disjunction

If the decision δ concerns a defence of a disjunction, a new play $\mathcal{P}_{m=n+1}$ should be opened, where the move uses the other decision option, following:

- The repetition rank of **P** might be changed.

- Take the left-decision if $\mathcal{P}_n$ is a right-decision and take the right decision if $\mathcal{P}_n$ is a left-decision. In this way, both sides of the disjunction ends up being defended by two different plays, $\mathcal{P}_n$ and $\mathcal{P}_m$.

5.2. Standard dialogical logic

- The decision in $\mathcal{P}_m$ should be labelled $[\delta_m, \delta_n]$ in the case of a left-decision and $[\delta_n, \delta_m]$ in the case of a right-decision. This labelling shows that both available options have been used in the decision.

- The new play continues as if the challenge of the conjunction or existential had not taken place in $\mathcal{P}_n$.

- The moves in $\mathcal{P}_n$ previous to the decision δ_n should be imported in the new play.

- Go to step 3 if the new play is **O**-terminal and if not, go to step 1.

Step 2.3: Decision concerning an implication

In the case that **O**'s implication is attacked, **O** has a choice whether to defend the implication, by providing the consequent, or to counter-attack, by challenging the antecedent provided by **P**. This provides a branching where we have two subplays, and not two new plays as in the case for conjunction, existential and disjunction.

- **O** may choose to *counterattack* the implication. This is done by starting a new subplay $\mathcal{P}_{n.L}$ with all moves that depend on the counterattack of **O**. If this subplay makes $\mathcal{P}_n$ **O**-terminal, go to step 3 and if not, go to step 1.

- **O** may choose to *defend* the implication. This is done by starting a new subplay $\mathcal{P}_{n.R}$ with all moves that depend on the defence of **O**. If this subplay makes $\mathcal{P}_n$ **O**-terminal, go to step 3 and if not, go to step 1.

Step 3: O-terminal plays

$\mathcal{P}_m$ is **O**-terminal if there are no remaining unused decisions to be taken in $\mathbf{P}_m$. The process should then stop and start again at step 0 with a different play $\mathcal{P}'_0$ such that it is won by **P**. If it is not possible to find such a play, **O** has a way to win and **P** has lost.

Step 4: Stopping the process
If **O** does not have any remaining unused decisions in play $\mathcal{P}_m$, $\mathcal{P}_m$ is **P**-terminal. The process should then stop and **P** has a winning strategy. (Rahman, McConaughey, et al. 2018, pp. 96-99)

Graphic presentation of the core
The graphical presentation can represent the same choices as in the procedure, but because of its tree structure it makes it more comprehensible when there are several **O**-choices to be made. This tree structure also simplifies the metalogical correspondences with sequent calculus and CTT demonstrations.

Graphic presentation without heuristic procedure
We can make a graphic tree presentation of the core where the nodes represent the players' moves as vertical sequences of **P**-steps and **O**-steps. In the case of an **O**-decision, we branch the tree in different plays.

We can describe the development in the following way:

1. The thesis forms the root of the tree.

2. **O** will state any initial concessions and challenge the thesis.

3. The tree will develop with moves of dialogical **P**-steps and **O**-steps until there is a decision to be made by **O**.

4. In the case of a decision of **O**, the tree branches and the sequence continues with one of the options.

5. In the case that **O** wins, that the branch ends with an **O**-move, the procedure terminates.

6. Otherwise, the sequence should continue with the other decision alternative until the end.

5.2. Standard dialogical logic

We might say that this graphic presentation of the core is a description that is built from top to bottom. This means that it starts with the first decision and not the last decision of the first play. This is opposed to the heuristic method presented previously. We can see that we in some sense have two levels to operate with. First we have a tree presentation of the demonstration, and second we have the table presentation of the dialogical background. However, both levels are important for the dialogical approach. We should not consider them as simply two distinct levels, one for the plays and one for the strategies. They should be united and this is what is shown by the heuristic procedure. The link between plays and strategies is what distinguishes the dialogical approach from proof theory. (Rahman, McConaughey, et al. 2018, pp. 104-106)

The tree-shaped graphic presentation of the core
We will assume that the heuristic procedure has been carried out and that we have found and ended up with the core of a **P**-strategy. A graphic tree presentation will then simply be a new way to expose the core. The same assumptions as found in the heuristic procedure will be assumed and we will be able to provide instructions for translating the core of the heuristic table presentation to a graphic tree representation. (Rahman, McConaughey, et al. 2018, pp. 104-106)

To build the graphic presentation of the core, we take the collection of plays that is yielded by the heuristic procedure. The procedure should start with the first play and go on until the last play and for every play it should start at the top and go to the bottom. This should provide a way to go back and forth between the two different expositions of the core without losing important information. The repetition ranks are left implicit, but are still counting in the graphic presentation. The procedure can be described in the following way:

1. The tree begins with the number for the move of the thesis, namely 0;

2. To the right of the move, place the name of the player, namely **P**;

3. To the right of the player, place:

    a) '! *proposition*' when the move is a statement, where *proposition* is the proposition stated or

    b) '? *request*' when the move is a request, where *request* is the matter of the request;

4. Proceed by following the order of the moves and writing each player's move according to the same notation as in step 1 to 3:

    [number of move][**P/O**][! *proposition*/? *request*];

5. To the right of each proposition, place the following:

    a) For a move that is a challenge, place [?*n*], where *n* corresponds to the number of the move that is challenged;

    b) For a move that is a defence, place [!*n*], where *n* corresponds to the number of the move that launched the challenge that this move defends;

6. In the case of a **O**-decision, place between the move and the challenge or defence, the indication of the **O**-decision from the heuristic procedure and branch the tree in the following way:

    a) In the left branch, continue with the play by using **O**'s left decision option;

    b) In the right branch, continue with the play by using **O**'s right decision option.

5.3 Dialogues with play objects

The interpretation of CTT in the dialogical system is called immanent reasoning and implements play objects into dialogues. Dialogues with play objects have been developed in Clerbout and Rahman (2015), but it has been further refined in Rahman, McConaughey, et al. (2018). It is this last work that will be used here and it is also where we get the notion of *immanent reasoning*. This section will be based on that work and we will explain the framework of immanent reasoning in order to have a theoretical foundation for implementing analogical arguments.

The choice of using CTT in the dialogical framework is not random. The constructive type-theoretical approach to meaning does seem to be closely related to its dialogical or game-theoretical counterpart. In CTT, what we might call metalogical features are made explicit on the object language level. The dialogical approach to meaning considers meaning as something that is created during an interaction and all aspects that are used in this constitution should be made explicit in the object language and not on some other meta level. By implementing CTT in the dialogical approach, we might consider the metalogical features as constituting the meaning of the language. By combining CTT and dialogical logic, one seems to agree with two of later Wittgenstein's claims, that one cannot position oneself outside the language in order to determine meaning and his claim for language-games being constitutive of meaning. Language-games are supposedly solving the problem of studying language while still acknowledging the use of the language in the study and therefore its internalised feature. This notion of language-games provides the essence of the dialogical approach since all relevant speech-acts are made explicit. (Rahman, McConaughey, et al. 2018, pp. 112-114)

The local and the global level

The local level

Local reasons

By introducing local reasons, we can explicitly represent the reason for the defence of the particular statement. This is useful in the representation of elementary statements. If the Proponent states an elementary proposition A, he can in the same time provide the reason for his defence of this statement. The Socratic rule is what determines the local reason that is particular to this A. The local reasons do not only provide the foundation of formal truth, but also for material truth in material dialogues. A formal truth is based on a local reason that is established by the dialogue itself, while a material truth is established and is specific for the particular proposition. (Rahman, McConaughey, et al. 2018, pp. 114-115)

Claiming some material truth is done by displaying the local reason that is particular for the given proposition. If for example the Proponent states that 1 is an odd number, the Opponent might challenge this by asking **P** to find a natural number n such that $1 = 2.n + 1$. Assuming that **O** already stated that 0 is a natural number, **P** can use 0 to produce the material truth of the initial statement that 1 is an odd number.

The local reason that is produced is constituted by the material dialogue and this is the essence of the normative approach to meaning that we find in the dialogical framework and in immanent reasoning. The dialogical interaction provides the notion of use for the meaning of both logical constants and elementary propositions. The meaning of an elementary proposition might be said to amount to the role that the Socratic rule prescribes to that particular proposition. Material dialogues are therefore important for the normativity of logic together with the use of language with content. (Rahman, McConaughey, et al. 2018, p. 115)

5.3. Dialogues with play objects

For formal dialogues, the formulation of the Socratic rule is of a form where only the logical constants involved provide the basis for the interaction. It does not depend on the meaning of the particular elementary propositions. For formal dialogues, the local reason is therefore also left to be decided by the Opponent and not created by the Proponent as in the case of material dialogues. We might therefore say that in formal dialogues, the Socratic rule is general, meaning that it is not specific for any particular elementary proposition.

For the local reason of a proposition A, the synthesis and analysis depend on the actions that are determined by the Socratic rule for whether it is a formal or material kind of play. In the case that the play is material, the Socratic rule will describe an action specific to the A's formation. In the case that the play is formal, the Socratic rule allows **O** to bring forward the relevant local reasons in the development of the play.

In the case of formal dialogues, the thesis is assumed to be well-formed until the logical constants, so that the formation of the elements is displayed during the course of the dialogue and depends on the authority of **O**. The formation for elementary statements therefore takes place at the level of global meaning rather than local meaning. The work of Rahman, McConaughey, et al. (2018, p. 116) that this chapter is based upon focuses mainly on the formal dialogues, rather than the material ones, though highlights the importance of implementing the material dialogues in future work.

Local meaning

The local meaning is provided by rules of three different kinds, the formation rules, the synthesis rules and analysis rules of local reasons.

In the standard dialogical framework, a statement is a proposition together with a reason for that proposition, though the reasons for each statement are left implicit in the notation. A statement might be of the form **X** ! A, where A is an elementary proposition and it is stated by a player **X**. In immanent reasoning, the reason can be displayed explicitly in the notation in the form **X** $a : A$, where a should be considered as the local reason that **X** has for stating A. Even though this is possible in immanent reasoning, we might also include statements of the first form, **X** ! A, where the reason for A is left implicit. That the reason is implicit is shown by the exclamation mark in the second variant. (Rahman, McConaughey, et al. 2018, p. 117)

In immanent reasoning, we might have statements of the form:

X ! $\pi(x_1, ..., x_n)[x_i : A_i]$,

where π is some statement where $(x_1, ..., x_n)$ occurs and $[x_i : A_i]$ is some conditions that $\pi(x_1, ..., x_n)$ depends on. This statement should then be read as:

X states $\pi(x_1, ..., x_n)$ under the condition that the antagonist concedes $x_i : A_i$.

This form of statements, $[x_i : A_i]$, are called required concessions since the antagonist accepts the statement through his challenge of the original statement. Concessions of the thesis are called initial concessions and might include formation statements, for example $A : prop, B : prop$ for a thesis $A \supset B : prop$. (Rahman, McConaughey, et al. 2018, p. 117)

As mentioned earlier, there are three kinds of rules, formation rules, synthesis rules and analysis rules. The first kind of rules that is explained is the formation rules. These rules are based upon the descriptions found in Rahman, McConaughey, et al. (2018, pp. 118-136).

5.3. Dialogues with play objects

Formation rules

In classical logic and the standard dialogical system, it is presupposed that the players only use well-formed formulas, often called wff. Their formation can be described by a meta-language where it can be controlled whether the formulas actually satisfy the definitions for the wffs. In CTT and therefore also in immanent reasoning, this is possible to do in the object language by allowing the players to challenge the formations of each others statements. The formation rules describe the formation of the logical constants without utilising a meta-language. In the case of elementary propositions, this is governed by the Socratic rule. The Opponent might therefore verify the well-formation of the thesis stated by the Proponent before its actual validity is verified. An important thing to note, and mentioned earlier, is that the formation rules are particle rules, which together with the synthesis rules and the analysis rules provide the local meaning for the logical constants. (Rahman, McConaughey, et al. 2018, p. 118)

In Table 5.4, we are give the formation rules for the logical constants, together with falsum. In the case of falsum $\bot : prop$, it cannot be challenged since it by definition is a proposition.

Constant	Move	Challenge	Defence
Conjunction	**X** $A \wedge B : prop$	**Y** ? $F_{\wedge 1}$ or **Y** ? $F_{\wedge 2}$	**X** $A : prop$ respectively **X** $B : prop$
Disjunction	**X** $A \vee B : prop$	**Y** ? $F_{\vee 1}$ or **Y** ? $F_{\vee 2}$	**X** $A : prop$ respectively **X** $B : prop$
Implication	**X** $A \supset B : prop$	**Y** ? $F_{\supset 1}$ or **Y** ? $F_{\supset 2}$	**X** $A : prop$ respectively **X** $B : prop$
Universal quantification	**X** $(\forall x : A)B(x) : prop$	**Y** ? $F_{\forall 1}$ or **Y** ? $F_{\forall 2}$	**X** $A : set$ respectively **X** $B(x) : prop[x : A]$
Existential quantification	**X** $(\exists x : A)B(x) : prop$	**Y** ? $F_{\exists 1}$ or **Y** ? $F_{\exists 2}$	**X** $A : set$ respectively **X** $B(x) : prop[x : A]$
Subset separation	**X** $\{x : A | B(x)\} : prop$	**Y** ? F_1 or **Y** ? F_2	**X** $A : set$ respectively **X** $B(x) : prop[x : A]$
Falsum	**X** $\bot : prop$	–	–

Table 5.4: Dialogical formation rules

In order to perform a formation play for dependent statements, we need a substitution rule. The substitution rule is not a formation rule, but is needed in order to apply the formation rules for dependent statements as for example, $B(x) : prop[x : A]$. It is given as the following:

	Move	Challenge	Defence
Subst-D	**X** $\pi(x_1, ..., x_n)[x_i : A_i]$	**Y** $\tau_1 : A_1, ..., \tau_n : A_n$	**X** $\pi(\tau_1, ..., \tau_n)$

5.3. Dialogues with play objects

where π is a statement. τ_i is a local reason of the form of $a_i : A_i$ or $x_i : A_i$. (Rahman, McConaughey, et al. 2018, pp. 132-133)

Synthesis rules
The second kind of particle rules is called *synthesis rules*. They decide how to produce local reasons for statements. The synthesis rules show what kind of move and what kind of action that should be performed in order to produce a local reason for that proposition or set. (Rahman, McConaughey, et al. 2018, pp. 135-136)

The general structure of synthesis rules for a local reason for a constant $\mathcal{K}$ is described by Table 5.5 and the synthesis rules of local reasons for the logical constants are found in the Table 5.6.

	A constant $\mathcal{K}$
Move	$\mathbf{X} \; ! \; \varphi[\mathcal{K}]$
	X claims that φ.
Challenge	**Y** asks for the reason for that claim.
Defence	$\mathbf{X} \; p : \varphi[\mathcal{K}]$
	X states that the local reason p for $\varphi[\mathcal{K}]$, according to the rules for the synthesis of local reasons prescribed for $\mathcal{K}$.

Table 5.5: Structure of synthesis rules for a local reason

Constant	Move	Challenge	Defence
Conjunction	$\mathbf{X}\ !\ A \wedge B$	$\mathbf{Y}\ ?\ L^{\wedge}$ or $\mathbf{Y}\ ?\ R^{\wedge}$	$\mathbf{X}\ p_1 : A$ respectively $\mathbf{X}\ p_2 : B$
Existential quantification	$\mathbf{X}\ !\ (\exists x : A)B(x)$	$\mathbf{Y}\ ?\ L^{\exists}$ or $\mathbf{Y}\ ?\ R^{\exists}$	$\mathbf{X}\ p_1 : A$ respectively $\mathbf{X}\ p_2 : B(p_1)$
Subset separation	$\mathbf{X}\ !\ \{x : A | B(x)\}$	$\mathbf{Y}\ ?\ L$ or $\mathbf{Y}\ ?\ R$	$\mathbf{X}\ p_1 : A$ respectively $\mathbf{X}\ p_2 : B(p_1)$
Disjunction	$\mathbf{X}\ !\ A \vee B$	$\mathbf{Y}\ ?^{\vee}$	$\mathbf{X}\ p_1 : A$ or $\mathbf{X}\ p_2 : B$
Implication	$\mathbf{X}\ !\ A \supset B$	$\mathbf{Y}\ p_1 : A$	$\mathbf{X}\ p_2 : B$
Universal quantification	$\mathbf{X}\ !\ (\forall x : A)B(x)$	$\mathbf{Y}\ p_1 : A$	$\mathbf{X}\ p_2 : B(p_1)$
Negation	$\mathbf{X}\ !\ \neg A$ also expressed $\mathbf{X}\ !\ A \supset \bot$	$\mathbf{Y}\ p_1 : A$	$\mathbf{X}\ !\ \bot$ ($\mathbf{X}$ gives up)

Table 5.6: Synthesis rules for local reasons

5.3. Dialogues with play objects

Analysis rules

The analysis rules provide the third kind of rules for explaining the local meaning of the logical constants. The analysis rules of local reasons explain how we should parse the complex local reasons. It describes how to take apart a local reason into its consisting elements. In order to give the analysis of local reasons, we need some new operators that are called *instructions*. These instructions have the following form, when we speak about a conjunction, $L^{\wedge}(p)$ and $R^{\wedge}(p)$. The first is a left-instruction of p and the second is a right-instruction of p. For each logical constant, there are distinct instruction operators, so that a right-instruction for a conjunction is not the same as a right-instruction for a disjunction. (Rahman, McConaughey, et al. 2018, pp. 121-122)

Instructions contain an interaction procedure that might be described by the following three steps:

1. **Resolution of instructions:** This describes how to carry out the instructions and provides an actual local reason;

2. **Substitution of instructions:** This describes how when one instruction has been carried out by a local reason, every other time this instruction occurs, it will be substituted by the very same local reason;

3. **Application of the Socratic rule:** The Socratic rule describes how the resolution and substitution of instructions provide equality and thereby link the synthesis with the analysis.

By the new operator for instructions we might provide the analysis rules for the logical constants. The superscript following the instructions shows what player that has the choice for which local reason to use. (Rahman, McConaughey, et al. 2018, p. 136) The analysis rules are then given by in Table 5.7.

Constant	Move	Challenge	Defence
Conjunction	$\mathbf{X}\ p : A \wedge B$	$\mathbf{Y}\ ?\ L^{\wedge}$ or $\mathbf{Y}\ ?\ R^{\wedge}$	$\mathbf{X}\ L^{\wedge}(p)^X : A$ respectively $\mathbf{X}\ R^{\wedge}(p)^X : B$
Existential quantification	$\mathbf{X}\ p : (\exists x : A)B(x)$	$\mathbf{Y}\ ?\ L^{\exists}$ or $\mathbf{Y}\ ?\ R^{\exists}$	$\mathbf{X}\ L^{\exists}(p)^X : A$ respectively $\mathbf{X}\ R^{\exists}(p)^X : B(L^{\exists}(p)^X)$
Subset separation	$\mathbf{X}\ p : \{x : A | B(x)\}$	$\mathbf{Y}\ ?\ L$ or $\mathbf{Y}\ ?\ R$	$\mathbf{X}\ L^{\{\ldots\}}(p)^X : A$ respectively $\mathbf{X}\ R^{\{\ldots\}}(p)^X : B(L^{\{\ldots\}}(p)^X)$
Disjunction	$\mathbf{X}\ p : A \vee B$	$\mathbf{Y}\ ?^{\vee}$	$\mathbf{X}\ L^{\vee}(p)^X : A$ or $\mathbf{X}\ L^{\vee}(p)^X : B$
Implication	$\mathbf{X}\ p : A \supset B$	$\mathbf{Y}\ L^{\supset}(p)^Y : A$	$\mathbf{X}\ R^{\supset}(p)^Y : B$
Universal quantification	$\mathbf{X}\ p : (\forall x : A)B(x)$	$\mathbf{Y}\ L^{\forall}(p)^Y : A$	$\mathbf{X}\ R^{\forall}(p)^Y : B(L^{\forall}(p)^Y)$
Negation	$\mathbf{X}\ p : \neg A$ also expressed $\mathbf{X}\ p : A \supset \bot$	$\mathbf{Y}\ L^{\neg}(p)^Y : A$ $\mathbf{Y}\ L^{\supset}(p)^Y : A$	$\mathbf{X}\ R^{\neg}(p)^X : \bot$ $\mathbf{X}\ R^{\supset}(p)^X : \bot$

Table 5.7: Analysis rules for logical constants

Reasons and equality

Dialogical logic has a notion of formality that is not purely syntactical. The Socratic rule in immanent reasoning and the Copy-cat rule in standard dialogical logic restrict the Proponent to play an elementary proposition to only when the Opponent has already played it. This provides an internal explanation of elementary propositions that is not found in other dialogical approaches. It makes it possible to account for elementary propositions without referring to metalogical explanations, but rather explaining elementary propositions in terms of interaction. This dialogical approach does

5.3. Dialogues with play objects

therefore not depend on a model-theoretical approach to meaning. Dialogical logic does not treat formal reasoning and formality in general as something that is independent of content. This view can be traced back to Plato's and Aristotle's descriptions of formal arguments. In this way, formal reasoning is not static or empty of meaning. In the standard dialogical logic, there is no way of asking for reasons for elementary propositions and this means that it cannot express the meaning of such propositions in the object language. Immanent reasoning however, renders this asking and giving of reasons explicit. Immanent reasoning is made up of CTT, where a statement consists of both a proposition and the reason in defence of this proposition. This enables the Proponent to not only copy the elementary statement of the Opponent, the Copy-cat rule, but to provide the very same local reason as introduced by the Opponent in defence of the proposition. A formal play in immanent reasoning therefore shows the root of the content of the proposition rather than a syntactic manipulation of it. (Rahman, McConaughey, et al. 2018, pp. 123-124)

Global meaning in immanent reasoning

In dialogical logic, there is a distinction between local and global meaning. The local meaning provides the rules for the logical constants and describes the different moves that the players might do. The global meaning provides the structural rules that dialogues are made by. The global meaning for formal dialogues is made up by structural rules of three kinds, starting rules, the Socratic rules and global rules. (Rahman, McConaughey, et al. 2018, p. 138)

Structural rules

The structural rules for immanent reasoning resembles the structural rules for standard dialogical logic, though the structural rules for immanent reasoning also include rules for formation dialogues, instructions and the Socratic rule that replaces the Copy-cat rule. The following structural rules for immanent reasoning are described in Rahman, McConaughey, et al. (2018, pp. 138-144).

SR0: Starting rule

The first structural rule is the starting rule. It describes how to start a formal dialogue of immanent reasoning. The start of such dialogue is a move where the Proponent, **P**, states the thesis. The thesis might include certain initial concessions that the Opponent, **O**, is committed to. The thesis will then have the form of $! A[B_1, ..., B_n]$, where $B_1, ..., B_n$ are statements that will correspond to the initial concessions and where they might have implicit local reasons, and A is a statement with an implicit local reason. In the case, and only in the case, that **O** accepts these conditions, $B_1, ..., B_n$, the dialogue starts. **O** then states these conditions as initial concessions in moves numbered $0.1, ..., 0.n$, before the choice of repetition ranks. Beginning with **O**, each player in turn chooses a positive integer to be their repetition rank. The repetition rank is the upper limit for the number of attacks and defences the player might do in response to each move in the play.

SR1: Development rule

There are two kinds of development rules. In the case that the game uses intuitionistic logic, SR1i should be used and in the case that the game uses classical logic, SR1c should be used.

5.3. Dialogues with play objects

SR1i: Intuitionistic development rule
The players move alternately one move each. The moves should be either an attack or a defence as described by the particle rules and stay coherent with the other structural rules. If there is a constant in the thesis that is not described by the rules for describing the local meaning, the table must be enriched to include that constant or there must be introduced some other nominal definition in the play.

A player can only answer to the last non-answered challenge of the other player. This condition is called the Last-Duty-First condition and its addition makes the game being based on intuitionistic logic rather than classical logic.

SR1c: Classical development rule
The players move alternately one move each. The moves should be either an attack or a defence as described by the particle rules and stay coherent with the other structural rules. If there is a constant in the thesis that is not described by the rules for describing the local meaning, the table must be enriched to include that constant or there must be introduced some other nominal definition in the play.

SR2: Formation rules for formal dialogues
Since the framework of immanent reasoning permits reasoning on the formation of thesis, formation dialogues are launched as a beginning step of the play.

SR2i: Starting a formation dialogue
The first step of the formation play is that **O** challenges the thesis with a formation request **O** $?_{prop}$, and **P** must defend this challenge by stating that the thesis is indeed a proposition.

SR2ii: Developing a formation dialogue

The following step of a formation play is that **O** uses the formation rules to arrive at the elementary constituents of the proposition. **O** might then use the particle rules in accordance with the structural rules.

SR3: Resolution of instructions

A player might ask for an instruction to be carried out. This procedure should also be applied for functions.

1. The instruction might be challenged by the demand of a resolution. The defender then has to replace the instruction with a suitable local reason for defending the proposition. An instruction is resolved when it has been replaced with such local reason.

2. Whether it is the defender or the challenger that has the choice for the local reason is decided by the superscript following the instruction, so that:

    - In the case that an instruction $\mathcal{I}$ for a logical constant $\mathcal{K}$, has the following form: $\mathcal{I}^{\mathcal{K}}(p)^{\mathbf{X}}$, and the request is from **Y**, of the following form: $\mathbf{Y}?.../\mathcal{I}^{\mathcal{K}}(p)^{\mathbf{X}}$, **X** chooses the local reason;

    - In the case that an instruction $\mathcal{I}$ for a logical constant $\mathcal{K}$, has the following form: $\mathcal{I}^{\mathcal{K}}(p)^{\mathbf{Y}}$, and the request is from **Y**, of the following form: $\mathbf{Y}?p_i/\mathcal{I}^{\mathcal{K}}(p)^{\mathbf{Y}}$, **Y** chooses the local reason.

3. If there is a sequence of instructions $\pi[\mathcal{I}_i(...(\mathcal{I}_k(p))...)]$, we should start by the inside resolving $(\mathcal{I}_k(p))$ and go on until resolving $(\mathcal{I}_i)$.

5.3. Dialogues with play objects

SR4: Substitution of instructions
Whenever an instruction $\mathcal{I}^{\mathcal{K}}(p)^{\mathbf{X}}$ has been resolved by using a local reason b, if $\mathcal{I}^{\mathcal{K}}(p)^{\mathbf{X}}$ again occurs, the players can demand that this very same instruction should be replaced by the same local reason b, by the substitution request $?b/\mathcal{I}^{\mathcal{K}}(p)^{\mathbf{X}}$. It cannot be chosen a different term for substitution when an instruction has already been resolved. As for SR3, this rule should also apply for functions.

SR5: Socratic rule and definitional equality
SR5.1, SR5.2, SR5.3, SR5.3.1, and SR5.3.2 are parts related to the Socratic rule.

SR5.1: Restriction of P-statements
Except for the first step in the thesis, **P** is not allowed to state an elementary statement unless **O** has already stated it. An elementary statement is an elementary proposition either with an implicit local reason or an explicit local reason. Instructions do not count as local reasons here.

SR5.2: Challenging elementary statements in formal dialogues
Elementary statements with implicit local reasons can be challenged in the following way:

$\mathbf{X} \,!\, A$

$\mathbf{Y} \,?_{reason}$

$\mathbf{X} \, a : A$,

where A is an elementary proposition and a is the local reason for A. **P** can only challenge the elementary statements of **O** if the elementary statement is an initial concession with an implicit local reason or related to transmission of equality. In the first case, **P** might ask for an explicit local reason for the initial concession.

SR5.3: Definitional equality

It is possible for **O** to challenge the elementary statements of **P**. The defence for **P** of such challenge is to state a definitional equality between a local reason and an instruction where both the local reason and the instruction are introduced by **O**, or a reflexive equality of the local reason, also introduced by **O**. There are therefore two cases of the Socratic rule, non-reflexive cases and reflexive cases.

SR5.3.1: Non-reflexive cases of the Socratic rule

P may respond to the challenge by stating that **O** gave the same local reason for the proposition as in the resolution of an instruction $\mathcal{I}$, and we are in this situation in a non-reflexive case of the Socratic rule. The non-reflexive cases of the Socratic rule can be described by three different moves in Table 5.8.

	Move	Challenge	Defence
SR5.3.1a	**P** $a : A$	**O** $? = a$	**P** $\mathcal{I} = a : A$
SR5.3.1b	**P** $a : A(b)$	**O** $? = b^{A(b)}$	**P** $\mathcal{I} = b : D$
SR5.3.1c	**P** $\mathcal{I} = b : D$	**O** $? = A(b)$	**P** $A(\mathcal{I}) = A(b) : prop$

Table 5.8: Non-reflexive cases of Socratic rule

For the defences of **P** in the three rules, there are certain presuppositions about the earlier development of the play.

SR5.3.1a: The defence can only be stated by **P** if **O** has already stated A or $a = b : A$ by a substitution of the instruction $\mathcal{I}$ in $\mathcal{I} : A$ or $\mathcal{I} = b : A$.

SR5.3.1b: The defence can only be stated by **P** if **O** has already stated A and $b : D$ by a substitution of the instruction $\mathcal{I}$ in $a : A(\mathcal{I})$.

5.3. Dialogues with play objects

SR5.3.1c: P $\mathcal{I} = b : D$ should be the result from applying the rule SR5.3.1b. The rule shows the equality in *prop*, that substitution of instruction by a local reason gives an equal proposition as before the instruction was replaced. The defence can only be stated by **P** if **O** has already stated $A(b) : prop$ or $A(\mathcal{I}) = A(b) : prop$.

The statements of **P** that are results of the defence of elementary statements cannot be attacked again by the Socratic rule or by substitution of instructions, where SR5.3.1c is an exception.

SR5.3.2: Reflexive cases of the Socratic rule

P may respond to the challenge by stating that **O** gave the same local reason for the same proposition and this is not a result of a substitution or resolution of instructions. We are in this situation in a reflexive case of the Socratic rule. The moves are the same as in SR5.3.1 and the defences of **P** presuppose that the same statement or the same equality has been stated by **O**. The statements of **P** that are results of the defence of elementary statements cannot be attacked again by the Socratic rule.

SR6: Transmission of definitional equality

There are two kinds of transmission of definitional equality, where the first is substitution within dependent or independent statements. The second one shows the reflexivity, symmetry and transitivity. A *type* is in this situation either a *prop* or a *set*.

The rules for transmission of definitional equality 1, substitution within dependent or independent statements, is given by Table 5.9 and the rules for transmission of definitional equality 2, reflexivity, symmetry and transitivity, is given by Table 5.10.

Move	Challenge	Defence
X $b(x) : B(x)[x : A]$	**Y** $a = c : A$	**X** $b(a) = b(c) : B(a)$
X $b(x) = d(x) : B(x)[x : A]$	**Y** $a : A$	**X** $b(a) = d(a) : B(a)$
X $B(x) : type[x : A]$	**Y** $a = c : A$	**X** $B(a) = B(c) : type$
X $B(x) = D(x) : type[x : A]$	**Y** $?_{B(x)=D(x)} a : A$ or **Y** $?_{B(x)=D(x)} a = c : A$	**X** $B(a) = D(a) : type$ or **X** $B(a) = D(c) : type$
X $A = B : type$	**Y** $?_{A=D} a : A$ or **Y** $?_{A=D} a = c : A$	**X** $a : B$ or **X** $a = c : B$

Table 5.9: Transmission of definitional equality 1

	Move	Challenge	Defence
Type-reflexivity	**X** $A : type$	**Y** $?_{type} - refl$	**X** $A = A : type$
Type-symmetry	**X** $A = B : type$	**Y** $?_B - symm$	**X** $B = A : type$
Type-transitivity	**X** $A = B : type$ **X** $B = C : type$	**Y** $?_A - trans$	**X** $A = C : type$
Reflexivity	**X** $a : A$	**Y** $?_a - refl$	**X** $a = a : A$
Symmetry	**X** $a = b : A$	**Y** $?_b - refl$	**X** $b = a : A$
Transitivity	**X** $a = b : A$ **X** $b = c : A$	**Y** $?_a - trans$	**X** $a = c : A$

Table 5.10: Transmission of definitional equality 2

5.3. Dialogues with play objects

SR7: Winning rule for plays
The last rule is the winning rule for plays. The winner is the player that makes the last move. In the case that the last move is **O** stating $\bot$, **P** can use $you_{gave\ up}(n)$ as a local reason for any challenge that is not defended before **O** stated $\bot$. (Rahman, McConaughey, et al. 2018, pp. 138-144)

Strategy level and example

Remarks for developing a strategy
In a similar way as in the standard dialogical framework, the strategy level in dialogues of immanent reasoning is included in order to enable the consideration of all possible plays. The procedure is to find the core of the **P**-strategy and from that find all relevant plays related to a given thesis. The procedure and assumptions are the same as for standard dialogical logic, though there are some differences in application because of instructions and the explicit local reasons. (Rahman, McConaughey, et al. 2018, pp. 146-149) The description of strategies for standard dialogical logic will therefore hold here has well, though with the following remarks:

Addition to the assumptions for move preferences of O
The following presuppositions should be added to the move preferences of **O**:

1. In the case that **O** will choose a local reason, **O** will choose a new, unused one;

2. If there are any instructions, **O** will challenge those before doing other moves. This means that if **P** has challenged an implication or universal quantification, **O** will counterattack the instructions $L^{\supset}$ or $L^{\forall}$ before defending the challenge.

Avoiding infinite ramifications

When resolving a previously unresolved instruction, **O** has to choose a local reason that might be a member of some infinite set. However, when the local reason is chosen for a certain instruction, **O** has to stay with that local reason for the rest of the play. The repetition rank limits the number of times a player can challenge or defend a certain move and since the repetition rank is finite, the play will also stay finite.

Proof objects and reasons

In CTT we speak about proof objects and they are not corresponding to local reasons in immanent reasoning. Immanent reasoning also include what is called strategic reasons which is the correspondence to proof objects in CTT. A strategic reason is made by finding a **P**-winning strategy, a way that **P** can win no matter what **O** does.

Disregarding formation plays

By the formation rules, immanent reasoning allows the players to challenge based on the formation of the expressions. The strategy level is concerned with validity of propositions and formal plays. In developing a strategy, the formation plays will be disregarded and it will be presupposed that the expressions are well typed when speaking about formal plays.

Disregarding the order of O-moves

In developing a **P**-winning strategy we have to consider every possible way that **O** might play and this also holds for what order **O** plays the moves. **O** should not play the moves in such a way that **O** loses because of playing badly. In the intuitionistic framework, **O** can only defend the last non-answered challenge, because of SR1i. This means that **O** should defend a challenge immediately, so that **O** does not risk to lose the chance to defend at a later stage and thereby loose the play. This avoids the problem of **O** losing because of playing the moves in a bad order.

5.3. Dialogues with play objects

By using these presuppositions, together with the presuppositions for standard dialogical logic, we can end up with a demonstration that is the core of a strategy. (Rahman, McConaughey, et al. 2018, pp. 146-149)

Strategic reasons in immanent reasoning
Strategic reasons in immanent reasoning can be described as a recapitulation of the potential development given a particular thesis. It provides a global view over all possible plays though these reasons still belong to the object language. It provides the link between dialogical strategies and CTT demonstrations. Strategic reasons are what corresponds to proof objects in CTT. The strategic reasons are provided by synthesis and analysis rules, corresponding to CTT-introduction and -elimination rules with recovered proof objects.[9]

Example of dialogue in immanent reasoning

We may illustrate dialogues in immanent reasoning by an example. The chosen thesis is $A \supset (A \vee B)$. First there should be a formation play. In the first formation play, the Opponent challenges the left part of the thesis. This is given in Play 4.

	O			P	
0.1	$A : prop$				
0.2	$B : prop$		$A \supset (A \vee B) : prop$		0
1	$n := 1$		$m := 2$		2
3	$?_{F \supset 1}$	0	$A : prop$		4

Play 4: Formation play 1

---

[9]For a detailed account over strategic reasons and their synthesis and analysis rules, see Rahman, McConaughey, et al. (2018, pp. 169-179)

In move 0, the Proponent states the thesis. In move 1 and 2, the players choose their repetition ranks r, n for the Opponent and m for the Proponent. In move 3, the Opponent challenges the implication in move 0 by a formation challenge of the first part. In move 4, the Proponent defends the challenge in move 3 with the formation of the first part of the implication, $A : prop$. The Proponent can do that because the Opponent states the same in move 0.1. After move 4, the Opponent does not have any possible moves to do and the play is won by the Proponent. The Opponent could have challenged the second part of the implication in move 3. This provides us with the second formation play, given in Play 5.

O			P	
0.1	$A : prop$			
0.2	$B : prop$		$A \supset (A \vee B) : prop$	0
1	$n := 1$		$m := 2$	2
3	$?_{F \supset 2}$	0	$(A \vee B) : prop$	4
5	$?_{F \supset 1}$	4	$A : prop$	6

Play 5: Formation play 2

The first moves are the same as in the first formation play. In move 3, the Opponent challenges the implication in move 0 by formation challenge of the second part. In move 4, the Proponent defends the challenge in move 3 with the formation of the second part of the implication, $A \vee B : prop$. In move 5, the Opponent challenges the disjunction in move 4 by a formation challenge of the first part of the disjunction. In move 6, the Proponent defends this challenge by stating the formation of the first part of the disjunction, $A : prop$, that had already been stated by the Opponent in move 0.1. After move 6, the Opponent does not have any possible moves to do and the play is won by the Proponent. The Opponent could have challenged the second part of the disjunction in move 5. This provides us with the third formation play, given in Play 6.

5.3. Dialogues with play objects

	O			P	
0.1	$A : prop$				
0.2	$B : prop$			$A \supset (A \vee B) : prop$	0
1	$n := 1$			$m := 2$	2
3	$?_{F\supset 2}$	0		$(A \vee B) : prop$	4
5	$?_{F\supset 2}$	4		$B : prop$	6

Play 6: Formation play 3

The first moves are the same as in the second formation play. In move 5, the Opponent challenges the disjunction in move 4 by a formation challenge of the second part of the disjunction. In move 6, the Proponent defends this challenge by stating the formation of the second part of the disjunction, $B : prop$, that had already been stated by the Opponent in move 0.2. After move 6, the Opponent does not have any possible moves to do and the play is won by the Proponent. This shows all possible ways the Opponent could challenge the formation of the thesis. After the formation plays, the dialogue consists of a play with particle rules, given in Play 7.

	O			P	
				$a : A \supset (A \vee B)$	0
1	$n := 1$			$m := 2$	2
3	$a_1 : A$	0		$a_2 : A \vee B$	4
5	$?_\vee$	4		$a_1 : A$	6

Play 7: Particle play

In move 0, the Proponent states the thesis. In move 1 and 2, the players choose their repetition ranks r, n for the Opponent and m for the Proponent. In move 3, the Opponent challenges the implication in move 0 by the implication challenge. This is done by stating a play object for the antecedent $a_1 : A$. In move 4, the Proponent defends the challenge in move 3 by stating an object for the consequent, $a_2 : A \lor B$. In move 5, the Opponent challenges the disjunction. In move 6, the Proponent defends the challenge in move 5 by stating an object for the first part of the disjunction, $a_1 : A$. The Proponent can do that because the Opponent states the same in move 3. After move 6, the Opponent does not have any possible moves to do and the play is won by the Proponent.[10]

The Opponent did not have any choice, so this also constitutes a winning strategy for the Proponent in the following way:

P $a : A \supset (A \lor B)$
O $n := 1$
P $m := 2$
O $a_1 : A$
P $a_2 : A \lor B$
O $?_\lor$
P $a_1 : A$

---

[10] See Rahman, McConaughey, et al. (2018, pp. 179-183) for examples for developing a strategic reason.

Chapter 6
Imperatives, precedents and relations

6.1 Implementing imperatives

Deontic logic can be said to be the logical study of how we ought to act. From a legal point of view, the typical way to understand this is to create a logical system that manages to interpret deontic notions. Based on immanent reasoning by Rahman, McConaughey, et al. (2018), there have been several implementations of deontic notions in this dialogical framework. We have the implementation of parallel reasoning in Islamic jurisprudence by Rahman and Iqbal (2018) and the implementation of heteronomous imperatives by Rahman and Granström (2019).

The implementation of the heteronomous imperatives will be explained here as this will be used for developing a more general framework of legal reasoning by combining it with the notion of analogy.

The area of deontic logic is full of potential paradoxes and much of the effort, at least in recent years, has been on finding ways around these paradoxes. (Navarro and Rodríguez 2014) The centre of these many paradoxes seems to be the challenges of combining the deontic notions with the modal notions. The deontic notions seem to be somehow similar while still somehow different from their ontological counterparts. The challenge for deontic logic might therefore be to provide a framework that can deal with both the deontic notions and their modal counterparts without reducing one into the other.

Heteronomous imperatives

The work on heteronomous imperatives can very briefly be described as the attempt of developing a logic of norms based on the analysis of the following deontic notions:

- Obligatory;
- Forbidden;
- Permissible;
- Facultative.

This is sometimes described as the essential project of deontic logic. The work of Rahman and Granström is based on Ibn Ḥazm's deontic notions that intend to tie the deontic notions to their performance being either rewarded, sanctioned or neither of the two. In a general setting, we can use law-abiding, law-breaking and legally neutral in their place. From a value-approach, we might use the terms legally worthy, legally unworthy and legally worth-neutral. (Rahman and Granström 2019, p. 1)

Description of heteronomous imperatives

Leibniz stated a link between the modal and deontic concepts by means of intelligibility, described by Table 6.1.[1]

---

[1] See (Rahman and Granström 2019, p. 5) for details about this and its relation to legal reasoning.

6.1. Implementing imperatives

Modal	Deontic
Possible, it is intelligible	Permissible (licitum)
Necessary, its negation is not intelligible	Obligatory (debitum)
Possibly not, its negation is intelligible	Omissible (indebitum)
Impossible, it is not intelligible	Forbidden (illicitum).

Table 6.1: Linking modal and deontic concepts

However, the origins of linking the deontic concepts with their modal counterparts, can historically be traced back to Ibn Ḥazm and al-Fārābī from the 10th and 11th century. (Rahman and Granström 2019, p. 6)

Defining heteronomous imperatives and their conditions

According to Ibn Ḥazm, we can identify five forms of deontic qualifications. In this context an action can be either rewarded or sanctioned, but it might also be neither. Reward and sanction are therefore incompatible, though not contradictory and there is a distinction between an action being rewarded and an action being neither rewarded nor sanctioned. The five forms of deontic qualifications are then the following:

1. Obligatory action:
  If we do it, we are rewarded;
  If we do not do it, we are sanctioned;

2. Forbidden action:
  If we do it, we are sanctioned;
  If we do not do it, we are rewarded;

3. Recommended permissible action:
  If we do it, we are rewarded;
  If we do not do it, we are neither sanctioned nor rewarded;

4. **Reprehended permissible action:**
   If we do it, we are neither sanctioned nor rewarded;
   If we do not do it, we are rewarded;

5. **Evenly permissible action:**
   If we do it, we are neither sanctioned nor rewarded;
   If we do not do it, we are neither sanctioned nor rewarded.

The performance of an action can based on these categories be judged in three different ways. It can be rewarded, it can be sanctioned and it can be neither. By introducing these categories into a contemporary debate regarding legal reasoning, we might consider it problematic to introduce the notions of 'sanction' and 'reward' in this way. The notion of 'sanction' does not in itself seem problematic, as we would expect an illegal action to be legally sanctioned in most legal systems. However, the notion of 'reward' seems more problematic. In a religious context, the notion of 'reward' could be well understood and clearly distinct from the notion of 'neutrality'. Theologically, one could consider that an action could be rewarded in the sense that it is a good action that will motivate some positive reaction in the afterlife (or in this life, for that matter). From this point of view, it seems clearly distinct from the neutral actions. A neutral action is in this sense an action that will not motivate some reaction, neither positive nor negative. The first point is that it seems rather unclear exactly what such reward should look like in the context of contemporary law. In the analysis we will therefore substitute the notions of 'sanction' and 'reward' with the notions of 'law-breaking' and 'law-abiding' to use more neutral variants than the ones described by Ibn Ḥazm. (Rahman and Granström 2019, pp. 8-9)

However, this does not remove all the theological "flavour" found in these deontic imperatives. By substituting 'rewarding' with 'law-abiding' we seem to erase or at least blur the distinction between an action being law-abiding and an action being neutral, meaning neither law-breaking nor law-abiding. We could connect the law-

6.1. Implementing imperatives

abidingness or reward to the advantages the agent receives by being a lawful citizen of the state. However, most of these advantages do not seem to be dependent on performing certain actions. They are given to you *unconditionally*, which here means that you do not have to do something to earn these advantages. They might though be taken away from you if you act illegally. The point is that one does not seem to require the citizens of the state to act in a special law-abiding or rewarding way to acquire these advantages. It is sufficient to refrain from breaking the law. And one cannot normally increase ones advantages by acting in a law-abiding way. This means that the distinction between law-abiding or rewarding actions and neutral actions seems to disappear if we understand reward in this way.

Another way to understand the difference could be from the point of view of morality or society. That an action is rewarded could then be understood as being morally good or that the performer could enjoy respect from their fellow citizens. By entering the context of morality, one seems to in the same time leave the context of legality. The legal system is normally not intended to reflect questions about morality and this kind of interpersonal exchange. By understanding reward in this way, we seem to admit that non-legal factors play a role in the legal framework which again seems go against the independency of the law. It seems difficult to make sense of the distinction between law-abiding or rewarding actions on one side and neutral actions on the other side without stepping out from the legal domain. In this sense, the law's intention is distinguishing legal from illegal actions, not good from neutral actions. For these reasons, we will in this analysis consider rewarding and neutral actions together. Recommended, reprehended and evenly permissible actions will therefore be considered as a single category of permissible actions.

If one still wishes to maintain all five deontic categories, the analysis can easily changed, and with some very minor adjustments be adapted to accommodate all five.[2] In this work, we therefore operate with the following three deontic categories:

1. **Obligatory action:**
   If we do it, we are law-abiding;
   If we do not do it, we are law-breaking;

2. **Forbidden action:**
   If we do it, we are law-breaking;
   If we do not do it, we are law-abiding;

3. **Permissible action:**
   If we do it, we are law-abiding;
   If we do not do it, we are law-abiding.

Ought presupposes can

For the deontic imperatives, there has to be an ability and a choice involved in the performance of them. For us to speak about an action being of a deontic character, there has to be a choice related to whether the action is performed or not. In addition to this, the qualification of the performed action should depend on the choice that is made. This means several things. First, only actions that could have been chosen to be performed or not to be performed should be included in the deontic qualifications. Second, it includes a notion of responsibility. A person that is responsible for his or her actions should be liable to law-abidingness and law-breakingness. That a person is responsible, means that he or she can choose to perform or refrain from performing some action. It is only in this sense that we should speak about law-breakingness or law-abidingness. However, a person might also refrain from choosing

---

[2]See Kvernenes (2021) for a CTT analysis of Ibn Ḥazm's five deontic categories.

6.1. Implementing imperatives

at all and thereby rejecting the choice. The action is therefore contingent on the person choosing. This seems to correspond well with the ethical context. These presuppositions can be formulated in the following way:

1. A person performing an action is legally accountable;

2. The person had a liberty of choosing whether to perform or refrain from performing the action in question.

Different to the principle *ought implies can* from Kant, we end up with a principle for deontic qualifications that *ought presupposes can*. We could understand *can* as some kind of permissibility, so that obligatory actions presuppose that the actions are permissible, but then we would need some alternative definition of permissibility since permissible actions (as defined earlier) and obligatory actions are mutually incompatible. Another way to understand *can* is to look at it as a modal notion, namely the ability to fulfil. This means that for something that ought to be done, it should be possible to actually do it. (Rahman and Granström 2019, p. 10)

The logical structure of such deontic imperatives should therefore have the form of a hypothetical in such a way that a person can choose whether to perform a certain action or not, and the action should be considered law-abiding or law-breaking according to the choice made. Since there is a choice involved, the hypothesis in the hypothetical should be of the form of a disjunction of performing an action and not performing the action. In this way, the law-abidingness or law-breakingness of the action will depend on the actual choice of the performance of the action. And the law-abidingness or law-breakingness will not be decided before the person actually has chosen. The liberty of choosing the performance of an action of type A will then be a hypothetical with a constructivist disjunction $A \vee \neg A$ as a hypothesis.

Logical analysis of heteronomous imperatives

The logical analysis of heteronomous imperatives by Rahman and Granström (2019, pp. 15-19) is based on CTT, where the notion of reward of a certain performance is represented by a hypothetical judgment of the form:

$$b(x) : R(x)(x : A),$$

which reads *The function b is evidence for the proposition that the performance x will be rewarded.* x in this case stays hypothetical and in the case of an actual performance a of the action A such that $a : A$, we can infer that this performance a will be rewarded, $b(a) : R(a)$. This can be explained by the following inference:

$$\frac{a : A \quad b(x) : R(x)(x : A)}{b(a) : B(a).}$$

And similar to the case of reward, we might represent sanctions by $c(z) : S(z)(z : \neg A)$ and the inference of performing the action by $u : \neg A$. This can then be explained by the following inference:

$$\frac{u : \neg A \quad c(z) : S(z)(z : \neg A)}{c(u) : S(u).}$$

Based on these two hypothetical judgments, we can by the existence of b and c represent that the action A is obligatory. However, this is not enough since we should also try to capture that this reward (or sanction) is dependent on a future contingent action. This means simply that the action has not happened yet and that there is a choice for the agent. As mentioned previously, this choice has the structure of a constructivist disjunction. Because of this, we will always know whether it is the left side or the right side that made the disjunction true. The head of the hypothetical judgment therefore has the following form:

$$x : A \vee \neg A.$$

6.1. Implementing imperatives

x is understood as evidence for either carrying out the action, A, or not carrying out this action, $\neg A$. Because of the constructivity, this is not assumed to be true as such and only in the case that we have some actual evidence for this judgment we will know whether it was fulfilled by the left side, A, or the right side, $\neg A$. It will therefore always be possible to trace back whether x is a result of A or of $\neg A$ in judgments that depend on x. To fulfil A is understood as performing the action, while to fulfil $\neg A$ is understood as frustrating the performance of the action A. This corresponds well with the constructivist implementation of negation as the abortion of a process. (Rahman and Granström 2019, p. 16)

As explained previously, there are several kinds of actions that should be analysed in different ways. However, they all seem to have a similar structure so the general structure will be explained for obligatory actions, though this structure will also hold for the other kind of actions. That an action is obligatory is understood in the following way:

> If there is some evidence that the individual g made the choice to perform an action of type A (i.e., if there is evidence that he made the choice for the **left side** of the disjunction), then he is rewarded (for this performance);

> If there is some evidence that the individual g made the choice to omit performing an action of type A (i.e., if there is evidence that he made the choice for the **right side** of the disjunction), then he is sanctioned (for this omission).

The corresponding analysis in CTT, by combining it with the previously described head of the hypothetical and by using $\{H\}$ as an abbreviation for $x : A \vee \neg A$, is then:

$$b(x) : [(\forall y : A)\mathbf{left}^\vee(y) =_{\{H\}} x \supset R(y)]$$
$$\wedge\, [(\forall z : \neg A)\mathbf{right}^\vee(z) =_{\{H\}} x \supset S(z)](x : A \vee \neg A).$$

$\text{left}^\vee(y)$ and $\text{right}^\vee(z)$ are injections that make the disjunction $x : A \vee \neg A$ true. In the first case it is A that makes the disjunction true and in the second case it is $\neg A$ that makes the disjunction true.

$\text{left}^\vee(y) =_{\{H\}} x$ means that the evidence for the action that makes the disjunction true is identical to the evidence for the action of that type, here the case of A. $(\forall y : A)\text{left}^\vee(y) =_{\{H\}} x \supset R(y)$ means that any performance y of the type of action A that is identical to the action that is chosen for x should be rewarded. Correspondingly, $(\forall z : \neg A)\text{right}^\vee(z) =_{\{H\}} x \supset S(z)$ means that any performance z of the type of action $\neg A$ that is identical to the action that is chosen for x should be sanctioned. This provides a structure that can represent the choice that is made, whether performing the action or not, and that the representation does not presuppose that this choice has already been taken. (Rahman and Granström 2019, pp. 17-18)

Particularly in the case of Islamic Law and Civil Law there might be exceptions for the sanctioning of not performing actions. They might be called excuses, E, and can be implemented in the framework[3] in the following way:

$$b(x) : [(\forall y : A)\text{left}^\vee(y) =_{\{H\}} x \supset R(y)]$$
$$\wedge [(\forall z : \neg A)(\neg E(z) \wedge \text{right}^\vee(z) =_{\{H\}} x \supset S(z))](x : A \vee \neg A).$$

If we ignore excuses, we can provide an analysis of the heteronomous imperatives, depending on the result of performing the action in the following way:

1. Obligatory action:
If we do it, we are rewarded;
If we do not do it, we are sanctioned,

$$b_1(x) : [(\forall y : A_1)\text{left}^\vee(y) =_{\{H1\}} x \supset R_1(y)]$$
$$\wedge [(\forall z : \neg A_1)\text{right}^\vee(z) =_{\{H1\}} x \supset S_1(z)](x : A_1 \vee \neg A_1);$$

---

[3]Though as remarked in Rahman and Granström (2019, p. 17), this will lead to defeasibility.

2. Forbidden action:
If we do it, we are sanctioned;
If we do not do it, we are rewarded,

$$b_2(x) : [(\forall y : A_2)\mathbf{left}^\vee(y) =_{\{H2\}} x \supset S_2(y)]$$
$$\wedge [(\forall z : \neg A_2)\mathbf{right}^\vee(z) =_{\{H2\}} x \supset R_2(z)](x : A_2 \vee \neg A_2);$$

3. Recommended permissible action:
If we do it, we are rewarded;
If we do not do it, we are neither sanctioned nor rewarded,

$$b_3(x) : [(\forall y : A_3)\mathbf{left}^\vee(y) =_{\{H3\}} x \supset R_3(y)] \wedge [(\forall z : \neg A_3)$$
$$\mathbf{right}^\vee(z) =_{\{H3\}} x \supset (\neg S_3(z) \wedge \neg R_3(z))](x : A_3 \vee \neg A_3);$$

4. Reprehended permissible action:
If we do it, we are neither sanctioned nor rewarded;
If we do not do it, we are rewarded,

$$b_4(x) : [(\forall y : A_4)\mathbf{left}^\vee(y) =_{\{H4\}} x \supset (\neg S_4(z) \wedge \neg R_4(z))]$$
$$\wedge [(\forall z : \neg A_4)\mathbf{right}^\vee(z) =_{\{H4\}} x \supset R_4(z)](x : A_4 \vee \neg A_4);$$

5. Evenly permissible action:
If we do it, we are neither sanctioned nor rewarded;
If we do not do it, we are neither sanctioned nor rewarded,

$$b_5(x) : [(\forall y : A_5)\mathbf{left}^\vee(y) =_{\{H5\}} x \supset (\neg S_5(z) \wedge \neg R_5(z))]$$
$$\wedge [(\forall z : \neg A_5)\mathbf{right}^\vee(z) =_{\{H5\}} x \supset (\neg S_5(z) \wedge \neg R_5(z))]$$
$$(x : A_5 \vee \neg A_5).$$

In addition to provide analyses of different kind of actions, we might also use a very similar structure to explain the more general terms as *obligatory, forbidden* and *permissible*. The only change is to go from a hypothetical to a universal quantification. (Rahman and

Granström 2019, p. 19) They can then be used to build propositions. For example, *obligatory* can be defined in the following way:

$$(\forall x : A_1 \vee \neg A_1)\{[(\forall y : A_1)\mathbf{left}^{\vee}(y) =_{\{H1\}} x \supset R_1(y)] \\ \wedge [(\forall z : \neg A_1)\mathbf{right}^{\vee}(z) =_{\{H1\}} y \supset S_1(z)]\}true.$$

As mentioned previously in the discussion related to reasoning in contemporary legal systems, there only seems to be two legal responses for actions. This means that the three variants of permissible actions can be reduced to a single one. In this analysis, we will also substitute the notions of 'sanction' and 'reward' with the notions of 'law-breaking' and 'law-abiding'. The three imperatives that will ground the present analysis are then formalised in the following way:

1. Obligatory action:
If we do it, we are law-abiding;
If we do not do it, we are law-breaking,

$$b_1(x) : [(\forall y : A_1)\mathbf{left}^{\vee}(y) =_{\{H1\}} x \supset LA_1(y)] \\ \wedge [(\forall z : \neg A_1)\mathbf{right}^{\vee}(z) =_{\{H1\}} x \supset LB_1(z)](x : A_1 \vee \neg A_1);$$

2. Forbidden action:
If we do it, we are law-breaking;
If we do not do it, we are law-abiding,

$$b_2(x) : [(\forall y : A_2)\mathbf{left}^{\vee}(y) =_{\{H2\}} x \supset LB_2(y)] \\ \wedge [(\forall z : \neg A_2)\mathbf{right}^{\vee}(z) =_{\{H2\}} x \supset LA_2(z)](x : A_2 \vee \neg A_2);$$

3. Permissible action:
If we do it, we are law-abiding;
If we do not do it, we are law-abiding,

$$b_3(x) : [(\forall y : A_3)\mathbf{left}^{\vee}(y) =_{\{H3\}} x \supset LA_3(y)] \\ \wedge [(\forall z : \neg A_3)\mathbf{right}^{\vee}(z) =_{\{H3\}} x \supset LA_3(z))](x : A_3 \vee \neg A_3).$$

Conditionals and heteronomous imperatives

The analyses of heteronomous imperatives have provided a way to handle and interpret actions of different kinds when they are imperative. From this point of view, obligatory actions should be performed and forbidden actions should not be performed. However, there are also certain actions that depend on other actions or events. The question whether these actions should be performed or not depends on whether the other action or event that they depend on has happened or been performed or not. Based on this, we might distinguish two different kinds of conditionals. We have conditional obligations where an action ought to be performed under the assumption that some other action has been performed. And we have conditional right, where some action ought to be performed under the assumption that some other event has happened. (Rahman and Granström 2019, p. 25)

Conditional obligations
Conditional obligations can be explained as it ought to be that if some action x makes A be performed, $B(x)$ ought also to be performed. There might correspondingly be an obligation of not performing $B(x)$ under the assumption that there is some action x that makes A performed. This yields a similar structure. It is important to note that since we speak about action in the case of conditional obligations, A will itself have a deontic character and will also be obligatory, forbidden or permitted in itself. The difference between the conditional obligations and the non-conditional obligations is that the question whether B should be performed or not depends on whether A was actually performed. In a similar way as mentioned previously, we might speak about conditional forbidden or conditional permissible actions and they will have a similar structure as the conditional obligatory actions. (Rahman and Granström 2019, p. 25)

Chapter 6. Imperatives, precedents and relations

The formulation of non-conditional obligation, that performing A is law-abiding and omitting A is law-breaking, is given in the following way:

$$(\forall x : A \vee \neg A)\{[(\forall y : A)\textbf{left}^{\vee}(y) =_{\{H1\}} x \supset LA_1(y)]$$
$$\wedge [(\forall z : \neg A)\textbf{right}^{\vee}(z) =_{\{H1\}} x \supset LB(z)]\}true.$$

In order to represent conditional obligations, we need to make a slight refinement in the notation for the law-breakingness and law-abidingness. LA_A reads that A is law-abiding and correspondingly, LB_A reads that A is law-breaking. We will in this way always specify what kind of action that is under the deontic qualification. The conditional obligation, where A is obligatory and B is obligatory under the assumption that A has been performed can be represented in the following way:

$$(\forall x : A \vee \neg A)\{(\forall y : A)[\textbf{left}^{\vee}(y) =_{\{H1\}} x \supset (\forall w : B \vee \neg B)$$
$$\{(\forall u : B)[\textbf{left}^{\vee}(u) =_{\{H2\}} w \supset LA_A(y) \wedge LA_B(y, u)] \wedge (\forall v : \neg B)$$
$$[\textbf{right}^{\vee}(v) =_{\{H2\}} w \supset LB_B(y, v)]\}] \wedge (\forall z : \neg A)$$
$$[\textbf{right}^{\vee}(z) =_{\{H1\}} x \supset LB_A(z)]\}true.$$

Based on this, we see that the conditional obligation can be said to have an embedded obligation. The obligation of B only comes into play in the case that A is performed. If A is not performed, there is never any obligation of B. This does not mean that B cannot be obligatory if A is not performed, but in that case, the obligation of B has to be covered by some other rule and its performance is outside this scope. Similarly, the obligation of B could be embedded in the obligation of omitting the performance of A. That A is obligatory and B is obligatory if A is not performed, would give the following

6.1. Implementing imperatives

formulation:

$$(\forall x : A \vee \neg A)\{(\forall y : A)[\textbf{left}^\vee(y) =_{\{H1\}} x \supset LA_A(y)] \wedge$$
$$(\forall z : \neg A)[\textbf{right}^\vee(z) =_{\{H1\}} x \supset (\forall w : B \vee \neg B)$$
$$\{(\forall u : B)[\textbf{left}^\vee(u) =_{\{H2\}} w \supset LA_A(y) \wedge LA_B(y,u)] \wedge (\forall v : \neg B)$$
$$[\textbf{right}^\vee(v) =_{\{H2\}} w \supset LB_B(y,v)]\}\}true.$$

As additional variations on these formulations, both A and B might be obligatory, forbidden or permissible. For example, B might be forbidden under the performance of a permissible A. The dependency formulation must then be adapted according to this. (Rahman and Granström 2019, pp. 25-26) It is a further extension of this form of conditional obligation that will be used as a foundation for the analysis of analogical reasoning in the present work.

Conditional right

The notion of conditional right is very important within legal reasoning. Here, it is understood as an obligation of performing an action that is dependent upon a certain condition. The structure resembles the ones of conditional obligations, but when the obligation of an action in a conditional obligation depends on another obligation, the obligation of an action in a conditional right depends on an event. The most famous example of conditional right was the example analysed by Leibniz, coming from Roman Law.[4] In this example Secundus, beneficiary, has the right to receive a certain sum of dinar from Primus, benefactor, in the case that a ship arrives from Asia. In the case that there is evidence that a ship actually arrives from Asia, the condition is satisfied and Primus must pay Secundus. In the case that there is evidence of no ship arriving from Asia, the condition is not satisfied, and Primus does not have to pay Secundus. In conditional right, the condition is called fact and the conditioned is called jus. (Rahman and Granström 2019, p. 27)

---

[4] A more detailed discussion related to this example and what Leibniz called *moral conditionals* is found in section 9.2.

Contrary to conditional obligations, the arrival of a ship from Asia, or more generally the fact, is not an action. It is an event or a fact of some other kind. Typically, a conditional right can be seen as a particular form of agreement between two parties, the beneficiary and the benefactor. For us to speak about a conditional right from a legal point of view, it also has to satisfy some other conditions. The most important condition was described by Leibniz and states that the antecedent, fact, must not be known to be fulfilled at the moment of the contract. This is called the suspensive clause and is what defines the notion of conditional right for Leibniz.[5]

If the fact in a conditional right is known not to be satisfied, the jus is not legally enforceable. This is represented by the introduction of a new predicate, $NLB(x, y)$, that means that the instance of not paying cannot be law-breaking and that they are not legally enforceable. A conditional right can then be formulated in the following way:

$$\{(\forall y : A)[\textbf{left}^\vee(x) =_{\{H1\}} y \supset (\forall w : B \vee \neg B)$$
$$\{(\forall u : B)[\textbf{left}^\vee(w) =_{\{H2\}} u \supset LA_B(y, u)] \wedge (\forall v : \neg B)$$
$$[\textbf{right}^\vee(w) =_{\{H2\}} v \supset LB_B(y, v)]\}] \wedge (\forall z : \neg A)(\forall n : \neg B)$$
$$[\textbf{right}^\vee(x) =_{\{H1\}} z \supset NLB_B(z, n)]\} true(x : A \vee \neg A).$$

If the benefactor performs the jus despite that the fact was not satisfied, the performance is considered as beyond the terms of the agreement. However, it does not break the terms of the contract. The benefactor has the right to perform the jus no matter whether the fact was satisfied or not, but is only obliged to do so when the fact is satisfied. (Rahman and Granström 2019, p. 28)

---

[5] A thorough analysis of this suspensive clause can be found in Magnier (2015)

6.2 Capturing the notion of precedent

A model of analogy

In this section, the notion of analogy will be discussed based on the terminology that is given in the following model by Bartha (2010): This model seems to provide a very good and intuitive description

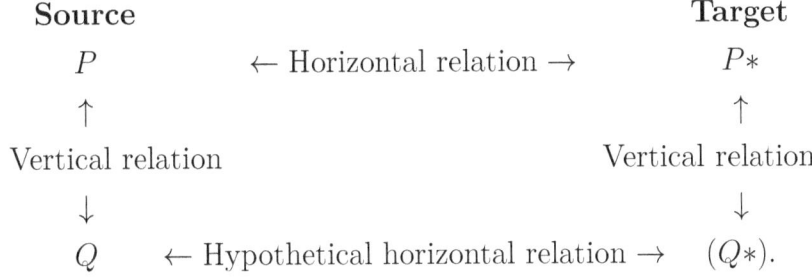

of an analogy. As mentioned, all the described theories of analogy in chapter 2 ascribe importance to both the horizontal relations and to the vertical relations in the representations. They vary slightly in their description, but one might say that the horizontal relations correspond to some kind of similarity, while the vertical relations correspond to some kind of relevancy. Different theories uses different terminology to describe analogies. Here, we will use the term *occasioning characteristic* for the notions that provide the foundation for the analogy (P and P* in the described model) and *entailed characteristic* for the result that the analogy provides (Q and Q* in the model).

The notion of a case

Source and target

In order to develop a theory of analogy, we seem to depend heavily on the notions of 'precedent' or 'source case'. An essential part of this project is therefore the implementation of the notion of case into the framework. Dialogically, a case should be considered a judgment that has already been demonstrated by an earlier play. In constructive type theory, a case can therefore be represented as a hypothetical judgment.

Precedent-based reasoning might be said to be reasoning from one case to another case based on some similarity between the two cases. In an analogy, we usually speak about at least two cases, the source case and the target case. The target case is our case at hand, what we want to find out something about. The source case is the (accepted) background that we use in order to develop our argumentation in the target case.

In this work a similar notion of case as described by Prakken and Sartor (1998) will be used, namely that a case has a dialectic structure. This means that a case does not only consist of a decision, but also contains the argumentation supporting this decision together with argumentation attacking this supportive argumentation and argumentation counter-attacking this attacking argumentation and so on. This means that a case can contain the argumentation for its conclusion. In CTT terms, we might call this its *construction*.

Cases as decisions and argumentation

We might distinguish between the decision, the head, and the argumentation, the tail. The argumentation provides the reason for the decision. A decision is then the result of the legal process and has the form of a proposition. In some sense we can consider it as the goal for the legal process in the first place. This decision should be backed up by some argumentation. This argumentation should ideally consist of judgments that logically imply the decision

6.2. Capturing the notion of precedent

and it is represented as the tail of the hypothetical judgment. The argumentation should have a dialectical structure, which means that it is not only the reasons that support the decision that should be included, but also reasons that challenge the reasons for the conclusion and the defence and attack of these reasons and so on.

This provides the general structure of cases, though it does not explain what kind of rules that might be included in the argumentation. We might make a further distinction within the argumentation between the *facts* and the *rules* of a case. A fact can be considered as a case-specific proposition about a contingent feature of the case. That facts are case-specific means that they cannot normally be directly transferred to another case. A fact is a description of the actual situation that we have in this particular case. A rule of a case can be considered as a general aspect of the law that is applied to the case at hand. Rules can therefore consist of amongst others, laws, values, norms, legal assumptions and definitions. By the distinction between facts and rules, we also have a distinction between what is particular for a case and what holds more generally for a group of cases. Facts do also seem to contain some empirical aspect that is not immediate for rules. Because of the particular nature of facts, the facts do seem to depend on an empirical observation, even though they might also be dependent on other legal assumptions or definitions.[6]

---

[6]Immanent reasoning opens up for distinguishing between facts and rules by an implementation of empirical quantities, though we do not include this distinction explicitly in the analysis provided here. See Rahman, McConaughey, et al. (2018, pp. 261-268) for a description of empirical quantities. A further implementation that combines this notion with probabilities is currently being developed in Rahman and Kvernenes (2021). See also section 9.2 for a brief description and discussion of relevant features related to this approach. Utilising empirical quantities to provide a distinction between rules and facts in the description of cases does however seem like a natural continuation of the current project.

Cases as hypothetical judgments

In CTT we can describe a case as a hypothetical judgment, where have the decision as the head and its justification as the tail. Let D be a decision and A be the argumentation for the decision. A case can then be represented in the following way:

$$d(x) : D(x : A).$$

By this representation we have captured the dependency of D on A. $d(x)$ is a demonstration of D under the assumption that x is A. Here we have only one explicit argument for the decision, namely A. A might have a deeper logical structure, where it is explicit that the argument actually depends on some other judgments. A further dependency can be represented in the following way:

$$d(y(x)) : D(x : B, y(x) : A).$$

This shows a deeper structure of A compared to the first formula, namely that it depends on B. Even though we can represent a structure of dependencies in an explicit way by the CTT interpretation, it does not really make clear the dialectical structure of the argumentation. It only displays what arguments it depends on, not their counter-arguments. Immanent reasoning combines CTT and the game-theoretical approach to meaning. In dialogical logic, meaning is provided by how it can be challenged. In CTT, a proof of a proposition is a construction that is given explicitly as an element of that proposition. A proof in immanent reasoning is a demonstration by an Opponent that challenges the thesis of a Proponent. This demonstration provides the dialectical meaning structure of the proposition in question. In other words, the dialectality of a proposition is inherent in its demonstration by the notion of strategies. The dialectical aspect of an argument is found in its element. If we take the judgment $d(y(x)) : D(x : B, y(x) : A)$, we have a dialectical understanding of the demonstration of D from B and A. This demonstration is made explicit by the proof object

6.2. Capturing the notion of precedent

$d(y(x))$ in D. The potential attacks, counter-attacks and defences are inherent to the demonstration itself. In a similar way, $y(x)$ is a dialectical demonstration of A from B, with all potential attacks, counter-attacks and so on.

A source case and a target case therefore has the same fundamental structure where their difference lies in what role they play in the particular context. A case that is a target case in one context might very well be a source case in another. This seems to also fit well with how cases actually behave. After the closing of a case, it might serve as a precedent for other cases and in this way we can represent not only the internal dependency we find in a particular case, but the general dependency that cases might have on each other, which is the goal of a theory of precedents.

Initial conditions

In none of the described theories of analogy in chapter 2 we find formalisations of any initial conditions to be met for performing analogical reasoning in the first place. Brewer (1996, p. 963) mentions that analogies should be performed in a *context of doubt* and explains that analogical argumentation becomes relevant when for example a legal concept is *actively vague*. However, it is not given any place in his formal theory. It is assumed to be part of the context where an analogy might be introduced. Similar points are also indicated by Woods (2015). The other presented theories are remarkably silent regarding this point. Though, as we can see from Langenbucher (1998), often there actually are restrictions on the use of analogies. The precise content of these restrictions differ between the kind of analogical argument we have and whether we are in a system of Common Law or Civil Law.

Langenbucher (1998) argues that for analogies in both Common Law and Civil Law, there should be a *negative-answer question*. In the *rule-based analogies* (the standard case of Civil Law and exception case of Common Law), this is understood as the existence of a *lacuna* in the law, meaning that the problem that the proposed analogy intends to provide an answer to is not already answered by other parts of the law. In the *principle-based analogies* (the standard case of Common Law and the exception case of Civil Law), this is understood as a requirement for there not to be any law that motivates a conclusion contrary to the solution established by the analogical argument. The negative-answer question seems to corresponds well together with what Brewer calls a context of doubt. The second initial restriction mentioned by Langenbucher is particular to rule-based analogies (and potentially an aspect specific for civil law systems and civil law aspects found in some common law systems). This is the requirement for there not to be any constitutional restrictions that would prohibit the use of analogies in this specific context.

The use of analogy in legal reasoning might then be restricted, not only in terms of horizontal and vertical relations, but also by initial conditions concerning the use of analogy in the first place. We can then see that there are at least two potential restrictions that might be considered:

1. The negative-answer question;

2. Constitutional restrictions.

We do not claim that this list should be exhaustive in any way, nor do we enter the discussion on the precise content of these restrictions. We simply notice that the use of analogical argumentation might be restricted or blocked in certain situations like the ones previously mentioned. In other words, analogical reasoning might only occur in situations where it is *permitted*. This is reflected in the analysis by the introduction of the permitted-analogy assumption in the context of an analogical argument. The introduction of permissibility will show to be one of the particularities with the present analysis

6.3. Explaining relations

of analogical reasoning, not found other contemporary theories concerning analogies in law. It will indeed provide a possibility to include such initial restrictions in the formal framework with reference in the object language.[7]

6.3 EXPLAINING RELATIONS

Horizontal relations

The horizontal relations are seemingly the easiest to give an account for as they express a *similarity* relation. P in the source and $P*$ in the target should be similar. A natural way, and how it will be done in this work, is to understand similarity as being two instances of the same category. This means that if we have a category A, a is similar to b if both a and b belong to the category A. Similarity is then understood by the notion of a property or a predicate. To say that a is similar to b means that both a and b have some property P.

In some sense, this seems like a very weak definition of similarity. The only requirement for two things to be similar is that they share some characteristic. In logical terms, an individual might even have an infinite amount of different characteristics if we understand it as predicates. Because of our understanding of similarity as being two instances of the same category, everything seems somehow similar to everything if we are just clever enough to find a proper predicate. This might cause some problems for arguments by analogy. If everything can be similar to everything, how can some similarities be somehow "better" than others?

In all the described theories, it is a combination of the horizontal and the vertical relations, together with the source and the target, that justifies the analogy. Some other theories for analogy do not include the notion of vertical relations, only the horizontal relations

---

[7]Note that this notion of *permitted* analogies should not be confused with the deontic notion of *permission of actions*.

and thereby measures the analogy only based on the similarities. However, they often end up with the problem that was described earlier, namely that everything is similar to everything in some way. One could imagine this to be solved by measuring the amount of similarities, but by a closer look we can see that not only is everything similar to everything in some way, but everything seem similar to everything in an infinite number of ways.[8] This makes it difficult to measure the degree of similarity in this way. One way to solve this problem could be to reject some predicates when describing the similarity. An attempt could be to distinguish positive predicates, characteristics actually present, from negative predicates, the negation of the presence of certain characteristics. This however, does seem like a difficult task.[9] Based on the reasons mentioned, it would seem virtuous to consider the vertical relations together with the horizontal relations when describing analogies.

---

[8]Think for example of the predicate 'being non-identical to the number 1'. We might attribute this predicate to all individuals that are not identical to the number 1, meaning most individuals. In a similar way we might take the predicate: 'being non-identical to the number 2'. This applies to all individuals that are not identical to the number 2. This includes the number 1, since if something is identical with the number 1, it is not identical to the number 2. We might continue in a similar way with 'being non-identical to the number 3' and 'being non-identical to the number 4' and so on. By this way, we might create a potentially infinite amount of predicates that will apply to any individual that we speak about, including the numbers 1, 2, 3, ... and so on. The point is that, for every two individuals, we might find some predicate that are shared by both.

[9]In the previously mentioned example, we used predicates of the form 'being non-identical to ...' and 'non-identicality' might be said to contain a negation and therefore be somehow a negative predicate. However, this seems to only be an aspect of language. We could also have used a predicate of 'difference', where the negation is not clearly present. In general, it does seem difficult to properly define a notion of positivity and negativity for predicates so that it would be sufficient for using them as a foundation for analogies. Even if we would manage to create such definition, it is not sure that it would solve the problem as we still miss a way to handle properties that does not have anything to do with the inference in question. Should all properties count equally, should

6.3. Explaining relations

The horizontal relations display a similarity between the source and the target. They attach characteristics of the source to characteristics of the target by means of some measurement of similarity. The most natural way to understand similarity in this sense is as tokens of a type. Characteristic a is similar to characteristic a' if there is a type A, so that both a and a' are elements of A. In CTT, this similarity relation should be understood as an identity judgment, $a = a' : A$. This reads that a and a' are equal elements of A, namely that they can be reduced to the same canonical element.

The similarity requirement is therefore that two elements are the same relevant to a type. The type that this similarity is relative to will have to be explicitly stated in the representation. A similarity therefore has to be relative to a specified type, and they must be reducible to the same canonical object of this type. To take an example, the number 1 might be similar to the number 2 in the sense that both are positive, but they are still distinct natural numbers, meaning that they are different canonical elements in the set $\mathbb{N}$.

This notion of similarity restricts our theory in several ways. First, we have to be specific about what is similar between two cases and why they are similar. This means that we cannot have similarity without explicitly stating what this similarity consists in. Second, we have restricted our notion of similarity to only permit identical canonical elements. In some sense this provides the essence of the similarity relation. The notion of similarity is linked to the notion of identity in the theory.[10] This enables us to not only express similarity between things relevant to some type, but also to include

---

we distinguish very important properties from not-so important properties or should we further restrict what properties that should qualify? If we choose the last alternative, the approach seems to collapse into an inclusion of vertical relations.

[10]In the case of numbers, 1 and 2 are not identical canonical elements of $\mathbb{N}$ even though they are both clearly numbers. We therefore have to define specifically the type that provides the identity of 1 and 2, for example by creating a new set *number* that only has one canonical element.

an explicit notion of difference. We can say that two things are different if they can be reduced to different canonical elements. In both the case of similarity and of difference, this can be expressed relative to a type, such as a proposition.

Vertical relations

The vertical relations provide links between characteristics within in each case. We might call these links relations of *relevancy*. All theories of analogy presented in chapter 2 emphasise the importance of these vertical relations. This is partly as a result of the problem of similarity that was mentioned. Common for all theories is that it is the vertical relations that provide the real strength of the analogy. In short, a good analogy has a strong vertical relation. However, it is less clear how one ought to measure the strength of these vertical relations.

Relevancy seems to be a slightly more complicated notion than similarity, which also explains the described theories' focus on this aspect. In a legal analogy, the most common situation would seem to be that the relevancy should go from the occasioning characteristic to the entailed characteristic, that P is relevant for Q and that $P*$ is relevant for $Q*$.[11]

If we try to make a general definition of relevancy, we would likely end up with either a definition that is too general to be applicable or too narrow to include everything we would like. Relevancy seems to be a philosophical notion that to a great extent resists proper definitions. This however, does not mean that we have nothing to say about the vertical relations. In all the described theories there are restrictions on the vertical relations. The different authors uses different terms and implements the vertical relations in

---

[11]Bartha (2010) also mentions some other alternatives, but particularly since we speak about a legal context, the most natural focus would be that P is relevant for Q and not that they are relevant for each other or that Q somehow is relevant for P. Q can be considered as the decision where P is the background or reason for that decision.

6.3. Explaining relations

different ways, but we will describe it based on the term *efficiency requirement*, taken from the Islamic model. (Rahman and Iqbal 2018) The efficiency requirement might be considered as a twofold condition. The first part is the condition of co-extensiveness, for all cases where P is present, Q is also present. The second part is the condition of co-exclusiveness, for all cases where P is absent, Q is also absent. All described theories seem to explicitly or implicitly accept at least the first part as a condition on the vertical relations. This simply states that there should be no counterexample to the analogy where we have the occasioning characteristic present, but where the entailed characteristic is absent. The second part also seems acceptable, though slightly more controversial. It states that there should be no counterexample to the analogy where the occasioning characteristic is absent, but where the entailed characteristic is present.[12]

---

[12] One might wonder whether this second part of the efficiency requirement really is an acceptable requirement at all. Let us use the **Adams v. New Jersey Steamboat Co.** as an example. A counterexample by the first part of the efficiency requirement would be a case where *the client paid for a room for some specified reasons and that the company has tempting opportunity for fraud and plunder of the client*, while the company still was not held *strictly liable for the theft of valuables from its customers*. This would seem to be an acceptable counterexample to the case, as it undermines the relevancy of the occasioning characteristic. The occasioning characteristics might be wrong or they might need a specification. A counterexample to the second part of the efficiency requirement would seem to be a case where a company was held *strictly liable for the theft of valuables from its customers* without that *the client paid for a room for some specified reasons and that the company has tempting opportunity for fraud and plunder of the client*. Intuitively, this seems strange. You surely have other situations where a company is *strictly liable for the theft of valuables from its customers*, where the condition is not satisfied, say for example a company providing safe deposit boxes. They do not satisfy the condition, since they do not provide a room at all, but would still be *strictly liable for the theft of valuables from its customers*. One alternative (that would seem like the alternative suggested by Brewer) would be to consider it as extending the notion of 'room' in the occasioning characteristic so that it would be interpreted to also cover safe deposit boxes.

Because of CTT's notion of dependent hypothetical judgments, this framework allows for an explicit representation of the dependency of the entailed characteristics on the occasioning characteristics. This makes the requirement of co-exclusiveness more acceptable. The representation in CTT makes it explicit that the absence of Q *depends* on the absence of P, not only that they have the same extension. We do not claim that this is not possible to represent in other logical frameworks, only that an explicit representation of the dependency makes the requirement of co-exclusiveness acceptable and that we have a simple way to do this in CTT.

The vertical relations might be said to display the relevance the occasioning characteristics have for the entailed characteristics. This is done in order to ensure that the analogy is justified. As explained earlier, everything might be considered to be be similar to everything in some ways and we therefore need a way to decide which characteristics that are relevant for this particular inference. We might therefore restrict these vertical relations in certain ways, for example by imposing a condition of efficiency.

Other relations?

When we have described the horizontal relations and the vertical relations there is a question that comes to mind; are there other relations than the horizontal and the vertical ones? The horizontal relations are in some sense similarity relations, while the vertical relations might be said to be relevancy relations. We might also speak about another kind of horizontal relations, namely the *similarity of the vertical relations*. In all described theories, it is required that there is a P in the source and a $P*$ in the target such that P is similar to $P*$. A corresponding point holds for Q in the source and $Q*$ in the target. They also require P to be somehow relevant for Q and $P*$ to be somehow relevant for $Q*$. What none of them mentions explicitly is a requirement for $P*$ to be relevant for $Q*$ in the

6.3. Explaining relations

same way as P is relevant for Q. This seems to be a condition that should be imposed on the analogy, but is not explicitly mentioned in any of the theories. We can describe this relation in the following way:

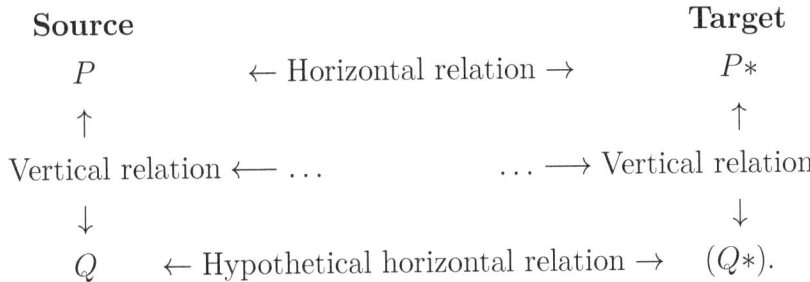

Does this horizontal relation of vertical relations captures something that is not captured by the vertical and horizontal relations alone? The horizontal vertical relation captures the notion that the source domain and the target domain are similar, not just that they have some similar properties. This might sound like a play with words that has no actual effect on the analysis, but we will argue that this is an important aspect to include when speaking about analogies. However, this notion of horizontal vertical relations seems present, though left implicit, in the different theories.

By going back again to antiquity, this relation seems to be accurately captured by the notion of *proportionality*. Proportionality is described by Aristotle in the Nicomachean Ethics as:

> *For proportion is equality of ratios, and involves four terms at least ([...]); and the just, too, involves at least four terms, and the ratio is the same for there is a similar distinction between the persons and between the things. As the term A, then, is to B, so will C be to*

> D, and therefore, alternando, as A is to C, B will be to
> D. Therefore also the whole is in the same ratio to the
> whole; and this coupling the distribution effects, and, if
> the terms are so combined, effects justly.

Aristotle (Ethica Nicomachea, V.3,1131b,1-10)

This principle provides a theoretical foundation for the notion of equality, and more precisely for the concept equality of the law. It grounds what was identified by Hart (1958, pp. 623-624) as a fundamental principle of justice of *treating like cases alike*. A similar principle was furthermore expressed by Lord Hoffmann as an advice in *Matadeen v. Pointu* [1998]:

> [...] treating like cases alike and unlike cases differently is a general axiom of rational behaviour.

Lord Hoffmann (*Matadeen v. Pointu*, 1 AC 98, 109)

The principle of proportionality has throughout the history been fundamental for a great variety of disciplines, including the notion of analogy. The principle of proportionality does not attempt to describe only that there is a relation from A to B and from B to C, and a relation from A to C and from B to D, but that the relation from B to D bears the *same* relation as the relation from A to C. It does not only speak about relations, but the relation between two relations.

From Aristotle's definition, we see that a proportion is an equality of *ratios*. So we might have an equality of two ratios between A and B and C and D,

$$
\begin{array}{ccc}
A & \leftarrow ratio \rightarrow & B \\
& \uparrow & \\
& equality & \\
& \downarrow & \\
C & \leftarrow ratio \rightarrow & D.
\end{array}
$$

6.3. Explaining relations

Based on such relation, by the principle of proportionality we can also say that there is an *equality* between the ratios A and C and B and D,

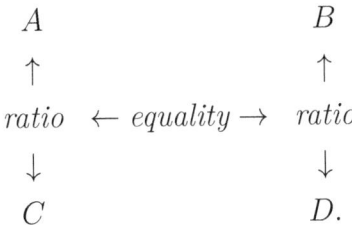

This looks remarkably close to a representation of analogies, though we see that the principle of proportionality is concerned not with what we have called the horizontal and vertical relations, but rather the *horizontal vertical relation*, or to put it in other terms the *similar relevancy*.

The contemporary theories of analogy described in chapter 2 seem to have implemented this notion. In the both the Islamic model and the dialogical model by Prakken and Sartor (1996), the horizontal vertical relation is the judgment that the source case and the target case should be equal elements in the analogy and particularly for the occasioning characteristic. In the Islamic model, this is called the juridical law, *Usul al-fiqh*. The procedure to develop an analogy in this model is to first state the presence of the ruling in the target. The next step is to develop a source case together with an occasioning factor. The third step is generalise the relation between the occasioning factor and the ruling to a universal, an instance of the juridical law. The last step is to use the universal to develop justification for the application of the ruling in the target case. In this theory, the horizontal vertical relations are provided by the universal, or more precisely the instantiation by the cases in the universal. The universal acts as the reference for the similarity between the source and the target. Because of the choice of CTT, the Islamic model does indeed show such dependency, even though it is not mentioned explicitly. In the articulation model by Bartha

(2010), the vertical relations are called *prior associations*. The horizontal vertical relation is in this theory displayed as six different categories of analogies. The categories are defined by what kind of prior association they use. Since an analogy occurs within a certain category, we will end up with the same kind of prior association in the target as we have in the source. This restriction is what we might identify as the horizontal vertical relation in the articulation model. It restricts the analogy to consist of similar prior associations in the source and in the target.

In the schema-based theories, the horizontal vertical relation is not as clearly expressed as they typically represent the horizontal and the vertical relations as two distinct tacit premises. This does not mean that it is not there. The reason for this lack of clarity is the slightly diffuse definition of *schema*. A schema can be anything that makes the derivation valid and still satisfies the requirement of efficiency. However, the schemas must be a quantified formula of some kind, as they would need to cover some particular facts in both the source and the target case. If the schema is not a quantification, it seems to either beg the question, be inconsistent or to be not necessary for the derivation.[13] The horizontal vertical relation is then a result of linking the vertical relations in the source and the vertical relations in the target by this quantified formula in the schema. Based on this, we can see that the schema-based theories do indeed share their explanation of the horizontal vertical relation with the Islamic model.

---

[13]We assume that neither Brewer (1996), Alchourrón (1991) nor Woods (2015) would accept an inconsistent schema since one could use that to derive anything, not only the intended result. We also assume that they would not accept begging the question in the sense that the schema would speak about the individuals in question. It would eventually make them applicable only to some specific cases and this does not seem to be acceptable by the equality of the law. If the schema is not necessary for the derivation, it would seem that we have another variant of begging the question, namely that the conclusion is already included in one of the other premises. The point here is that a schema would seem to be a quantifier of some sort.

6.3. Explaining relations

However, should we have an explicit description of these horizontal vertical relations? If we imagine that we do not have any condition of similarity of the vertical relations, we could end up with analogies where the source is significantly different from the target. This can be explained in terms of the articulation model as analogies where the source would have one prior association and the target would have another, which is an evident, but nonetheless implicit assumption. This point is less clear in the other theories as they only intend to capture legal reasoning and operate therefore within only one category (namely the one of jurisprudence). In some sense they force the analogy to have one 'standard of comparison'. This might work fine when using only one kind of vertical relations. However, being explicit about this notion might first enable us to later implement different categories of analogy in our theory and second, make clear that what actually is going on is a comparison of relations.

As we have seen, the main motivation for speaking about *similar relevancy* instead of *similarity* and *relevancy* is not a logical one, but it does seem to be a more precise way to describe the kind of inference we consider. CTT allows for representing dependency of elements, and it is this aspect that will be used for explaining the notion of similar relevancy by letting the source case be dependent on the target case. This is closely related solution we find in the Islamic model by Rahman and Iqbal (2018). Throughout the analysis, we will still use the notions of horizontal and vertical relations in order to keep in line with the contemporary terminology and for simplicity purposes. The purpose of this section is to precise that reducing analogical reasoning into a question of similarity and relevancy (or horizontal and vertical relations) does not seem to give a precise description of the meaning explanations in the process. We might in many situations consider these two things separately, but ultimately what we are after is the notion of *similar relevancy*, not simply similarity *and* relevancy.

Part III
Analysing analogy

Chapter 7
CTT ANALYSIS

We might distinguish two kinds of analogical argumentation or reasoning with precedents. We have reasoning about heteronomous imperatives, together with the more general reasoning about characteristics. The difference between the two is what kind of result we achieve from the analogical argument. In the case of reasoning about heteronomous imperatives, the result of the argument should be an imperative, understood as a decision whether the performance of a certain action is law-breaking or law-abiding. In reasoning about characteristics, the result is whether a certain situation has a given property. Typically, this is the situation for reasoning about definitions or borderline rules. In the intuitionistic framework, imperatives seem to be a special kind of predicate. Reasoning about heteronomous imperatives is therefore considered to be a special kind of reasoning about characteristics.

The requirement of efficiency consists of two conditions, the condition of co-extensiveness and the condition of co-exclusiveness. It is meant to provide restrictions on the choice of the occasioning characteristic. The occasioning characteristic should be so that in all cases where we have this occasioning characteristic, we also have the entailed characteristic, and in all cases where we do not have this occasioning characteristic, we do not have the entailed characteristic either. Instead of being implemented explicitly, the condition of efficiency is included in the procedure as a whole. This analysis will be not be based on the requirement of efficiency as such, but rather a variant of the *Proportionality-principle*, namely:

Treat like cases alike and unlike cases differently.

This is a principle that can be traced back to Aristotle's *Nicomachean Ethics* (V.3,1131a10-b15) and provides a fundamental notion regarding equality, based on the notion of proportionality. It is often considered to be the foundation of analogical reasoning and reasoning with precedents, or sometimes even as a fundamental principle of law. It also provides justification for the principle of *stare decisis*. We can see that this principle actually consists of two parts, what we will call the *Alike-principle* and *Differently-principle*. The first can be described as:

Alike-principle: *Treat like cases alike.*

That a case is like another is understood as it being similar to the other. All cases are similar in one way or another and we cannot include all ways cases can be like each other. In order for this principle to be meaningful, we must therefore speak about *relevant similarities* or *similar relevancies*. A similarity is then based upon a relevant characteristic, shared by both cases and this characteristic should be the reason for its precise treatment.

We can easily see how this principle relates to analogical reasoning as an analogy is provided by two things that are similar in some aspect. If we have decided that a case is similar to another one, we should by the principle of equality, treat the first case in the same way as we treated the other. This provides the justification for arguments based upon similarity, namely positive analogies. However, we do also want to include arguments based upon differences, namely negative analogies. For this we would need to rely on the second part of the Proportionality-principle, which will be called the *Differently-principle*,

Differently-principle: *Treat unlike cases differently.*

At first sight, this is a seemingly more controversial principle than the previous. However, we seem to have good reason also to accept this principle if we accept the first. Seemingly, no cases are the same; all cases are different to each other in some way or another. As with the first principle, we would therefore be inclined to speak about *relevant differences*, or *different relevancies*. That a case A is different from another case B is understood as A not sharing the relevant aspect with B that caused B being treated in the way it was. This means that there was some aspect in B that was the reason for this particular treatment and this aspect was not found in A. When we do not have the reason for this particular treatment, the treatment is seemingly groundless and therefore not applicable. That the treatment is not applicable means that we will have to find some other treatment, namely to treat it differently.

Together, these two principles provide justification for this analysis of analogical reasoning. The two principles seem to reflect the requirement of efficiency, though the Proportionality-principle is formulated closer to Aristotle's original analysis. By distinguishing the Proportionality-principle into the Alike-principle and the Differently-principle, we also provide the grounds for distinguishing between positive and negative analogies. This principle will be used to reflect the last step of the analysis performed here, namely the application to the target case.

7.1 General precedent-based reasoning

Performing analogical reasoning

The first step in the analysis will be to describe an informal seven-step procedure for how to perform general analogical reasoning with characteristics. The last step of the procedure might be said to be the most complex and controversial step as it involves the application to the target case. This step is a twofold step where the first part involves what we might call a standard or positive analogy (based on the Alike-principle), while the second part involves what we might call a negative analogy (based on the Differently-principle).

Procedure for performing analogical reasoning:

1. Include a target case where the presence or absence of some (consequent) characteristic has to be decided.

2. Find a relevant (occasioning) characteristic that will be chosen for reaching a decision in the target case.

3. Make sure that the terms are well-defined and that the use of the analogical argument is legally acceptable in this particular situation.

4. Decide whether this occasioning characteristic is present in the target case or not.

5. Find some source case and decide whether this occasioning characteristic is present in the source case or not.

6. Decide whether the entailed characteristic is present in the source case or not.

7.1. General precedent-based reasoning

7. Decide whether the occasioning characteristic has the same status in both the target case and the source case (that it is present or absent). This is a twofold step:
    a) If the occasioning characteristic has the same status in both the source case and the target case (that it is present or absent):
        i. the status of the entailed characteristic in the source case can be transferred directly to the target case;
    b) If the occasioning characteristic has a different status in the source case and the target case (that it was present or absent):
        i. the status that the entailed characteristic has in the source case should not be the situation in the target case (its negation can be transferred to the target case).

Explaining the procedure

The first step is the foundation for the argument in the first place as there has to be some particular case that motivates the introduction of the argument. This is the target case, which essentially can be described as a problem that has to be solved.

The second step is the most difficult and controversial step when speaking about analogical reasoning. This step corresponds to what Brewer (1996) refers to as an abductive step, as it is the introduction of the occasioning characteristic. The choice of relevant occasioning characteristic seems to depend on some creative or intuitive aspect that cannot be fully described by a procedure. We might use constraints similar to ones developed for abductive inferences, like simplicity, generality, coherence and possibly particular constraints related to legal reasoning, but even with such constraints it seems difficult or impossible to describe an efficient procedure for choosing such characteristic. However, if we have found a potential characteristic, we might reject it if it does not give a coherent result. This might motivate us to go back to change or revise the originally chosen characteristic. This is a result of the efficiency requirement that is implemented in the analysis by means of the Proportionality-principle.

The third step is the starting point for the analysis. The occasioning characteristic chosen in the second step has to be well-defined, which in CTT means to be well-typed. The legal result of the occasioning characteristic and its negation must be type-declared. We need to declare a set for the accepted source cases. We must also declare that the legal system permits the use of analogical reasoning in this particular situation. This can involve the proposed requirements mentioned earlier, but they can also be different.

The fourth step is the decision of whether the occasioning characteristic or its negation is present in the target case. This is the first *investigation* that is represented in the analysis.

The fifth step refers to the source case. The same investigation has to be performed in the chosen source case, whether the chosen occasioning characteristic or its negation is present in the source case.

The sixth step is a second investigation in the source case and creates the foundation for the decision in the target case. This investigation relates to whether the presence of the occasioning characteristic, or the absence of the occasioning characteristic, provides the presence or absence of the entailed characteristic in the source case.

The seventh step is the most complex step as it is the application of a consequence in the target case. It is a twofold step where the first part explains what should happen if the occasioning characteristic either is present in both the target case and the source case or is absent in both the target case and the source case. In this situation, we might directly transfer the presence/absence of the entailed characteristic from the source case to the target case. This is what might be called a positive analogy. It is a result of the Alike-principle, to treat like cases alike. The second alternative

7.1. General precedent-based reasoning

describes a negative analogy where the occasioning characteristic is present in either the target case or in the source case and it is absent in the other. In this situation we might infer that the negation of the presence or absence of the entailed characteristic in the source case, holds in the target case. This is a result of the Differently-principle, to treat unlike cases differently. It is in the interpretation of this step that we notice a difference between intuitionistic and classical logic. Since in classical logic we have the elimination rule of double negation, we might infer that when the entailed characteristic is absent in the source case, it should be *present* in the target case. This is not the case in intuitionistic logic. Intuitionistically, we can only infer that the entailed characteristic should *not be absent*, and this is not the same as to say that it should be present.

Positive and negative analogies

Positive analogies occur when the status of the chosen occasioning characteristic is shared between the source and the target. We can then infer that the entailed characteristic has the same status in the target case as it had in the source case. If the entailed characteristic is present in the source case, we can infer that it should be present in the target case. While if the entailed characteristic is absent in the source case, we can infer that it should be absent also in the target case.

Negative analogies occur when the status of the chosen occasioning characteristic is different in the source and the target case. For negative analogies, when the entailed characteristic is present in the source case, we can infer that this characteristic should be absent (its negation should be present) in the target case. Similarly, if the negated entailed characteristic is present in the source case, we can infer that this negated characteristic should be absent (its negated should be present) in the target case. We assume that the absence of a characteristic is the same as the presence of the negated characteristic. That a characteristic is present is denoted as $B(x)$ while that a characteristic that is absent is denoted as $\neg B(x)$. In negative analogies, when we have a presence, $B(x)$, of an entailed characteristic in the source case, we can infer that this characteristic should be absent, $\neg B(x)$, in the target case. A particular situation occurs when we have an absence, $\neg B(x)$, of an entailed characteristic in the source case. We can then infer that this (absent) characteristic should be absent, $\neg\neg B(x)$, in the target case. This is not the same as saying that the entailed characteristic should be present in the target case, as we then end up with a double negated characteristic in the target case. Since we are in an intuitionistic framework, we cannot infer the non-negated characteristic from this. This means that in negative analogies, we end up with a double negated characteristic in the target case when we have a negated characteristic in the source case.

The meaning of this double negated characteristic might seem slightly unclear at first sight. However, by a closer look this distinction seem to be rather natural in the legal context. Since the framework of immanent reasoning is constructive, the notion of truth is connected to its provability. That something is true means that it can be proven. That a negation is true means that the non-negated is not provable (that the attempt of proving is aborted). That a double negation is true means that the negated is not provable. In a legal context, this means that we have a refutation of the negation, but not an explicit proof for a (non-negated) decision. We are then provided with a distinction between reasons in favour of some claim and reasons against rejecting a claim. Negative analogies will generally provide reasons of the last kind.

7.1. General precedent-based reasoning

Restricted and unrestricted analogies

The informal description describes how to reason when including one source case. This means that the result depends on the situation in a single source case, independently of what are the situations in all other source cases. Usually in legal reasoning, we would like to base the arguments on what generally holds, not only the situation of a particular source case. This can be included by restricting the analysis to include not a single source case, but all source cases.

Based on this, we can make a distinction between what we might call *restricted* and *unrestricted* analogical reasoning. The informal analysis of the procedure describes what happens in the unrestricted variant of analogical reasoning. This distinction can then be expressed in the following way:

Unrestricted analogy: An unrestricted analogy is an inference based on a single source case that share (or differ based on) a characteristic with the target case;

Restricted analogy: A restricted analogy is an inference based on all source cases that share (or differ based on) a characteristic with the target case.

The difference between the restricted and the unrestricted analogical reasoning is whether we require the analogy to hold for all cases or only for a single case, irrespective of all other cases. An unrestricted analogy is based on simply a similarity or difference between the source and the target. Since it does not limit the point of reference for the similarity or the difference, it is also vulnerable to the previously described argument of a potential infinite amount of similarities (or differences). This means that it can be used as an argument for any proposition, and that it therefore hardly can be used as a reference for the use of analogical reasoning in a legal context.

Since the unrestricted analogy only requires one source case, it is considered to be weaker than the restricted form. In ordinary life outside of the context of legal reasoning, it is the form that we often refer to when we speak about analogy. Because of this generality, an unrestricted analogical argument does not seem to provide very strong justification for its result. In short, the unrestricted analogy does not seem to include anything that corresponds to the requirement of efficiency.

A restricted analogy will provide a stronger justification and is also the form that is used in the legal context. Instead of being an analogy over a single source case, it quantifies over all source cases so that all source cases that are similar (or different) to the target case should be coherent in regard to the entailed characteristic of the analogy. However, it is important to note that also in a restricted analogy, the analogy depends on particular source cases and should not necessarily be considered dependent on the generalisation as such. This shows that there seem to be some tension inside the restricted analogy, whether we speak about a particular source case or a generalisation. The framework of immanent reasoning seems capable of capturing this in a rather subtle way as it allows the analogical argument to based upon a particular case, though captures the general aspect by the ability to *choose*. One could have chosen differently, but end up with the same result and after the choice is made, the analogy is dependent on the particular case that was chosen. In this way, immanent reasoning is able to capture both the particular and the general aspect of restricted analogical reasoning.

Imposing conditions on analogical reasoning

A widespread condition for analogical reasoning is the condition of efficiency. There is no explicit implementation of this condition in the process, but the condition of efficiency can be introduced by restricting step 5 to 7 to hold not only for one source case, but for all source cases, so that we speak about a *restricted* analogy. If

7.1. General precedent-based reasoning

no decision can be reached based on all source cases, one has to go back to step 2, choose another characteristic and continue the process from there. Other conditions regarding the use of analogical reasoning can be implemented in step 3, as they will be analysed as formation conditions. The logical analysis provided in this work describes and analyses step 3 to step 7.

In the third step, the conditions regarding the formation of an analogy are implemented. This step could be said to consist of several substeps. The first is the type declaration of the proposition or characteristic. We represent the propositions and characteristics as the standard type *prop*. For some proposition A, we would need to suppose:

$A : prop.$

The source cases have to be declared as a set. It means that we have some defined and accepted source cases that might be used in the analogy.[1] This can be represented in the following way:

$Source : set.$

In addition, we have to declare that the intended entailed characteristic is a proposition. This proposition is also dependent on both the proposition A and on the set *Source*, introduced in the following way:

$B(x, s) : prop(x : A, s : Source).$

The last part is the inclusion of the permission in the legal system of utilising analogical reasoning in this particular situation. The permission of an analogy is rooted in its result in the target case, not in the proposition itself. This means that we will introduce

---

[1] In the CTT representation, we leave out the explicit representation of the target case as a set. This is to avoid further complexity and keep the analysis as simple as possible. In the dialogical analysis, complexity is however less of a problem and we will introduce the explicit set for the target case in this representation. See chapter 8 for details about the implementation of the target case set.

the permission of the analogy on the presence or absence of B. We therefore have four sets of permitted analogies, represented in the following way:

$$PA_1(z_1) : set(z_1 : (x_1 : A)B(x_1) \vee (x_2 : A)\neg B(x_2));$$
$$PA_2(z_2) : set(z_2 : (y_1 : \neg A)\neg B(y_1) \vee (y_2 : \neg A)\neg\neg B(y_2));$$
$$PA_3(z_3) : set(z_3 : (x_3 : A)\neg B(x_3) \vee (x_4 : A)\neg\neg B(x_4));$$
$$PA_4(z_4) : set(z_4 : (y_3 : \neg A)B(y_3) \vee (y_4 : \neg A)\neg B(y_4)).$$

The explicit permission of an analogy is introduced by the previously described judgments. These judgments can be produced by an instance of the elimination rule of the disjoint union. The instance for the first judgment is the following:

$$\frac{c : B \vee \neg B \quad \overset{(x:B)}{d(x) : PA(i(x))} \quad \overset{(y:\neg B)}{e(y) : PA(j(y))}}{D(c, (x)d(x), (y)e(y)) : PA(c),} \; PA$$

which reads that when we have an a that is a permitted analogy, it is justified by the proof object $D(c, (x)d(x), (y)e(y))$ that is produced when c is the proof object of the disjunction and $(x)d(x)$ is verified in the case of B, while $(y)e(y)$ is verified in the case of $\neg B$.

It is important to note that this does not explain the content of this requirement, for example that it should be a lacuna in the law and not undermine constitutional values, but is rather a representation of the result assessing this content.

For general analogies, we then end up with the following context:

$$A : prop,$$
$$Source : set,$$
$$B(x, s) : prop(x : A, s : Source),$$
$$PA_1(z_1) : set(z_1 : (x_1 : A)B(x_1) \vee (x_2 : A)\neg B(x_2)),$$
$$PA_2(z_2) : set(z_2 : (y_1 : \neg A)\neg B(y_1) \vee (y_2 : \neg A)\neg\neg B(y_2)),$$
$$PA_3(z_3) : set(z_3 : (x_3 : A)\neg B(x_3) \vee (x_4 : A)\neg\neg B(x_4)),$$
$$PA_4(z_4) : set(z_4 : (y_3 : \neg A)B(y_3) \vee (y_4 : \neg A)\neg B(y_4)).$$

7.1. General precedent-based reasoning

In the following sections, the explicit formulation of this context will be left out for the sake of simplicity.

Representing source cases

We can now describe how to reach a decision based on the available source cases at hand. Here, we suppose that the absence of a characteristic is the presence of its negation. That A is being absent will therefore be described as $\neg A$ being present. For a source case s, we then have several situations:

1. A is present in s,

    a) B is present in s,

    b) $\neg B$ is present in s;

2. $\neg A$ is present in s,

    a) B is present in s,

    b) $\neg B$ is present in s.

Depending on the source case s, we can use s as an argument for a certain standpoint in the target case. The standard form of analogical reasoning is based on A being present in both the source case and the target case and since B was present/absent in the source case, it should also be present/absent in the target case. If we assume that A is present in the target case, this can be represented in the following way, so that when there are two lines from a statement, it represents an implication of a conjunction:

```
For a source case s
└─ A is present in s
   ├─ B is present in s
   │  └─ B should be present in the target case
   └─ ¬B is present in s
      └─ ¬B should be present in the target
         case.
```

In addition to the standard form of analogical arguments, we also have what we called negative analogies. Instead of being based on the similarity between the target case and the source case, it depends on their difference. If A is present in the target case and not in the source case, and B is present in the source case, B should be absent in the target case. And if B is absent in the source case, B should not be absent in the target case. We can represent this in the following way, where we still suppose that A is present in the target case:

```
For a source case s
└─ ¬A is present in s
   ├─ B is present in s
   │  └─ ¬B should be present in the target
   │     case
   └─ ¬B is present in s
      └─ ¬¬B should be present in the target
         case.
```

By combining these two representations, we end up with a procedure for handling analogical reasoning when A is present in the target case. This yields the following form:

```
For a source case s
├─ A is present in s
│  ├─ B is present in s
│  │  └─ B should be present in the target case
│  └─ ¬B is present in s
│     └─ ¬B should be present in the target
│        case
└─ ¬A is present in s
   ├─ B is present in s
   │  └─ ¬B should be present in the target
   │     case
   └─ ¬B is present in s
      └─ ¬¬B should be present in the target
         case.
```

7.1. General precedent-based reasoning

Correspondingly, we can describe the process of analogical reasoning when $\neg A$ is present in the target case. If $\neg A$ is also present in the source case, we speak about a positive analogy since $\neg A$ is shared between the source and the target. The decision whether B is present or absent can be directly transferred from the source case to the target case. We suppose here that $\neg A$ is present in the target case. This transfer can be represented in the following way:

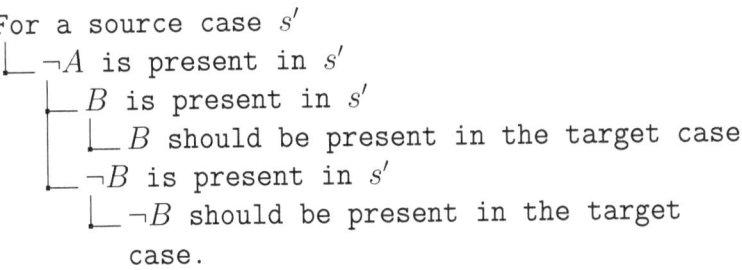

When $\neg A$ is present in the target case, we might also speak about negative analogies. The negative analogy occurs when A is present in the source case. The analogy is then based on some characteristic that is not shared between the source and the target. This can be represented in the following way, where it is supposed that $\neg A$ is present in the target case:

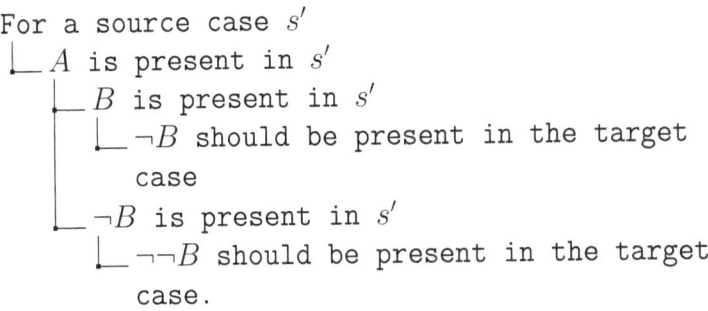

We then end up with a procedure for handling analogical reasoning when $\neg A$ is present in the target case. This yields the following form:

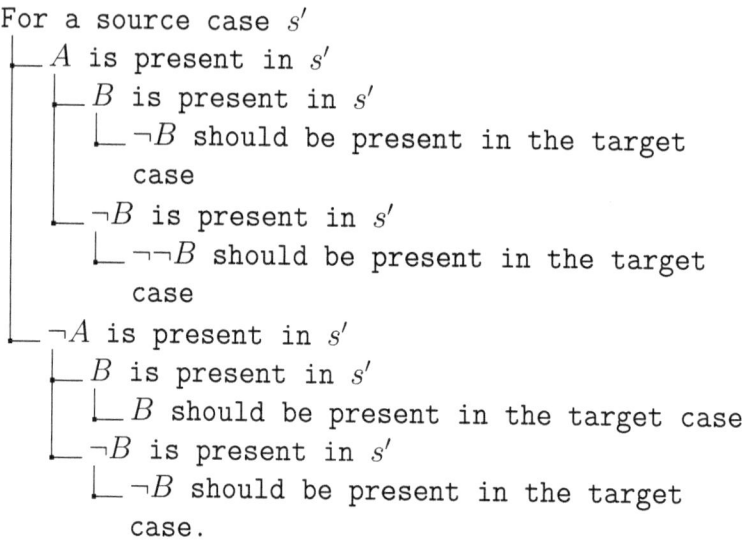

Representing the analogical procedure in CTT

By combining the procedures for handling analogies when A is present and when $\neg A$ is present in the target case, we end up with a description of the whole process for analogical reasoning. This can be represented by the following:

7.1. General precedent-based reasoning

```
For a target case where A ∨ ¬A is present
└─ A is present in the target case
   └─ For a source case s
      ├─ A is present in s
      │  ├─ B is present in s
      │  │  └─ B should be present in the target
      │  │     case
      │  └─ ¬B is present in s
      │     └─ ¬B should be present in the
      │        target case
      └─ ¬A is present in s
         ├─ B is present in s
         │  └─ ¬B should be present in the
         │     target case
         └─ ¬B was present in s
            └─ ¬¬B should be present in the
               target case
└─ ¬A is present in the target case
   └─ For a source case s'
      ├─ A is present in s'
      │  ├─ B is present in s'
      │  │  └─ ¬B should be present in the
      │  │     target case
      │  └─ ¬B is present in s'
      │     └─ ¬¬B should be present in the
      │        target case
      └─ ¬A is present in s'
         ├─ B is present in s'
         │  └─ B should be present in the target
         │     case
         └─ ¬B is present in s'
            └─ ¬B should be present in the
               target case.
```

This provides the foundation for its representation in CTT. The target case can be represented by a similar form as the conditional analysis described in Rahman and Granström (2019), though including an explicit dependency on the source case. In a similar way as previously described, we will use $\{H1\}, \{H2\}, \ldots$ as abbreviations for formulas like $A \vee \neg A$ in identity statements. We then use a conditional formulation to represent the inquiry of whether it is the right or the left side of this disjunction that makes it true in the target case. If it is the left side A, we continue with the source case s. If it is the right side $\neg A$, we continue with the source case s'. This yields the following, incomplete formula:

$$b(x) : [(\forall y : A)\mathbf{left}^{\vee}(y) =_{\{H1\}} x \supset (\forall s : Source)...] \wedge$$
$$[(\forall y' : \neg A)\mathbf{right}^{\vee}(y') =_{\{H1\}} x \supset (\forall s' : Source)...](x : A \vee \neg A).$$

In the tree structure, this formula receives the following notation:

$(x : A \vee \neg A)$
$b(x)$:

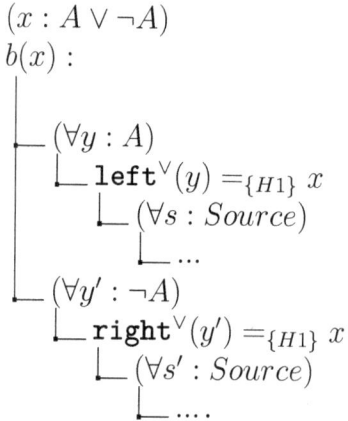

This formula is incomplete because it does not include the description of the source cases. They should be included in '...'. By understanding the target case in this way, we include a notion of *suspense*. Based on the procedure for performing analogical reasoning as described earlier, this representation will include a suspense on the decision of whether A or $\neg A$ is present in the target case. Essentially, this means that the presence or absence of A is not

7.1. General precedent-based reasoning

given by the target case, but is performed as an investigation into the target case when referring to an analogy. We might therefore say that the investigation or inquiry whether A or $\neg A$ is present in the target case comes after the target case itself. The source cases are implemented inside the formula after it has been decided whether A or $\neg A$ is present in the target case. The source cases are only introduced when trying to build an analogical argument after deciding the presence or absence of some proposition in the target case. The analysis therefore does not introduce the source cases before they are needed.

There are two '...' in the incomplete formula. The source cases are introduced in two parts, first when A is present in the target case and second when $\neg A$ is present in the target case. If A is present in the target case, the process can be formalised in the following way:

256   Chapter 7. *CTT analysis*

$(\forall s : Source)$
  $\llcorner (\forall z : A(s) \lor \neg A(s))$
     $\llcorner (\forall u_1 : A(s))$
        $\llcorner \text{left}^\lor(u_1) =_{\{H2\}} z$
           $\llcorner (\forall v_1 : B(s) \lor \neg B(s))$
               $\llcorner (\forall w_1 : B(s))$
                    $\llcorner \text{left}^\lor(w_1) =_{\{H3\}} v_1$
                       $\llcorner B$ should be present in the target case
               $\llcorner (\forall w_2 : \neg B(s))$
                   $\llcorner \text{right}^\lor(w_1) =_{\{H3\}} v_1$
                     $\llcorner \neg B$ should be present in the target case
     $\llcorner (\forall u_2 : \neg A(s))$
        $\llcorner \text{right}^\lor(u_2) =_{\{H2\}} z$
           $\llcorner (\forall v_2 : B(s) \lor \neg B(s))$
               $\llcorner (\forall w_3 : B(s))$
                    $\llcorner \text{left}^\lor(w_3) =_{\{H4\}} v_2$
                     $\llcorner \neg B$ should be present in the target case
               $\llcorner (\forall w_4 : \neg B(s))$
                 $\llcorner \text{right}^\lor(w_4) =_{\{H4\}} v_2$
                    $\llcorner \neg\neg B$ should be present in the target case.

Similarly, if $\neg A$ is present in the target case, the process can be formalised in the following way:

7.1. General precedent-based reasoning

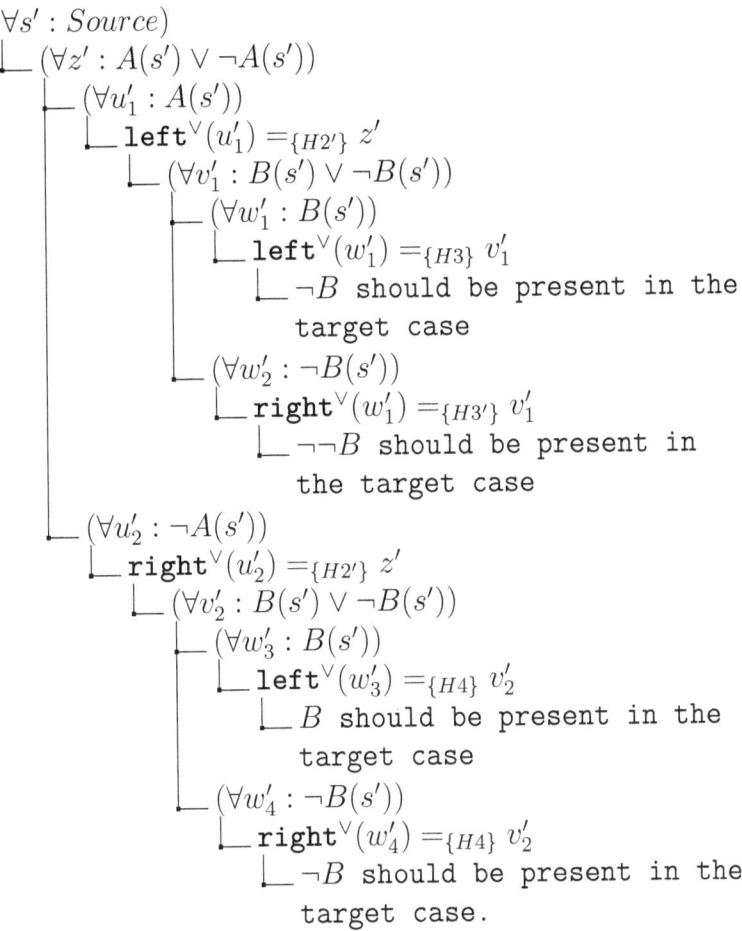

$(\forall s' : Source)$
$\quad\vdash (\forall z' : A(s') \vee \neg A(s'))$
$\quad\quad\vdash (\forall u'_1 : A(s'))$
$\quad\quad\quad\vdash \text{left}^\vee(u'_1) =_{\{H2'\}} z'$
$\quad\quad\quad\quad\vdash (\forall v'_1 : B(s') \vee \neg B(s'))$
$\quad\quad\quad\quad\quad\vdash (\forall w'_1 : B(s'))$
$\quad\quad\quad\quad\quad\quad\vdash \text{left}^\vee(w'_1) =_{\{H3\}} v'_1$
$\quad\quad\quad\quad\quad\quad\quad\vdash \neg B$ should be present in the target case
$\quad\quad\quad\quad\quad\vdash (\forall w'_2 : \neg B(s'))$
$\quad\quad\quad\quad\quad\quad\vdash \text{right}^\vee(w'_1) =_{\{H3'\}} v'_1$
$\quad\quad\quad\quad\quad\quad\quad\vdash \neg\neg B$ should be present in the target case
$\quad\quad\vdash (\forall u'_2 : \neg A(s'))$
$\quad\quad\quad\vdash \text{right}^\vee(u'_2) =_{\{H2'\}} z'$
$\quad\quad\quad\quad\vdash (\forall v'_2 : B(s') \vee \neg B(s'))$
$\quad\quad\quad\quad\quad\vdash (\forall w'_3 : B(s'))$
$\quad\quad\quad\quad\quad\quad\vdash \text{left}^\vee(w'_3) =_{\{H4\}} v'_2$
$\quad\quad\quad\quad\quad\quad\quad\vdash B$ should be present in the target case
$\quad\quad\quad\quad\quad\vdash (\forall w'_4 : \neg B(s'))$
$\quad\quad\quad\quad\quad\quad\vdash \text{right}^\vee(w'_4) =_{\{H4\}} v'_2$
$\quad\quad\quad\quad\quad\quad\quad\vdash \neg B$ should be present in the target case.

By combining both of these formulations, we end up with a CTT analysis of the process of analogical reasoning. The general formulation for analogical reasoning in CTT gives the following:

Chapter 7. CTT analysis

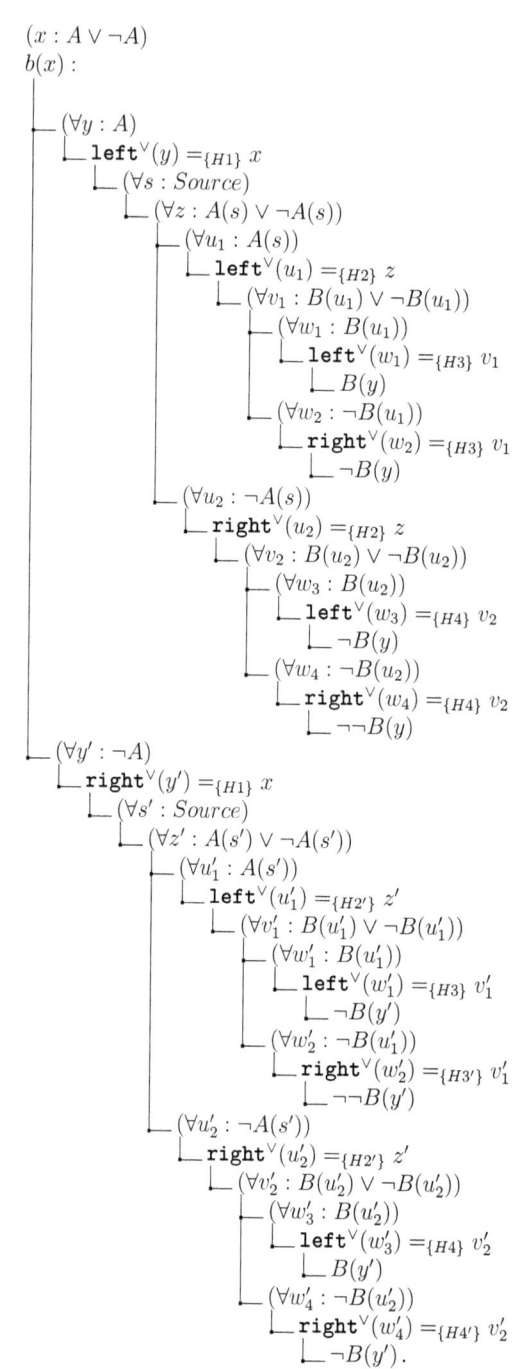

7.1. General precedent-based reasoning

This procedure is the CTT representation of step 4 to 7 in the description of the process of analogical reasoning. By including the context that was described earlier, we would also include step 3. When applying this formula to some particular case, every disjunction will play the role as a question, inquiry or investigation. After step 3, the first investigation that occurs is formalised as $x : A \vee \neg A$ and represents the decision whether the chosen characteristic is present or absent in the target case. After it has been decided whether A is present or absent in the target case, the source cases are introduced and for every source case the investigation whether the characteristic is present or absent in this source case is formalised $(\forall z : A(s) \vee \neg A(s))$ and $(\forall z' : A(s') \vee \neg A(s'))$. After deciding whether A is present or absent in the source case, the next investigation is whether the entailed characteristic is present or absent in the source case, which is represented as $(\forall v_1 : B(u_1) \vee \neg B(u_1))$, $(\forall v_2 : B(u_2) \vee \neg B(u_2))$, $(\forall v'_1 : B(u'_1) \vee \neg B(u'_1))$ and $(\forall v'_2 : B(u'_2) \vee \neg B(u'_2))$. If the occasioning characteristic is present in both the target case and the source case, the presence (or absence) of the entailed characteristic in the source case can be directly transferred to the target case. This is the situation for w_1, w_2, w'_3 and w'_4. This transfer is formalised by binding the entailed characteristic to the choice that was performed in the target case, y or y'. This corresponds to what we have called a positive analogy.

The other alternative is that the characteristic is present in either the target case or the source case and not present in the other. This is the foundation for what we have called negative analogies. Negative analogies are however slightly more complicate than positive analogies. The negative analogies occur in w_3, w_4, w'_1 and w'_2. In w_3, we have $\neg A$ and B in the source case, so since we also have A in the target case, we can infer $\neg B$ in the target case. In w_4, we have $\neg A$ and $\neg B$ in the source case, so since we also have A in the target case, we can infer $\neg \neg B$ in the target case. In w'_1, we have A and B in the source case, so since we also have $\neg A$ in the target case, we can infer $\neg B$ in the target case. In w_2', we have A and $\neg B$ in the source case, so since we also have A in the target case, we can infer $\neg\neg B$ in the target case.

We notice that since we operate within an intuitionistic framework, the notion $\neg\neg B$ is not equivalent or reducible to B. We do however claim that this distinction is important as it highlights the kind of evidence provided by such negative analogies. A source case, where the point of reference is not shared with the target case cannot be used to provide evidence for applying a notion not present in the source case to the target case. It seems all in all to correspond well together with legal practice regarding evidence as it highlights the difference of being evidence for a certain claim and being evidence against its negation.

7.2 Precedent-based reasoning with imperatives

Performing analogical reasoning

Procedure for performing analogical reasoning

A more specific variant of analogical reasoning is reasoning about heteronomous imperatives. What is understood by imperatives is discussed in section 6.1. When performing reasoning with precedents about imperatives we seem to be entitled to some further inferences compared to the situation with characteristics. In this representation, we will base it on the description on the three deontic categories described earlier. If we had included all five categories by Ibn Ḥazm, we would indeed arrive at a different process as there would be a distinction between an action being law-abiding and an action being legally neutral.[2] Note also that we here speak about *actions* rather

---

[2] For an analysis in the same system based on these five categories, see Kvernenes (2021).

7.2. Precedent-based reasoning with imperatives

than characteristics, as it is a condition for an imperative that the proposition describes an action, not a characteristic or property.[3] The descriptions of *positive/negative* and *unrestricted/restricted* analogies in section 7.1 also hold here.

We will use the notions 'law-abiding' and 'law-breaking' instead of 'reward' and 'sanction', as they seem to be more general in respect to different points of view on legal theory. Analogical reasoning based on the law-abidingness or law-breakingness of an action can be described as the following seven-step process:

1. Include a target case where some decision regarding the deontic status of an action has to be reached.

2. Find a relevant(occasioning) action-proposition that will be chosen for reaching a decision in the target case.

3. Make sure that the terms are well-defined and that the use of analogical reasoning is legally acceptable in this particular situation.

4. Decide whether this action, as it is described by the action-proposition, was performed in the target case or not.

5. Find some source case and decide whether this action was performed in the source case or not.

6. Decide whether the performance, or non-performance, was judged law-abiding or law-breaking in the source case.

7. Decide whether the action has the same status in both the target case and the source case (that it was performed/not performed). This is a twofold step:

    a) If the action has the same status in the source case and the target case (that it was performed/not performed):

---

[3]We could implement a new type of proposition specific for action-descriptions, though for the purposes in this analysis an explanation by the standard type *prop* seems sufficient.

i. the decision of the performance or non-performance of the action from the source case can be transferred directly to the performance or non-performance of the action in the target case;

b) If the action has a different status in the source case and the target case (that it was performed/not performed):

i. the performance/non-performance was law-abiding in the source case, and the opposite (that is the situation in the target case) should be law-abiding or law-breaking in the target case and;

ii. the performance/non-performance was law-breaking in the source case, and the opposite (that is the situation in the target case) should be law-abiding in the target case.

Explaining the procedure

Step one and two correspond to the procedure for general analogies.

In the third step, the action-proposition chosen in the second step has to be well-defined, which in CTT means to be well-typed. The law-abidingness and law-breakingness of the chosen action-proposition and its negation must be type declared. We need to declare a set for the accepted source cases. We must also assure that the legal system permits the use of analogical reasoning in this particular situation.

The fourth step is the decision of whether the chosen action-proposition or its negation can be used to describe the action that was performed in the target case. For simplicity, we will speak about action-propositions as being present or absent.

The fifth step refers to the source case. The same investigation has to be performed in the chosen source case, whether the chosen action-proposition or its negation can be used to describe the action in the source case.

7.2. Precedent-based reasoning with imperatives

The sixth step is a second investigation in the source case and creates the foundation for the decision in the target case. This investigation is whether the performance of this action (or the absence of the performance) was judged law-abiding or law-breaking in the source case.

The seventh step is a twofold step where the first part explains what should happen if the action-proposition either is present in both the target case and the source case or is absent in both the target case and the source case. In this situation, we might directly transfer the consequence from the source case to the target case. The second alternative is where the action-proposition is present in either the target case or the source case and it is absent in the other. In this situation, there are two alternatives. In the source case, the presence or absence of the action-proposition could be law-abiding or it could be law-breaking. If it was law-abiding, the opposite, what is the situation in the target case, can be either law-abiding or law-breaking in the target case. This can be explained by the deontic categories previously mentioned. If it was law-breaking, we can claim that the opposite should law-abiding in the target case.

Imposing conditions on analogical reasoning

In the third step, the conditions regarding formation of an analogy is implemented. This step could be said to consist of several substeps. The first is the type-declaration of the action-proposition. For some action A, we would need to suppose:

$A : prop.$

The source cases need to be declared a set. It means that we have some defined and accepted source cases that might be used in the analogy. This can be represented in the following way:

$Source : set.$

The permission of an analogy is rooted in its result, not in the action itself. This means that we will introduce the permission on the analogy on the law-abidingness or law-breakingness of the action. We will see that this closely relates to the deontic categories that are introduced. More precisely, we might say that the permission of using an analogical argument depends on the deontic categories that we include in our framework, not on the particular legal consequence.[4] We therefore have a set of permitted analogies, which might be represented in the following way:

$$PA_1(z_1) : set(z_1 : LA_A \vee LB_{\neg A});$$
$$PA_2(z_2) : set(z_2 : LB_A \vee LA_{\neg A});$$
$$PA_3(z_3) : set(z_3 : LA_A \vee LA_{\neg A}),$$

where LB and LA are abbreviations for the following:

LB_A	$(v_1 : A)LB(v_1);$
$LB_{\neg A}$	$(w_1 : \neg A)LB(w_2);$
LA_A	$(v_1 : A)LA(v_1);$
$LA_{\neg A}$	$(w_2 : \neg A)LA(w_2).$

The permission of an analogy can be produced by an instance of the elimination rule of the disjoint union. The instance that provides the permission of analogies for the first permission is

$$\frac{c : LA \vee LB \quad \overset{(x:LA)}{d(x) : PA(i(x))} \quad \overset{(y:LB)}{e(y) : PA(j(y))}}{D(c,(x)d(x),(y)e(y)) : PA(c),} PA$$

---

[4]If we want to include deontic categories with a possibility of legal reward, this could be done by introducing additional judgments here. However, such change will also have other effects on the procedure.

7.2. Precedent-based reasoning with imperatives

which reads that when we have an a that is a permitted analogy, it is justified by the proof object $D(c, (x)d(x), (y)e(y))$ that is produced when c is the proof object of the disjunction and $(x)d(x)$ is verified in the case of law-abidingness, while $(y)e(y)$ is verified in the case of law-breakingness.[5]

To represent analogical reasoning based on the deontic imperatives by choosing A as action-proposition, we end up with the following context:

$$A : prop,$$
$$Source : set,$$
$$PA_1(z_1) : set(z_1 : LA_A \vee LB_{\neg A}),$$
$$PA_2(z_2) : set(z_2 : LB_A \vee LA_{\neg A}),$$
$$PA_3(z_3) : set(z_3 : LA_A \vee LA_{\neg A}).$$

Representing source cases

For a source case s, we have several potential situations:

1. A is present in s,
   a) A was law-abiding in s;
   b) A was law-breaking in s;
2. $\neg A$ is present in s,
   a) $\neg A$ was law-abiding in s;
   b) $\neg A$ was law-breaking in s.

Depending on what is the situation for the source case s, we can use it as an argument for a certain standpoint in the target case. The standard form of analogical reasoning is based on that A is present in both the source case and the target case and since

---

[5] We here implicitly assume that law-abidingness and law-breakingness are defined as propositions over the chosen action-proposition A.

A was law-abiding/law-breaking in the source case, it should also be law-abiding/law-breaking in the target case. Assuming that A is present in the target case, this can be represented in the following way:

```
For a source case s
└─ A is present in s
   ├─ A was law-abiding in s
   │  └─ A should be law-abiding in the target
   │     case
   └─ A was law-breaking in s
      └─ A should be law-breaking in the target
         case.
```

We also have negative analogies. If the action A that is present in the target case is not shared by the source case so that $\neg A$ is law-abiding in the source case, A should be law-abiding or law-breaking in the target case. This means that we cannot decide on this basis whether A should be law-abiding or law-breaking. If A that is present in the target case and $\neg A$ is law-breaking in the source case, A should be law-abiding in the target case. Similarly, we can represent this in the following way, where we still suppose that A is present in the target case:

```
For a source case s
└─ ¬A is present in s
   ├─ ¬A was law-abiding in s
   │  └─ A should be law-abiding or
   │     law-breaking in the target case
   └─ ¬A was law-breaking in s
      └─ A should be law-abiding in the target
         case.
```

This can be explained by referring to the deontic categories. If $\neg A$ has been law-abiding, the deontic status of A can be either forbidden or permissible. The performance of A can be either law-breaking if it is a forbidden action or law-abiding if it is a

7.2. Precedent-based reasoning with imperatives

permissible action. If on the other hand $\neg A$ is law-breaking, the deontic status of A can only be that of an obligatory action. There are no other deontic categories where $\neg A$ is law-breaking. Since in obligatory actions, A is law-abiding we can include such inference in the representation.

By combining these two representations, we end up with a procedure for handling analogical reasoning when A is present in the target case. This yields the following form:

```
For a source case s
  A is present in s
    A was law-abiding in s
      A should be law-abiding in the target
      case
    A was law-breaking in s
      A should be law-breaking in the target
      case
  ¬A is present in s
    ¬A was law-abiding in s
      A should be law-abiding or
      law-breaking in the target case
    ¬A was law-breaking in s
      A should be law-abiding in the target
      case.
```

Correspondingly, we can describe the process of analogical reasoning when $\neg A$ is present in the target case. If $\neg A$ is also present in the source case, we speak about a positive analogy since $\neg A$ is shared between the target and the source case. The decision whether $\neg A$ was law-abiding or law-breaking can be directly transferred to the target case. We can represent this in the following way, where we suppose that $\neg A$ is present in the target case:

```
For a source case s'
└─ ¬A is present in s'
   ├─ ¬A was law-abiding in s'
   │  └─ ¬A should be law-abiding in the target
   │     case
   └─ ¬A was law-breaking in s'
      └─ ¬A should be law-breaking in the
         target case.
```

When ¬A is present in the target case, we might also speak about negative analogies. A negative analogy occurs when A is present in the source case. This can be represented in the following way:

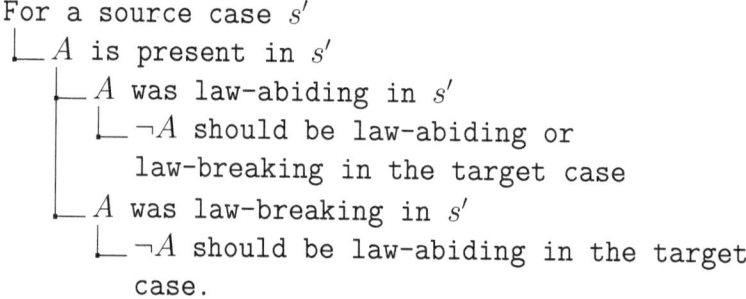
```
For a source case s'
└─ A is present in s'
   ├─ A was law-abiding in s'
   │  └─ ¬A should be law-abiding or
   │     law-breaking in the target case
   └─ A was law-breaking in s'
      └─ ¬A should be law-abiding in the target
         case.
```

If A is law-abiding in the source case, A can either be obligatory or permissible. This means that $\neg A$ can be either law-breaking if it is an obligatory action or law-abiding if it is a permissible action. If A is law-breaking, the deontic status of A can only be that of a forbidden action. There are no other deontic categories where A is law-breaking. Since in forbidden actions, $\neg A$ is law-abiding we can include this in the representation.

We then end up with a procedure for handling analogical reasoning when $\neg A$ is present in the target case. This yields the following form:

7.2. Precedent-based reasoning with imperatives

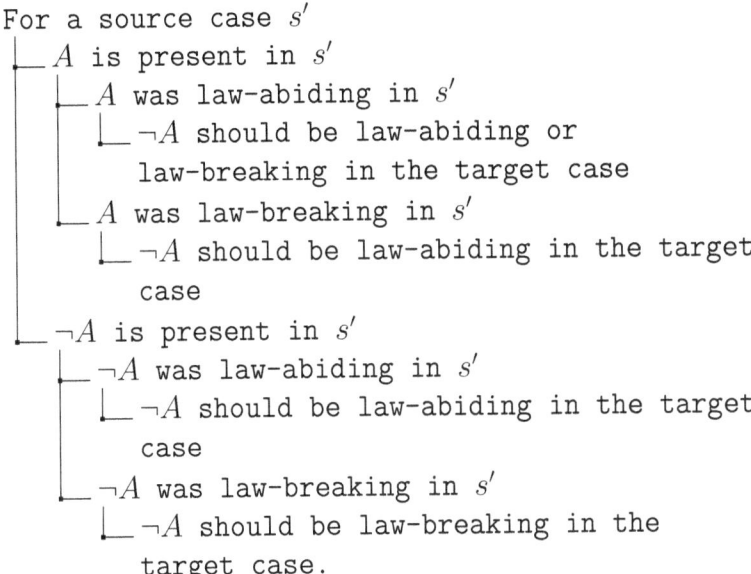

```
For a source case s'
├─ A is present in s'
│   ├─ A was law-abiding in s'
│   │   └─ ¬A should be law-abiding or
│   │      law-breaking in the target case
│   └─ A was law-breaking in s'
│       └─ ¬A should be law-abiding in the target
│          case
└─ ¬A is present in s'
    ├─ ¬A was law-abiding in s'
    │   └─ ¬A should be law-abiding in the target
    │      case
    └─ ¬A was law-breaking in s'
        └─ ¬A should be law-breaking in the
           target case.
```

Representing the analogical procedure in CTT

By combining the procedures for handling analogies when A is present and when $\neg A$ is present in the target case, we end up with a description of the whole process for analogical reasoning with imperatives. This can be represented by the following description:

For a target case where $A \vee \neg A$ is present
- A is present in the target case
  - For a source case s
    - A is present in s
      - A was law-abiding in s
        - A should be law-abiding in the target case
      - A was law-breaking in s
        - A should be law-breaking in the target case
    - $\neg A$ is present in s
      - $\neg A$ was law-abiding in s
        - A should be law-abiding or law-breaking in the target case
      - $\neg A$ was law-breaking in s
        - A should be law-abiding in the target case
- $\neg A$ is present in the target case
  - For a source case s'
    - A is present in s'
      - A was law-abiding in s'
        - $\neg A$ should be law-abiding or law-breaking in the target case
      - A was law-breaking in s'
        - $\neg A$ should be law-abiding in the target case
    - $\neg A$ is present in s'
      - $\neg A$ was law-abiding in s'
        - $\neg A$ should be law-abiding in the target case
      - $\neg A$ was law-breaking in s'
        - $\neg A$ should be law-breaking in the target case.

7.2. Precedent-based reasoning with imperatives

The structure of the formalisation follows the patterns as described for the general analogies. If A is present in the target case, the process can be formalised in the following way:

$(\forall s : Source)$
$\quad \llcorner (\forall z : A(s) \lor \neg A(s))$
$\quad\quad \llcorner (\forall u_1 : A(s))$
$\quad\quad\quad \llcorner \texttt{left}^\lor(u_1) =_{\{H2\}} z$
$\quad\quad\quad\quad \llcorner (\forall v_1 : LA_A(s) \lor LB_A(s))$
$\quad\quad\quad\quad\quad \llcorner (\forall w_1 : LA_A(s))$
$\quad\quad\quad\quad\quad\quad \llcorner \texttt{left}^\lor(w_1) =_{\{H3\}} v_1$
$\quad\quad\quad\quad\quad\quad\quad \llcorner$ A should be law-abiding in the target case
$\quad\quad\quad\quad\quad \llcorner (\forall w_2 : LB_A(s))$
$\quad\quad\quad\quad\quad\quad \llcorner \texttt{right}^\lor(w_1) =_{\{H3\}} v_1$
$\quad\quad\quad\quad\quad\quad\quad \llcorner$ A should be law-breaking in the target case
$\quad\quad \llcorner (\forall u_2 : \neg A(s))$
$\quad\quad\quad \llcorner \texttt{right}^\lor(u_2) =_{\{H2\}} z$
$\quad\quad\quad\quad \llcorner (\forall v_2 : LA_{\neg A}(s) \lor LB_{\neg A}(s))$
$\quad\quad\quad\quad\quad \llcorner (\forall w_3 : LA_{\neg A}(s))$
$\quad\quad\quad\quad\quad\quad \llcorner \texttt{left}^\lor(w_3) =_{\{H4\}} v_2$
$\quad\quad\quad\quad\quad\quad\quad \llcorner$ A should be either law-abiding or law-breaking in the target case
$\quad\quad\quad\quad\quad \llcorner (\forall w_4 : LB_{\neg A}(s))$
$\quad\quad\quad\quad\quad\quad \llcorner \texttt{right}^\lor(w_4) =_{\{H4\}} v_2$
$\quad\quad\quad\quad\quad\quad\quad \llcorner$ A should be law-abiding in the target case.

Similarly, if $\neg A$ is present in the target case, the process can be formalised in the following way:

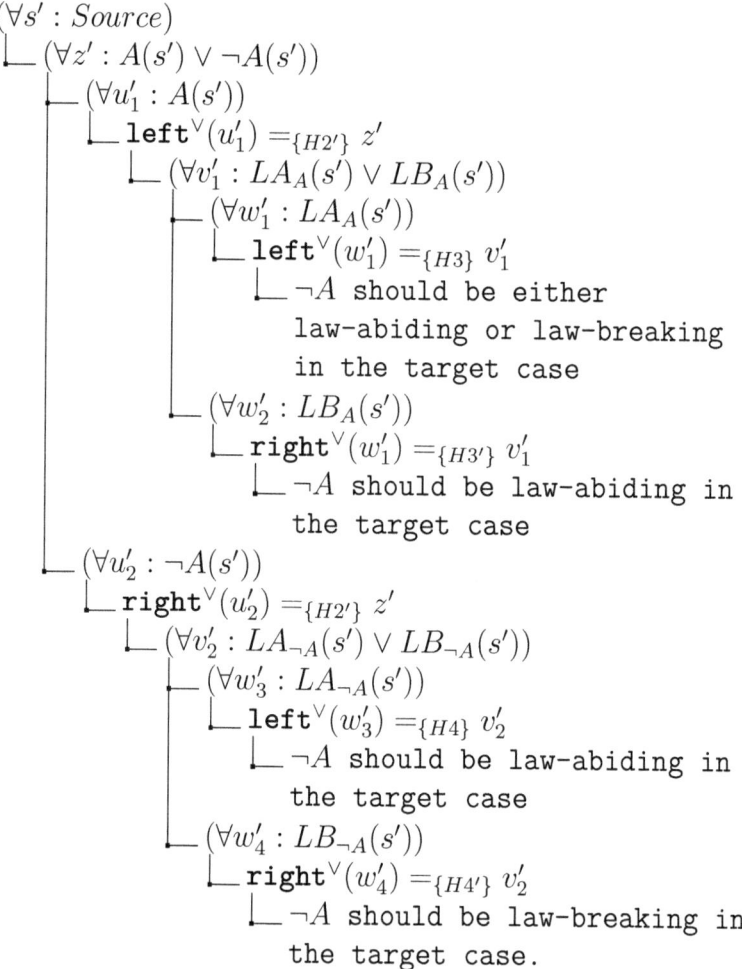

The complete analysis of analogical reasoning with imperatives in CTT yields the following formula:

7.2. Precedent-based reasoning with imperatives

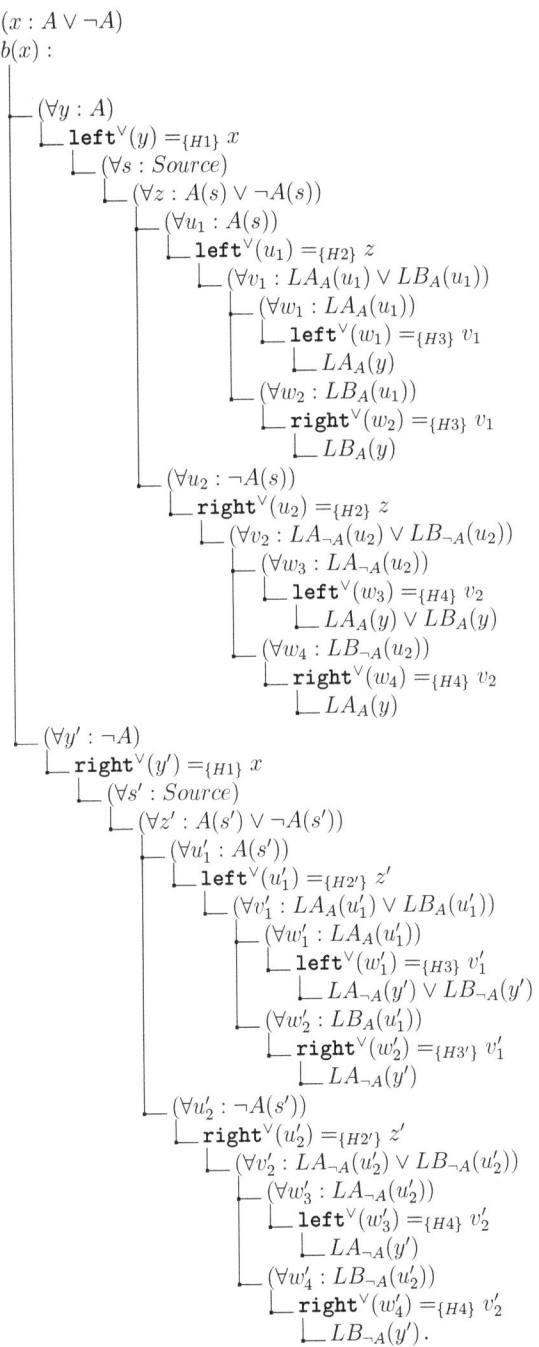

The formula that we end up with is the CTT representation of step 4 to 7 in the description of the process of analogical reasoning with imperatives. By including the context that was described earlier, we would also formalise step 3. After step 3, the first investigation that occurs is formalised as $x : A \vee \neg A$ and represents the investigation whether the chosen action-proposition is present or absent in the target case. After it has been decided whether A is present or absent in the target case, the source cases are introduced and for every source case the investigation whether the action-proposition is present or absent in this source case can be formalised as $(\forall z : A(s) \vee \neg A(s))$ and $(\forall z' : A(s') \vee \neg A(s'))$. When it is decided whether A is present or absent in the source case, the next question is whether this action was law-abiding or law-breaking in the source case, formalised as $(\forall v_1 : LA_A(u_1) \vee LB_A(u_1))$, $(\forall v_2 : LA_{\neg A}(u_2) \vee LB_{\neg A}(u_2))$, $(\forall v'_1 : LA_A(u'_1) \vee LB_A(u'_1))$ and $(\forall v'_2 : LA_{\neg A}(u'_2) \vee LB_{\neg A}(u'_2))$. If the action was performed (or not performed) in both the target case and the source case, the decision of law-abidingness or law-breakingness in the source case can be directly transferred to the target case. This is the situation for w_1, w_2, w'_3 and w'_4. Such transfer is formalised by binding the law-abidingness or law-breakingness to the choice that was performed in the target case, y or y', providing a positive analogy.

The other alternative is that the action was performed in either the target case or the source case and not performed in the other. This is the foundation for negative analogies. Since we describe analogy for deontic notions, namely law-abidingness and law-breakingness, this will be based upon the three previously described deontic categories. The negative analogies occur in w_3, w_4, w'_1 and w'_2. In w_3, $\neg A$ is law-abiding in the source case, $LA_{\neg A}(u_2)$, and A should therefore be either law-abiding or law-breaking in the target case, $LA_A(y) \vee LB_A(y)$. In w_4, $\neg A$ is law-breaking in the source case, $LB_{\neg A}(u_2)$, and A should therefore be law-abiding in the target case, $LA_A(y)$. In w'_1, A is law-abiding in the source case, $LA_A(u'_1)$, and $\neg A$ should therefore be either law-abiding or law-breaking in the target case, $LA_{\neg A}(y') \vee LB_{\neg A}(y')$. In w'_2, A is law-breaking in the source case, $LB_A(u'_1)$, and $\neg A$ should therefore be law-abiding in the target case, $LA_{\neg A}(y)$.

7.3 STEAMBOAT EXAMPLE

Assumptions and description of example

We will illustrate the procedure by a commonly used example in the literature, namely the steamboat example. It is taken from Brewer (1996, pp. 1003-1005) and is the case of *Adams v. New Jersey Steamboat Co.*, 151 N.Y. 163 (1896).

The example is a case about whether or not a certain steamboat owner is liable for a theft from a customer. *Adams* had rented a cabin in a steamboat owned by *New Jersey Steamboat Co.* and some of his valuables were stolen. The question was whether the steamboat company was strictly liable towards *Adams*. There were (at least) two references to older cases, one where an innkeeper had been held strictly liable for the thefts of valuables of a customer, and one where a railway company had not been held strictly liable for theft of valuables from an open-berth sleeping car. The question was therefore whether the steamboat was like a railroad or like an inn from a legal viewpoint. The judge decides that the steamboat was similar to an inn, and that the steamboat company therefore was strictly liable for the theft of valuables from its customer. The judge claimed that the relevant similarities were that *the client paid for a room for some specified reasons and that the company has tempting opportunity for fraud and plunder of the client*. The previous case with an inn was similar in both of these aspects, while the railroad case was not similar in either. (Brewer 1996, pp. 1003–1005, 1013–1015)

There are some preliminary remarks regarding the explanation of the example in the procedure. First, we suppose that there are only these two precedents, the inn-case and the railroad-case, to be considered in the present example. Second, we suppose that *New Jersey Steamboat Co.* refused to compensate *Adams* for his stolen valuables, which otherwise would not seem to be a legal case in the first place. The question is then whether *New Jersey Steamboat Co.*'s refusal to compensate was according to the law, whether it was law-abiding or law-breaking.

In the steamboat example, we have two different precedents that are considered to be potentially relevant for the case at hand, the innkeeper case and the railway case. We will consider both of these cases in the analysis. The relevant similarities that made the case be similar to the innkeeper case and not the railway case was that *the client paid for a room for some specified reasons and that the company has tempting opportunity for fraud and plunder of the client.* Brewer (1996, p. 1005) analyses this as two distinct requirements, by two different predicates. We might analyse it in a similar way, as a conjunction of two predicates, $(F' \wedge G') : prop$, though since they will always occur together in the argument, we choose to represent them by a single predicate, so that $F : prop$ stands for the proposition *refusing strict liability for the theft of valuables when the client paid for a room for some specified reasons and that the company has tempting opportunity for fraud and plunder of the client.* We will first show how the example can be explained in terms of the informal procedure and then show how it can be transformed into a CTT analysis.

Informal analysis

1. The first step is the creation of a target case, which is the disagreement because *New Jersey Steamboat Co.* refused to compensate *Adams* for the theft of his valuables.

7.3. Steamboat example

2. The second step is the choice of action-proposition, which in this case is *refusing strict liability for theft of valuables when the client paid for a room for some specified reasons and that the company has tempting opportunity for fraud and plunder of the client*. This was decided by the judge to be the relevant similarity and therefore also what caused that decision in the case.

3. The third step is about the well-definition of terms and the permissibility of analogical argumentation. We should know what it means for a case to be covered by the chosen action-proposition, namely that we can tell whether in a precedent there have been *refusing strict liability for theft of valuables when the client paid for a room for some specified reasons and that the company has tempting opportunity for fraud and plunder of the client* or not. We should also know what source cases or precedents we are bound by, here the innkeeper case and the railroad case. The last part is that we have to make sure that the framework allows for the use of analogical argumentation regardless of the deontic status of the action-proposition. In Common Law, the legal framework of this case, analogical argumentation lies in its core and the principle of stare decisis binds the judge to the legal result of the source cases. The judge is also in a context of doubt, meaning that there is no clear answer to this problem. Because of this, the use of analogical argumentation is assumed to be permitted.

4. The fourth step is the decision whether the action-proposition covers the target case or not. The question is then whether in the case at hand, *New Jersey Steamboat Co.* was *refusing strict liability for theft of valuables when the client paid for a room for some specified reasons and that the company has tempting opportunity for fraud and plunder of the client*. This action was performed in the target case.

5. At this step we should find some source case and decide whether or not the action was performed in this source case. In this situation we have two alternatives here, the innkeeper case and the railway case. This motivates two different paths ahead. We will start by the railway case.

The railway case:

   5. In the source case, the railway case, the action *refusing strict liability for theft of valuables when the client paid for a room for some specified reasons and that the company has tempting opportunity for fraud and plunder of the client* was not performed.

   6. In the source case, the railway company was not held strictly liable for the theft of valuables for its customer. It was not acting against the law by refusing to compensate its customer, which means that refusing compensation for a theft when *the client paid for a room for some specified reasons and that the company has tempting opportunity for fraud and plunder of the client* was not performed, was judged to be law-abiding in the source case.

   7. Since in the steamboat case, the action *refusing strict liability for theft of valuables when the client paid for a room for some specified reasons and that the company has tempting opportunity for fraud and plunder of the client* was performed while in the railway case it was not, the source case and the target case do not have the same status. The action was performed in the target case, while not performed in the source case. This means that we are in the situation of (b), a different status for the action-proposition in the source case and the target case. The non-performance in the source case was also judged to be law-abiding. This

7.3. Steamboat example

means that we are in the situation of i., that the case was law-abiding in the source case. We can therefore infer that the performance in the target case should be law-abiding or law-breaking. This means that this action could be either forbidden or legally permissible.

The innkeeper case:

5. In the source case, the innkeeper case, the action *refusing strict liability for theft of valuables when the client paid for a room for some specified reasons and that the company has tempting opportunity for fraud and plunder of the client* was performed.

6. In the source case, the innkeeper was strictly liable for the theft of valuables for its customer. It was acting against the law by refusing to compensate its customer. This means that refusing compensation for a theft when *the client paid for a room for some specified reasons and that the company has tempting opportunity for fraud and plunder of the client*, was judged to be law-breaking in the source case.

7. Since both in the case at hand and in the innkeeper case, the action *refusing strict liability for theft of valuables when the client paid for a room for some specified reasons and that the company has tempting opportunity for fraud and plunder of the client* was performed, the source case and the target case do have the same status. The action was performed both in the target case and in the source case. This means that we are in the situation of (a), the same status in the source case and the target case. The performance in the source case was also judged to be law-breaking,

and we can transfer the decision of the source case to the target case. We can therefore infer that the performance in the target case should be law-breaking and that the action is forbidden.

Based on the railway case, we can infer that the performance in the target case should be law-breaking or law-abiding, while based on the innkeeper case we can infer that the performance in the target case should be law-breaking. The railway case makes the grounds for what is called a negative analogy because it is based on a difference between the target and the source. The innkeeper case provides a positive analogy. The results of these two source cases are compatible, that an action is law-abiding or law-breaking is perfectly compatible with it being law-breaking. Based on the two source cases, we can say that the action is forbidden. Since the innkeeper case enables us to infer that the performance in the target case was law-breaking, we end up with the same result as the judge in the example, which was what we wanted.

Formal analysis

For the formal analysis of the argumentation process, the analysis starts at step 3. The first step is given by the conflict between *Adams* and *New Jersey Steamboat Co.*, for *refusing strict liability for the theft of valuables.* The second step is the selection of relevant action-proposition, which is given explicitly as *refusing strict liability for the theft of valuables when the client paid for a room for some specified reasons and that the company has tempting opportunity for fraud and plunder of the client.* We will therefore assume that this rule is occurs as an emergence in the legal context. What our analysis does is to show the inner structure that any such rule need to satisfy.

7.3. Steamboat example

Step three involves the well-definition of the terms. The first part is therefore to make sure that the action-proposition is well-defined. Let F represent *refusing strict liability for the theft of valuables when the client paid for a room for some specified reasons and that the company has tempting opportunity for fraud and plunder of the client*, so that:

$$F : prop.$$

The next part is the definition of source cases, which in this situation are the innkeeper case and the railway case. They are not introduced explicitly at this point, but we assure the well-definition of the set,

$$Source : set.$$

The last thing we need to assure is the permission of the use of analogy. As mentioned earlier, the principle of stare decisis in common law systems seems to permit the use of analogy to a great extent. The judge is also in a context of doubt. We then need to assure that the use of analogical reasoning is permitted for this particular action-proposition, no matter what deontic status the relevant action-proposition might have. This is done in the following way for the first deontic category, of obligatory actions:

$$PA_1(z_1) : set(z_1 : LA_F \lor LB_{\neg F}),$$

and similarly for the other deontic categories. We then end up with the following context for the steamboat example:

$$F : prop,$$
$$Source : set,$$
$$PA_1(z_1) : set(z_1 : LA_F \lor LB_{\neg F}),$$
$$PA_2(z_2) : set(z_2 : LB_F \lor LA_{\neg F}),$$
$$PA_3(z_3) : set(z_3 : LA_F \lor LA_{\neg F}).$$

Step four is deciding whether the action-proposition is present or absent in the target case. This will be represented by the following incomplete formula:

$(x : F \vee \neg F)$
$b(x) :$

$\quad \vdash (\forall y : F)$
$\quad \quad \vdash \texttt{left}^\vee(y) =_{\{H1\}} x$
$\quad \quad \quad \vdash \ldots$
$\quad \vdash (\forall y' : \neg F)$
$\quad \quad \vdash \texttt{right}^\vee(y') =_{\{H1\}} x$
$\quad \quad \quad \vdash \ldots .$

The complete formulation of the example is then the following:

7.3. Steamboat example

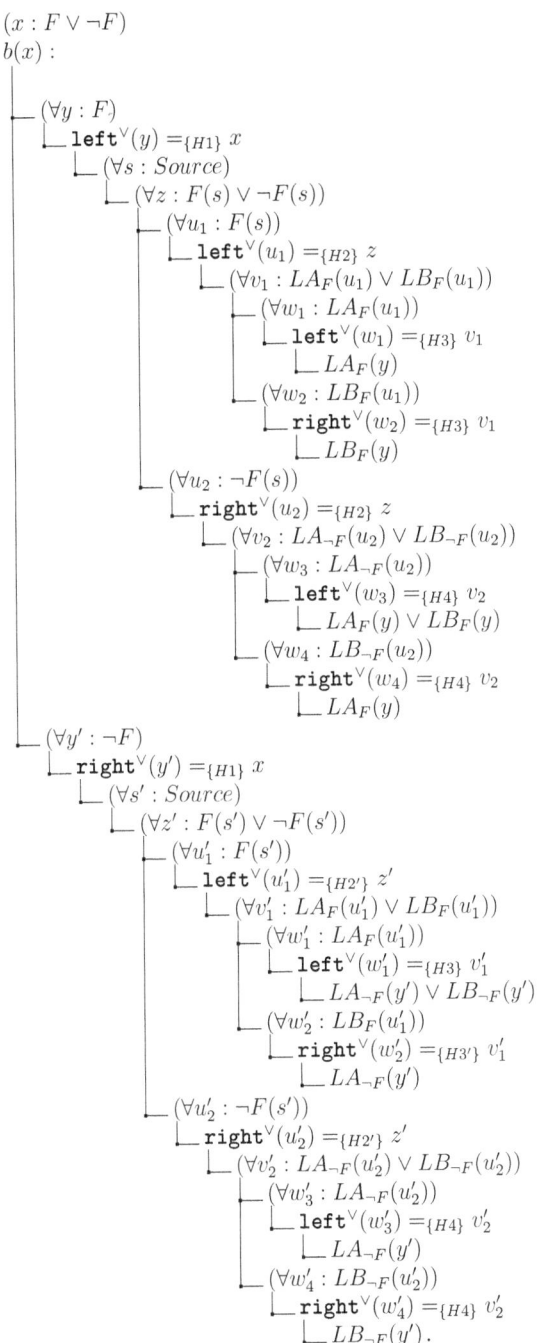

Regarding the fourth step, F is present, so the first alternative should be chosen:

$\llcorner (\forall y : F)$
$\quad \llcorner \mathbf{left}^\vee(y) =_{\{H1\}} x$
$\quad \llcorner \ldots .$

The fifth step depends on whether we use the railway case or the innkeeper case as a basis for the analysis. As with the informal representation, the formal analysis also takes different paths based on the two cases. The decision in the source case is represented by a quantification on the set of source cases,

$(\forall s : Source).$

This is followed up by an inquiry on whether the chosen action-proposition is present or absent in the source case. This inquiry is represented as:

$(\forall z : F(s) \vee \neg F(s)),$

which gives us the following procedure in the tree notation:

$\llcorner (\forall s : Source)$
$\quad \llcorner (\forall z : F(s) \vee \neg F(s))$
$\quad\quad \vdash (\forall u_1 : F(s))$
$\quad\quad\quad \llcorner \ldots$
$\quad\quad \llcorner (\forall u_2 : \neg F(s))$
$\quad\quad\quad \llcorner \ldots .$

It is in answering this inquiry that the two precedents differ.

The railway case
In the railway-case, the action-proposition is absent. This means that we will follow the path of u_2. The answer of this inquiry has the following form:

$(\forall u_2 : \neg F(s)) \mathbf{right}^\vee(u_2) =_{\{H2\}} z,$

7.3. Steamboat example

which is represented in the following way in the tree notation:

$\llcorner (\forall s : Source)$
$\quad \llcorner (\forall z : F(s) \vee \neg F(s))$
$\quad\quad \llcorner (\forall u_2 : \neg F(s))$
$\quad\quad\quad \llcorner \texttt{right}^{\vee}(u_2) =_{\{H2\}} z$
$\quad\quad\quad\quad \llcorner \ldots.$

The inquiry is answered by the proof object u_2 for $\neg F$.

The sixth step is deciding whether the action-proposition was judged law-abiding or law-breaking in the source case. The decision of the railway case was that the railway company was not held strictly liable for the theft of their customers. This means that the railway company was acting law-abiding when refusing this strict liability. The decision was not based on the absence of the action-proposition in particular, but since the action-proposition was absent in the source case, it implies that this absence was considered law-abiding. This decision is represented as an inquiry of the form:

$$(\forall v_1 : LA_{\neg F}(s) \vee LB_{\neg F}(s)).$$

As with the other inquiries, there are two potential answers, that it was law-abiding, $LA_{\neg F}(s')$, or that it was law-breaking, $LB_{\neg F}(s')$. In the railway case, the first alternative was the situation and this is represented in the following way:

$$(\forall w_3 : LA_{\neg F}(u_2))\texttt{left}^{\vee}(w_3) =_{\{H4\}} v_2,$$

which gives us the path of w_3 in the tree notation:

$\llcorner (\forall v_2 : LA_{\neg F}(u_2) \vee LB_{\neg F}(u_2))$
$\quad \llcorner (\forall w_3 : LA_{\neg F}(u_2))$
$\quad\quad \llcorner \texttt{left}^{\vee}(w_3) =_{\{H4\}} v_2$
$\quad\quad\quad \llcorner \ldots.$

The seventh and last step is the application to the target case. Since we have established that the action-proposition was present in the target case, while absent in the source case, the action has a different status in the target case and in the source case. We are therefore in the case of (b). The non-performance in the source case was judged law-abiding. We can infer from the analysis that the performance in the target case should be judged either law-abiding or law-breaking in the target case, namely the following:

$$LA_F(y) \vee LB_F(y),$$

which reads that the performance of F is either law-abiding or law-breaking in the target case. This corresponds to the result we ended up with in the informal description.

The innkeeper case
In the innkeeper case the action-proposition is present. This means that we will follow the path of u_1. The answer of this inquiry has the following form:

$$(\forall u_1 : F(s))\text{left}^\vee(u_1) =_{\{H2\}} z,$$

which is represented in the following way in the tree notation:

```
└ (∀s : Source)
   └ (∀z : F(s) ∨ ¬F(s))
      └ (∀u₁ : F(s))
         └ leftⱽ(u₁) ={H2} z
         └ ....
```

The inquiry is answered by the proof object u_1 for F.

The sixth step is deciding whether the action-proposition was judged law-abiding or law-breaking in the source case. The decision of the innkeeper case was that the innkeeper was held strictly liable for the theft of their customers. This means that the innkeeper was acting law-breaking when refusing this strict liability. This decision is represented as an inquiry of the form:

$$(\forall v_1 : LA_F(s) \vee LB_F(s)).$$

7.3. Steamboat example

As with the other inquiries, there are two potential answers, that is was law-abiding, $LA_F(s)$, or that it was law-breaking, $LB_F(s)$. In the innkeeper case, the second alternative was decided, and this is represented in the following way:

$$(\forall w_2 : LA_F(u_1))\mathbf{right}^\vee(w_2) =_{\{H4\}} v_1,$$

which gives us the path of w_2 in the tree notation:

$\llcorner (\forall v_1 : LA_F(u_1) \vee LB_F(u_1))$
  $\llcorner (\forall w_2 : LA_F(u_1))$
    $\llcorner \mathbf{right}^\vee(w_2) =_{\{H4\}} v_1$
    $\llcorner \ldots$

The seventh and last step is the application to the target case. Since we have established that the action-proposition was present both in the target case and in the source case, the action has the same status in the target case and in the source case. We are therefore in the situation of (a). The performance in the source case was judged law-breaking. We can infer from the analysis that the performance in the target case should be judged law-breaking, namely the following:

$$LB_F(y),$$

which reads that the performance of F is law-breaking in the target case. This corresponds to the result we ended up with in the informal description. Because of the similarity to the innkeeper case, its decision can be transferred to steamboat case, which is precisely the result that we expected. Note that this result if perfectly compatible with the result for the railway case, which said that the performance in the target case should be either law-abiding or law-breaking.

Chapter 8

Dialogical implementation

8.1 Precedent-based reasoning

Terminology

Until now the analysis has been described in type-theoretical terms. However, we will see that immanent reasoning provides a natural and comprehensible alternative explanation to the procedure previously described. The dialogical analysis of analogical reasoning will show us that we might consider analogy to consist of eight different dialogical rules, one for each form of analogy, instead of one complex framework. The dialogical framework enables us to do this because of the repetition ranks of the players. A repetition rank of 1 will provide us with an *unrestricted* analogy, as it does not enable the play to compare different source cases. For a *restricted* analogy, the players would need repetition ranks of 2 or higher. We will show that the repetition ranks will decide how many source cases that might be brought into the play. The repetition rank is a particularity of the dialogical framework that is not present in the general formulation of CTT. Since it is the repetition rank that enables us to separate analogical reasoning into different rules, we are only enabled to do so in this dialogical interpretation, not in the general CTT representation.

The dialogical representation will also enable us to express the permission of a particular analogy form only when this kind of analogy is actually utilised. This means that we are not bound to permit all forms of analogical arguments, but we can permit only the kinds that are introduced in the particular play. However, there is no logical reason that this can only be done in the dialogical implementation of CTT, though it facilitates the integration in a natural and comprehensible way. To integrate such dependent permission of analogical arguments without the dialogical framework would require a formalisation that is significantly more complex than what has previously been introduced.

Since we will introduce eight different forms of analogy, we will categorise them in a particular way. As previously mentioned, an analogy can be said to depend on three inquiries, namely:

1. the presence or absence of the occasioning characteristic in the target case;

2. the presence or absence of the occasioning characteristic in the source case;

3. the presence or absence of the entailed characteristic in the source case.

We might then categorise the three different steps, according to whether the characteristic is present or absent. An analogy where the occasioning characteristic is present both in the target case and in the source case, and where the entailed characteristic is present in the source case will be called a *Present-present-present-analogy*, or 'PPP-analogy' for short. An analogy where the occasioning characteristic is absent both in the target case and in the source case, and where the entailed characteristic is absent in the source case will be called a *Absent-absent-absent analogy* or 'AAA-analogy' for short. An analogy where the occasioning characteristic is present in the target case and absent in the source case, and where the entailed characteristic is present in the source case will be called a

8.1. Precedent-based reasoning

Present-absent-present analogy or 'PAP-analogy' for short. Similar descriptions hold for the other alternatives. This section will start by describing the general analogies that infer a property in the target case. Analogies with deontic qualifications will be introduced by simply adding two additional definitions.

To provide the dialogical implementation of the mentioned procedure, we will introduce two kinds of rules, challenge rules and explanation rules, together with corresponding formation rules. As mentioned, we can separate the analogical procedure into eight different forms of analogical argument and these rules are intended to provide a way to break the formula into different parts that can more easily be utilised in the dialogical framework. The expression 'Analogy$[A, B]$' can in some sense be understood as standing for the procedure of analogy described in section 7.1, where the presence or absence of A in the target case and the source case, together with the presence or absence of B in the target case, provide justification for the presence or absence of B in the target case. This complex expression can however be separated into different parts, described by the eight different forms of analogy. To do this operation, we have two Analogy Challenge Rules that can be used when a player has stated an analogy between A and B.

We previously argued for considering analogy to be a question of *similar relevancy* rather than similarity *and* relevancy. This dialogical approach takes this seriously and we can see that in the formulation of a particular analogy form, the dependency in the source case is connected to the dependency in the target case by an intuitionistic implication. It does not introduce any distinct notion of similarity and relevancy, but rather it considers the combined notion to be an aspect of a general dependency of dependencies. In such way, this approach seem to provide meaning explanations of an analogies closely related to the Aristotelean notion of proportionality.

Challenge rules

A player can propose that an analogy holds between A and B. This is done by the move '! Analogy$[A, B]$'. The general formation requirements for such statement is given in Scheme 1.

Move	Challenge	Defence
X Analogy$[A, B] : prop$	**Y** ? $F_{Analogy[A,B]1}$ Or	**X** $A : prop$
	Y ? $F_{Analogy[A,B]2}$ Or	**X** $Tar : set$
	Y ? $F_{Analogy[A,B]3}$ Or	**X** $Sou : set$
	Y ? $F_{Analogy[A,B]4}$	**X** $B(x,y) : prop[x : A \vee \neg A, y : Tar \vee Sou]$

Scheme 1: Analogy Formation Rule

There are here four formation requirements for this statement. If we had followed the previously described general CTT explanation, we could also introduce the permission of the analogies here. However, for the reasons mentioned earlier, these requirements are rather introduced for each individual analogy form. This is done in order to enable the formalisation to permit only those kind of analogies that are in play.

The statement of an analogy between A and B can be challenged in two ways. The first way is by asking the other player to show what way this analogy can be used to advocate a certain result in the target case. This is done by the demand '? AnForm$[A, B]$', which stands for *Analogy Form*. It is here up to the defender to choose what kind of analogy that will be presented. The Analogy Challenge Rule 1 is given in Scheme 2.

8.1. Precedent-based reasoning

Move	Challenge	Defence
X ! Analogy[A, B]	**Y** ? AnForm[A, B]	**X** ! PPP-Analogy[A, B] Or **X** ! PPA-Analogy[A, B] Or **X** ! PAP-Analogy[A, B] Or **X** ! PAA-Analogy[A, B] Or **X** ! APP-Analogy[A, B] Or **X** ! APA-Analogy[A, B] Or **X** ! AAP-Analogy[A, B] Or **X** ! AAA-Analogy[A, B]

Scheme 2: Analogy Challenge Rule 1

The second way to challenge an analogy statement is for the challenger to suggest a particular form of analogy. This is done after the first rule, as it is a way for the challenger to attack the proposed analogy by a counterexample. Notice that we use the term *counterexample* in a very broad way. The point is that when a player proposes an analogy between A and B, that player should also concede any analogy form, not only the form chosen by himself. This is a result of what is called the condition of efficiency or the Proportionality-principle. The defender will then be committed to the result of the analogy form chosen by the challenger. The challenge in this rule opens up a subplay where the challenger tries to either force the defender into an inconsistency or to make the defender unable to respond to the challenge. The Analogy Challenge Rule 2 is given in Scheme 3.

Move	Challenge	Defence
X ! Analogy[A, B]	**Y** ! PPP-Analogy[A, B] Or	**X** ! $B(x,t)[x : A, t : Tar]$
	Y ! PPA-Analogy[A, B] Or	**X** ! $\neg B(x,t)[x : A, t : Tar]$
	Y ! PAP-Analogy[A, B] Or	**X** ! $\neg B(x,t)[x : \neg A, t : Tar]$
	Y ! PAA-Analogy[A, B] Or	**X** ! $\neg\neg B(x,t)[x : A, t : Tar]$
	Y ! APP-Analogy[A, B] Or	**X** ! $\neg B(x,t)[x : \neg A, t : Tar]$
	Y ! APA-Analogy[A, B] Or	**X** ! $\neg\neg B(x,t)[x : \neg A, t : Tar]$
	Y ! AAP-Analogy[A, B] Or	**X** ! $B(x,t)[x : \neg A, t : Tar]$
	Y ! AAA-Analogy[A, B]	**X** ! $\neg B(x,t)[x : \neg A, t : Tar]$

Scheme 3: Analogy Challenge Rule 2

Regarding the Analogy Challenge Rule 2, it is restricted in the way that it can only be played after the Analogy Challenge Rule 1. This is to avoid the challenger to win the play, simply because the challenger never was forced to concede the defenders proposed analogy. Notice that this is a structural restriction, special to these analogy rules. This structural rule is described in Restriction 1.

8.1. Precedent-based reasoning

Whenever a player proposes an analogy, $\mathbf{X}$! Analogy$[A, B]$, the other player, $\mathbf{Y}$, can only challenge it with the Analogy Challenge Rule 2 after challenging $\mathbf{X}$'s defence in the Analogy Challenge Rule 1 with the corresponding explanation rule.

Restriction 1: Analogy Challenge Rule Restriction

The third kind of rules is the explanation rules. They make the challenger spell out the expression that is behind the form of analogy. These rules provide the meaning for each of the eight forms of analogy, and we therefore have eight different rules. We will describe each rule and provide the explanation rule related to each form of analogy. Since we distinguish the procedure for analogical reasoning into eight different forms, we are also able to attach the permission of the analogy to the formation requirement to the particular form of analogy that is utilised in the play. Notice that this approach presupposes that the players agree on the source cases. The relevant source cases are included in the initial conditions. The framework is not intended to provide a description of disagreements on the status of these source cases.

In terms of meaning explanation, the explanation rule challenge can be understood as the step where the initial concessions about the target and source cases are established. When a player plays an explanation rule, the player concedes a statement about some analogy relative to certain target and source cases. Whenever a player states a certain analogy form (for example PPP-analogy), this should be understood as a move that introduces some specified source cases together with the claim that this analogy form holds over these source cases. The analogy form statements should then be understood as: "given target case t and source case $s_1, s_2, ...$ this particular analogy form holds". This is also the reason for what at first sight seems to give the burden of proof to the challenger in these rules. Such challenge should not be understood as taking the responsibility for the proof of the analogy form, but as a challenge of some claim about this analogy form holding for certain cases.

The analysis then presupposes agreement on these source cases in the sense that they are added directly to the initial concessions.[1] The agreement regarding the target case is also presupposed in this analysis. However, we might consider the target case as a presupposition for the introduction of the analogy in the first place and therefore as an initial concession that is introduced before or at the same time as the proposed analogy. This discussion is anyway not immediately relevant here as the analysis presupposes agreement also on the target case.

A similar point as the previously mentioned also holds for the permission of the analogy. When a player suggests that a certain analogy form holds, the player should also ensure that the use of this particular analogy form in this particular situation is permitted. Whenever a player states a certain analogy form, one should consider that the permission of this analogy form should be added to the initial concessions as a precondition for performing the analogical argument in the first place.

Explanation rules

The introduction of analogy explanation rules requires some assumptions on their formulations. In the original CTT analysis, the analogical procedure is introduced with suspensions. This was done in order to implement the notion of an investigation or inquiry. We then introduced a formalisation that took account of the uncertainty regarding the fulfilment for each step. In the dialogical approach, this seems less pressing. Here, the notion of inquiry is directly implemented in the approach itself. The notion of 'challenge' seems to account well for the semantical notion of suspension that we wanted to introduce in the pure CTT analysis. This point, together

---

[1] A natural way to further extend this analysis would be to show how the players might disagree about the status of the source cases (that they might be rejected on the basis of for example inconsistency). This will however be outside the scope here and we will therefore presuppose agreement on the target and source cases.

8.1. Precedent-based reasoning

with the intention of avoiding very complex dialogical rules, the analogy explanation rules will be simplified compared to their CTT counterparts. Since the inclusion of suspensions in the formalisations seems less urgent than in the CTT analysis, we will leave them out in the dialogical implementation to avoid overly complex rules and a significant increase of moves in the plays. This is not to say that previously introduced suspensions cannot be included also in the dialogical approach, but simply that we will give priority to a simplified variant.

Particular to the dialogical approach is also the explicit introduction of the target case. There is no logical reason for not including it also in the non-dialogical CTT analysis, but a practical one to avoid an overly complex system. Dialogically, this practical matter is less pressing since we are able to distinguish the analysis into different explanation rules. In each explanation rule, we have therefore included explicit notions of both a source case and a target case.

Each analogy form consists of a formation rule and an explanation rule. The formation rules describe the corresponding permission of the analogy, attached to that particular analogy form. The explanation rules challenge the chosen analogy form by stating the inference of the result in the target case from the source case.

The formation rules attach the permission of the analogy form and represents the initial condition of the utilisation of analogy in this particular situation. In CTT, any hypothetical or categorical judgment must be preceded by a type declaration where its type is specified. By using PPP-analogies as an example, this means that we must assume:

$$\text{PPP-Analogy}[A, B] : prop.$$

The challenger can then attack this by demanding the defender to show that this kind of analogy is indeed permitted,

$$?\ F_{PPP-Analogy[A,B]}.$$

This provides the starting point for the formation rule, as the permission of the analogy can be introduced as a defence to this challenge. In section 7.1 we provide the corresponding formulations of the permission of the analogy. For this example the relevant permitted-analogy formulation is:

$$PA_1(z) : set[z : (x : A)B(x) \lor (y : A)\neg B(y)].$$

This reads that analogies showing that when A is present, B is either present or absent are permitted. This is then a requirement that does not bind the target case to any particular result, as it opens up for either B or $\neg B$ to be concluded. Each formation rule is shared with one other analogy form that provides an incompatible result. We might call this a *direct counterexample*. In this example, the formation rule is shared with the PPA-analogy.

After the permission of the analogy has been established, the play can continue by providing the explanation rule regarding the chosen analogy form. The explanation rules are based on the formulation of particular decisions in a case. Generally, we can then describe the structure of a case as a hypothetical judgment where the decision B is dependent on some A,

$$b : B(x : A).$$

Quantified by the Π-form, a decision in a case has the form of a universal,

$$(\forall x : A)B(x).$$

In order to distinguish between the target case and the source case, we also make the set that the decision belongs to explicit. The target case belongs to the set of target cases, $Tar : set$, and the source case belongs to the set of source cases, $Sou : set$. This inclusion is then done by introducing a subset separation on the set that the universal quantifies over. For the source case we get:

$$(\forall y : \{x : A | Sou(x)\})B(y),$$

8.1. Precedent-based reasoning

and for the target case we get:

$$(\forall z : \{x : A | Tar(x)\}) B(z).$$

This provides the foundation for the analysis that enables us to describe the dependency that the target case has on the source case by an implication,

$$(\forall y : \{x : A | Sou(x)\}) B(y) \supset (\forall z : \{x : A | Tar(x)\}) B(z).$$

The explanation rules describe the particular content of the analogy form. First a player places a certain analogy form into play,

! PPP-Analogy$[A, B]$.

The other player can then challenge this move by stating the particular content of this analogy form. For the PPP-analogy this is:

! $(\forall y : \{x : A | Sou(x)\}) B(y) \supset (\forall z : \{x : A | Tar(x)\}) B(z).$

which reads that we have an implication from the source case to the target case. The antecedent describes the source case and the consequent describes the target case. Both the target case and the source case are described by a universal that explains how the juridical decision B is dependent on the presence of A and the respective sets. The defence of this challenge is the result that is decided in the target case,

! $B(z)$.

In a play, this means that also the defender will be obliged to state that the resulting decision also holds in the target case. Here we have used PPP-analogy as an example, though similar points hold for all forms of analogy.

In this analysis, we depend on defining target case as a set, which opens up a possibility for multiple target cases. However, in many situations this is not a possibility that is needed or wished for as we might already have an established target case that is the case for discussion. In the examples here, we will therefore include the particular target case as an initial condition in the play. In order to distinguish the target case from the source cases in the initial conditions and in the same time ensure that they all are dependent on the same A (or eventually $\neg A$), they will both be dependent on a disjunction,

$$a : A \vee \neg A.$$

The source and target cases can then be formulated as either dependent on the left injection of a or on the right injection of a as for example

$$t : Tar(L^{\vee}(a))$$

and

$$s : Sou(R^{\vee}(a)).$$

This connects very closely to the approach in the non-dialogical CTT analysis. Since the different players agree on the source cases, we will also formulate the presence or absence of the entailed characteristic in the source cases in the initial conditions,

$$b : B(s).$$

By including such formulations as initial conditions, the players are restricted in choosing which target case and eventually which source cases that are brought into play.

PPP-analogies

The present-present-present analogy is the positive and standard form for analogy, where the occasioning characteristic is present in both the target case and the source case and where the entailed characteristic is present in the source case. Together with the PPA-analogy, the AAP-analogy and the AAA-analogy, the PPP-analogy

8.1. Precedent-based reasoning

is of the form that is called positive analogy. This means that the target case and the source case share the presence or the absence of some occasioning characteristic and that we transfer the presence or absence of the entailed characteristic in the source case to the target case. The analogy can be described in the following way, where the entailed characteristic is in parentheses:

$$
\begin{array}{ccc}
\text{Source} & & \text{Target} \\
A & & A \\
\downarrow & \leftrightarrow & \downarrow \\
B & & (B).
\end{array}
$$

For the moves, we will use **Mov**, **Cha** and **Def** as abbreviations for **Move**, **Challenge** and **Defence** respectively. The formation of the PPP-analogy is introduced in Scheme 4. The formation requirement for this form of analogy is shared with the PPA-analogy.

	PPP-Analogy Formation
Mov	X PPP-Analogy$[A, B]$: $prop$
Cha	Y ? $F_{PPP-Analogy[A,B]}$
Def	X $PA_1(z)$: $set[z : (x : A)B(x) \vee (y : A)\neg B(y)]$

Scheme 4: PPP-Analogy Formation Rule

The dialogical rule for performing PPP-analogies is given in Scheme 5.

	PPP-Analogy
Mov	X ! PPP-Analogy$[A, B]$
Cha	Y ! $(\forall y : \{x : A|Sou(x)\})B(y) \supset (\forall z : \{x : A|Tar(x)\})B(z)$
Def	X ! $B(z)$

Scheme 5: PPP-Analogy Explanation Rule

PPA-analogies

The present-present-absent analogy is a positive analogy, where the occasioning characteristic is present in both the target case and the source case and where the entailed characteristic is absent in the source case. This analogy form can be described in the following way:

$$\begin{array}{ccc} \text{Source} & & \text{Target} \\ A & & A \\ \downarrow & \leftrightarrow & \downarrow \\ \neg B & & (\neg B). \end{array}$$

The formation of the PPP-analogy is introduced in Scheme 6. The formation requirement for this form of analogy is shared with the PPP-analogy.

	PPA-Analogy Formation
Mov	X PPA-Analogy$[A, B]$: $prop$
Cha	Y ? $F_{PPA-Analogy[A,B]}$
Def	X $PA_1(z)$: $set[z : (x : A)B(x) \lor (y : A)\neg B(y)]$

Scheme 6: PPA-Analogy Formation Rule

The dialogical rule for performing analogies of this form is given in Scheme 7.

	PPA-Analogy
Mov	X ! PPA-Analogy$[A, B]$
Cha	Y $(\forall y : \{x : A\|Sou(x)\})\neg B(y) \supset (\forall z : \{x : A\|Tar(x)\})\neg B(z)$
Def	X ! $\neg B(z)$

Scheme 7: PPA-Analogy Explanation Rule

8.1. Precedent-based reasoning

PAP-analogies

The present-absent-present analogy is of the form of a negative analogy, where the occasioning characteristic is present in the target case, absent in the source case and where the entailed characteristic is present in the source case. This analogy form can be described in the following way:

$$\begin{array}{ccc} \text{Source} & & \text{Target} \\ \neg A & & A \\ \downarrow & \leftrightarrow & \downarrow \\ B & & (\neg B). \end{array}$$

The formation of the PAP-analogy is introduced in Scheme 8. The formation requirement for this form of analogy is shared with the PAA-analogy.

	PAP-Analogy Formation
Mov	X PAP-Analogy$[A, B]$: $prop$
Cha	Y ? $F_{PAP-Analogy[A,B]}$
Def	X $PA_3(z) : set[z : (x : A) \neg B(x) \vee (y : A) \neg \neg B(y)]$

Scheme 8: PAP-Analogy Formation Rule

The dialogical rule for performing analogies of this form is given in Scheme 9.

	PAP-Analogy
Mov	X ! PAP-Analogy$[A, B]$
Cha	Y ! $(\forall y : \{x : \neg A | Sou(x)\}) B(y) \supset (\forall z : \{x : A | Tar(x)\}) \neg B(z)$
Def	X ! $\neg B(z)$

Scheme 9: PAP-Analogy Explanation Rule

PAA-analogies

The present-absent-absent analogy is of the form of a negative analogy, where the occasioning characteristic is present in the target case, absent in the source case and where the entailed characteristic is absent in the source case. This analogy form can be described in the following way:

$$
\begin{array}{ccc}
\textbf{Source} & & \textbf{Target} \\
\neg A & & A \\
\downarrow & \leftrightarrow & \downarrow \\
\neg B & & (\neg\neg B).
\end{array}
$$

The formation of the PAA-analogy is introduced in Scheme 10. The formation requirement for this form of analogy is shared with the PAP-analogy.

	PAA-Analogy Formation
Mov	X PAA-Analogy$[A, B]$: $prop$
Cha	Y ? $F_{PAA-Analogy[A,B]}$
Def	X $PA_3(z) : set[z : (x : A)\neg B(x) \vee (y : A)\neg\neg B(y)]$

Scheme 10: PAA-Analogy Formation Rule

The dialogical rule for performing analogies of this form is given in Scheme 11.

	PAA-Analogy
Mov	X ! PAA-Analogy$[A, B]$
Cha	Y ! $(\forall y : \{x : \neg A | Sou(x)\})\neg B(y) \supset (\forall z : \{x : A | Tar(x)\})\neg\neg B(z)$
Def	X ! $\neg\neg B(z)$

Scheme 11: PAA-Analogy Explanation Rule

APP-analogies

The absent-present-present analogy is of the form of a negative analogy, where the occasioning characteristic is absent in the target case, present in the source case and where the entailed characteristic is present in the source case. This analogy form can be described in the following way:

$$
\begin{array}{ccc}
\text{Source} & & \text{Target} \\
A & & \neg A \\
\downarrow & \leftrightarrow & \downarrow \\
B & & (\neg B).
\end{array}
$$

The formation of the APP-analogy is introduced in Scheme 12. The formation requirement for this form of analogy is shared with the APA-analogy.

APP-Analogy Formation

Mov	X APP-Analogy$[A, B]$: $prop$
Cha	Y ? $F_{APP-Analogy[A,B]}$
Def	X $PA_2(z)$: $set[z : (x : \neg A)\neg B(x) \vee (y : \neg A)\neg\neg B(y)]$

Scheme 12: APP-Analogy Formation Rule

The dialogical rule for performing analogies of this form is given Scheme 13.

APP-Analogy

Mov	X ! APP-Analogy$[A, B]$
Cha	Y ! $(\forall y : \{x : A\|Sou(x)\})B(y) \supset (\forall z : \{x : \neg A\|Tar(x)\})\neg B(z)$
Def	X ! $\neg B(z)$

Scheme 13: APP-Analogy Explanation Rule

APA-analogies

The absent-present-absent analogy is of the form of a negative analogy, where the occasioning characteristic is absent in the target case, present in the source case and where the entailed characteristic is absent in the source case. This analogy form can be described in the following way:

$$\begin{array}{ccc} \textbf{Source} & & \textbf{Target} \\ A & & \neg A \\ \downarrow & \leftrightarrow & \downarrow \\ \neg B & & (\neg\neg B). \end{array}$$

The formation of the APA-analogy is introduced in Scheme 14. The formation requirement for this form of analogy is shared with the APP-analogy.

	APA-Analogy Formation
Mov	X APA-Analogy$[A, B]$: $prop$
Cha	Y ? $F_{APA-Analogy[A,B]}$
Def	X $PA_2(z) : set[z : (x : \neg A)\neg B(x) \vee (y : \neg A)\neg\neg B(y)]$

Scheme 14: APA-Analogy Formation Rule

The dialogical rule for performing analogies of this form is given in Scheme 15.

	APA-Analogy
Mov	X ! APA-Analogy$[A, B]$
Cha	Y ! $(\forall y : \{x : A|Sou(x)\})\neg B(y) \supset (\forall z : \{x : \neg A|Tar(x)\})\neg\neg B(z)$
Def	X ! $\neg\neg B(z)$

Scheme 15: APA-Analogy Explanation Rule

8.1. Precedent-based reasoning

AAP-analogies

The absent-absent-present analogy is a positive analogy, where the occasioning characteristic is absent in both the target case and the source case and where the entailed characteristic is present in the source case. This analogy form can be described in the following way:

$$
\begin{array}{ccc}
\text{Source} & & \text{Target} \\
\neg A & & \neg A \\
\downarrow & \leftrightarrow & \downarrow \\
B & & (B).
\end{array}
$$

The formation of the AAP-analogy is introduced in Scheme 16. The formation requirement for this form of analogy is shared with the AAA-analogy.

AAP-Analogy Formation	
Mov	X AAP-Analogy$[A, B]$: $prop$
Cha	Y ? $F_{AAP-Analogy[A,B]}$
Def	X $PA_4(z) : set[z : (x : \neg A)B(x) \vee (y : \neg A)\neg B(y)]$

Scheme 16: AAP-Analogy Formation Rule

The dialogical rule for performing analogies of this form is given in Scheme 17.

AAP-Analogy	
Mov	X ! AAP-Analogy$[A, B]$
Cha	Y ! $(\forall y : \{x : \neg A \mid Sou(x)\})B(y) \supset (\forall z : \{x : \neg A \mid Tar(x)\})B(z)$
Def	X ! $B(z)$

Scheme 17: AAP-Analogy Explanation Rule

AAA-analogies

The absent-absent-absent analogy is a positive analogy, where the occasioning characteristic is absent in both the target case and the source case and where the entailed characteristic is present in the source case. This analogy form can be described in the following way:

$$\begin{array}{ccc} \text{Source} & & \text{Target} \\ \neg A & & \neg A \\ \downarrow & \leftrightarrow & \downarrow \\ \neg B & & (\neg B). \end{array}$$

The formation of the AAA-analogy is introduced in Scheme 18. The formation requirement for this form of analogy is shared with the AAP-analogy.

AAA-Analogy Formation	
Mov	X AAA-Analogy$[A, B]$: $prop$
Cha	Y ? $F_{AAA-Analogy[A,B]}$
Def	X $PA_4(z) : set[z : (x : \neg A)B(x) \vee (y : \neg A)\neg B(y)]$

Scheme 18: AAA-Analogy Formation Rule

The dialogical rule for performing analogies of this form is given in Scheme 19.

AAA-Analogy	
Mov	X ! AAA-Analogy$[A, B]$
Cha	Y ! $(\forall y : \{x : \neg A \vert Sou(x)\}) \neg B(y) \supset (\forall z : \{x : \neg A \vert Tar(x)\}) \neg B(z)$
Def	X ! $\neg B(z)$

Scheme 19: AAA-Analogy Explanation Rule

8.2 Explaining and extending the analysis

Explanation of the dialogical approach

As mentioned in the beginning of chapter 8, this approach intends to reduce the procedure of analogical argumentation to standard dialogues of immanent reasoning. The goal of this section is then to explain how the different rules can work together in order to represent the procedure of analogical reasoning. In short, we might describe the development of the explanation play by the following procedure:

1. A player proposes that an analogy holds between A and B. This player is now called **X**.

2. The other player, **Y**, now has to challenge the claim of **X** by an Analogy Challenge Rule 1 (Scheme 2). This is because this rule forces **X** to choose the form of analogy that will be proposed, before **Y** chooses any analogy form intended to counter the first one. This is reflected in the Analogy Challenge Rule Restriction.

3. **X** now has to defend the challenge in the previous step. This is done by stating a chosen form of analogy. In this step, the source cases in support of **X**'s chosen analogy form are introduced in the initial concessions. Given these source cases, **X** claims that the chosen analogy form holds.

4. **Y** then challenges the previous step by stating the type-theoretical formulation of that particular analogy form. **Y** has to use the appropriate Analogy Explanation Rule corresponding to the chosen analogy form in the previous steps.

5. The play will then develop in a normal way, based on the earlier defence chosen by **X**.

6. If the analogy form holds, **Y** can force **X** to state the entailed characteristic in the target case as a result of defending the challenge in the previous step. If the chosen analogy form does not hold, this cannot be done.

7. In the next step, **Y** chooses to do the other alternative from step 2. This means to challenge the thesis by the Analogy Challenge Rule 2. This obliges **Y** to forward a particular analogy form. It is here up to **Y** to choose the analogy form that **X** should be committed to. This step introduces a subplay with the chosen analogy form as a thesis. We might say that the roles in a subplay are turned, so that the original challenger becomes the defender and opposite. This step corresponds to bringing forward a counterexample to the proposed analogy. In this step, the source cases in support of **Y**'s chosen analogy form are introduced in the initial concessions. Given these additional source cases, **Y** claims that the chosen analogy form holds. For **Y** to succeed with this, **Y** has to choose an analogy form that will be defendable and that will give an entailed characteristic that is incompatible with the entailed characteristic in the analogy form proposed by **X**.[2] For **Y** to win, **X** should not be able to defend this challenge as it is intended to provide an inconsistency in **X**'s concessions.

8. **X** then challenges the previous step by stating the type-theoretical formulation of that particular analogy form. **X** has to use the appropriate Analogy Explanation Rule corresponding to the chosen analogy form in the previous steps.

9. The play will then develop in a normal way, based on the earlier challenge chosen by **Y**.

---

[2]Notice that this step requires **Y** to have a repetition rank of 2 or higher. If **Y**'s repetition rank is 1, the analogy will be *unrestricted*.

8.2. Explaining and extending the analysis

10. Depending on **Y**'s choice in the Analogy Challenge Rule 2 and its success in the play, the result of the first analogy form might be incompatible with the result of the second analogy form. **X** will be committed to both results. In this way, **Y** might force **X** to posit an inconsistency and therefore win the play. This rejects the proposed analogy and might provide motivation for modifying the occasioning characteristic. This corresponds to showing that the proposed analogy does not satisfy the condition of efficiency or the principle of proportionality.

We will illustrate the functioning of these rules by a brief and simplified example in Play 8, where **P** proposes a PPP-analogy between A and B and where **O** finds a counterexample by a PPA-analogy. In this play, the formation play is ignored for simplicity reasons. The play is also simplified in the sense that it does not account for the interaction between synthesis rules and analysis rules by the substitution of introduced variables. The play objects are marked according to whether they provide justification related to the source cases, p^s, to the target cases, p^t, or to the counterexample, p^c. We see here that **P** is forced to give up as he is not able to respond.

- I to VI are the initial concessions that form the assumptions for that particular play. I formulates the disjunction of the occasioning characteristic and its negation. II states that A in I (the occasioning characteristic) holds in the target case. This is formulated as a left instruction on the disjunction $A \vee \neg A$. III to V are introduced as claims related to the suggested analogy forms. III states that s_1 is a source case and that A holds in this source case. IV states that B holds in the source case s_1. V states that s_2 is a source case and that A holds in this source case. Notice that in the situations of the target and source cases, t, s_1 and s_2, they are instructions on a, $t(L^\vee(a))$, $s_1(L^\vee(a))$ and $s_2(L^\vee(a))$.

	O			P	
I	$a : A \vee \neg A$				
II	$t : Tar(L^{\vee}(a))$				
III	$s_1 : Sou(L^{\vee}(a))$				
IV	$b : B(s_1)$				
V	$s_2 : Sou(L^{\vee}(a))$				
				! Analogy$[A, B]$	0
1	n:=2			n:=3	2
3	? AnForm$[A, B]$	0		! PPP-Analogy$[A, B]$	4
5	! $(\forall y : \{x : A\|Sou(x)\})B(y) \supset (\forall z : \{x : A\|Tar(x)\})B(z)$	4		! $B(p_2^t)$	12
9	$p_1^t : (\forall z : \{x : A\|Tar(x)\})B(z)$		5	$p_1^s : (\forall y : \{x : A\|Sou(x)\})B(y)$	6
7	$s_1 : \{x : A\|Sou(x)\}$	6		$b : B(s_1)$	8
11	$p_3^t : B(p_2^t)$		9	$p_2^t : \{x : A\|Tar(x)\}$	10
13	! PPA-Analogy$[A, B]$	0			
	[Opening of subplay]				
			13	! $(\forall y : \{x : A\|Sou(x)\})\neg B(y) \supset (\forall z : \{x : A\|Tar(x)\})\neg B(z)$	14
15	$p_1^c : (\forall y : \{x : A\|Sou(x)\})\neg B(y)$	14		$p_2^c : (\forall z : \{x : A\|Tar(x)\})\neg B(z)$	16
17	$p_4^t : \{x : A\|Tar(x)\}$	16			
19	$a : A$		17	?L	18
21	$t : Tar((L^{\vee}(a))$		17	?R	20
23	$b' : \neg B(p_3^c)$		15	$p_3^c : \{x : A\|Sou(x)\}$	22

Play 8: Example play with PPP-Analogy and PPA-Analogy

- Move 0 states the proposed analogy, that there is an analogical relation between A and B.

- In moves 1 and 2, the players choose their repetition ranks. Notice that the Opponent chooses a repetition rank that is at least 2. This is to ensure the ability to challenge the proposed thesis twice. It is this move that ensures that we are speaking about a *restricted* analogy.

8.2. Explaining and extending the analysis

- In move 3, **O** challenges the proposed analogy in move 0 by the Analogy Challenge Rule 1. The Opponent here asks the Proponent to choose one analogy form that he thinks can be defended. **O** cannot use the Analogy Challenge Rule 2 here as this would go against the Analogy Challenge Rule Restriction, which states that the second rule can only be played after the first rule has been played.

- In move 4, **P** chooses the analogy form to be a PPP-Analogy, where A is present in both the source case and the target case and where B is present in the source case. In terms of meaning explanations, it is here that the initial concessions III and IV are introduced.

- In move 5, **O** challenges **P**'s chosen analogy form in move 4 by its corresponding explanation rule, here the PPP-Analogy Explanation Rule.

- Moves 6 to 11 show a normal development according to the rules of immanent reasoning. In move 6, **P** challenges the statement in move 5 by stating that the presence of B in the source cases is dependent on the presence of A. **O** challenges this statement in move 7 by stating the source cases where A is present.[3] In move 8, **P** defends this challenge by stating the presence of B in the source case from IV. In move 9, **O** defends the challenge in move 6 by stating that the presence of B in the target case depends on the presence of A. move 10 establishes the presence of A in the target case by **P** challenging the statement in move 9. We let **O** choose to simply defend this challenge for simplicity reasons. **O** can choose to challenge

---

[3]We have chosen to let the Opponent counterattack in move 7 instead of defending the challenge from move 6. In this way, we are provided with the entailed characteristic in the source case before the introduction of the target case. Strategically, the order of the moves does not change anything for the development of the play, but it provides meaning explanations that seem more closely related to actual practice.

move 10 in a similar way as **P** challenges move 17 in move 18 and 20. This will however not add anything further to the play as **P** will simply respond based on the initial concessions in move I and II. **O** could play out also these moves by carefully choosing the target case formulation, though here we leave that implicit. In move 11, **O** defends the challenge in move 10 by stating the presence of B in the target case.

- In move 12, **P** then defends the challenge in move 5 by stating that B is present in the target case. **P** can do this because of **O**'s statement in move 11. This finishes the first analogy form.

- In move 13, **O** challenges the thesis in move 0 again. This can be done because of **O**'s choice of repetition rank in move 1. The challenge is by the Analogy Challenge Rule 2, which now can be used since **O** already challenged by the Analogy Challenge Rule 1. This enables **O** to bring up a counterexample to the proposed analogy. It is now up to **O** to choose an analogy form. In this example, **O** chooses the form PPA-analogy. This move also opens up a subplay where the proposed counterexample will be brought in. It is here that the initial concession V is introduced.[4]

- In move 14, **P** challenges the proposed analogy form in move 13 by the corresponding explanation rule, the PPA-Analogy Explanation Rule.

- Moves 15 to 23 follow normal development according the rules of immanent reasoning. In move 15, **O** challenges the statement in move 14 by claiming that the absence of B is dependent on the presence of A in the source cases. **P** defends this challenge in move 16 by stating that the absence of B

---

[4]Notice that since s_2 is brought in as a counterexample by **O** we do not include the entailed characteristic in s_2 in the initial concessions, but directly in **O**'s move 23.

is dependent on the presence of A also in the target case. **O** challenges this statement in move 17 by stating the presence of A in the target case. In moves 18 to 21, **P** demands **O** to show the presence of A in the target case. In move 22, **P** challenges the statement in move 15 by claiming the presence of A in the source cases. **O** directly responds to this as it will assure the winning of **O**, by stating the absence of B in the source case.

- **P** is not able to respond to the challenge in move 17 and **O**'s counterexample is therefore effective and **O** wins the play.

In this example it is assumed that the formations have already been set. Following the notational traditions in the contemporary literature, this step is given in a play of its own. In the following section we provide a separate formation play that describes the development of the presuppositions for the explanation plays.

Formation plays and permitted analogies

One of the particularities of the present approach is its ability to express the permission of the analogy (and other formations). This means that we are not only able to have plays about the content of the analogy, but also about the initial conditions that justifies performing analogical reasoning in the first place. Conceptually, such formation play is supposed to occur before every play to establish that the play is meaningful. Though in the contemporary literature, the formation plays are often left implicit or as separate plays.

As an example, we will use a play where the Proponent proposes an analogy between A and B, based on a PPP-analogy and where the Opponent suggests a PAP-analogy as a counterexample. We choose this because it illustrates the introduction of different forms of permitted analogies. In the example, given in Play 9, the description of development of the content will be left implicit.

O			P		
I	$A : prop$				
II	$Tar : set$				
III	$Sou : set$				
IV	$B(x,y) : prop[$ $x : A \vee \neg A, y : Tar \vee Sou]$				
V	$PA_1(z) : set[z : (x : A)B(x)$ $\vee (y : A)\neg B(y)]$				
			! $Analogy[A, B]$		0
1	n:=4		n:=5		2
3	$?_{prop}$	0	$Analogy[A, B] : prop$		4
5	? $F_{Analogy[A,B]1}$	4	$A : prop$		6
7	? $F_{Analogy[A,B]2}$	4	$Tar : set$		8
9	? $F_{Analogy[A,B]3}$	4	$Sou : set$		10
11	? $F_{Analogy[A,B]4}$	4	$B(x,y) : prop[$ $x : A \vee \neg A, y : Tar \vee Sou]$		12
13	? $AnForm[A, B]$	0	! $PPP\text{-}Analogy[A, B]$		14
15	$?_{prop}$	14	$PPP\text{-}Analogy[A, B] : prop$		16
17	? $F_{PPP-Analogy[A,B]}$	16	$PA_1(z) : set[z : (x : A)B(x)$ $\vee (y : A)\neg B(y)]$		18
[Play develops normally]					
19	! $PAP\text{-}Analogy[A, B]$	0			
21	$PAP\text{-}Analogy[A, B] : prop$		19	$?_{prop}$	20
23	$PA_3(z) : set[$ $z : (x : A)\neg B(x)$ $\vee (y : A)\neg\neg B(y)]$		21	? $F_{PAP-Analogy[A,B]}$	22
[Play develops normally]					

Play 9: Example play with formation

- I to V are the initial concessions that form the assumptions for that particular play. I states that A is a proposition. II specifies the set of target cases. III specifies the set of source cases. IV states that B is a proposition under the assumption that A or $\neg A$ is present in either a source case or a target case. V states that analogies where A is present in the target case are permitted. In terms of meaning explanations, V is introduced in move 14.

8.2. Explaining and extending the analysis

- Move 0 states the proposed analogy, that there is an analogical relation between A and B.
- In move 1 and 2, the players choose their repetition ranks.[5]
- In move 3, **O** demands **P** to show that the proposed analogy is a proposition. **P** defends this in move 4.
- In move 5 to 12, **O** challenges **P**'s claim in move 4 by each of the four different challenges in the Analogy formation Rule. **P** defends by the corresponding claims, given in I, II, III and IV.
- In move 13, **O** challenges the proposed analogy in move 0 by the Analogy Challenge Rule 1. The Opponent here asks the Proponent to choose one analogy form that he thinks can be defended.
- In move 14, **P** chooses the analogy form to be a PPP-Analogy, where A is present in both the source case and the target case and where B is present in the source case. This move also introduces the permission of the analogy in V.
- In move 15, **O** demands **P** to show that the proposed analogy form is a proposition. **P** defends this in move 16.
- In move 17, **O** challenges **P**'s chosen analogy form in move 16 by demanding **P** to show that the use of a PPP-analogy is permitted in the context of B being analogical with A. **P** defends by stating PA_1, already stated by **O** in V. The precise formation of PA_1 is left implicit, though can be formulated by A being a proposition and B being a proposition under the assumption of A.

---

[5]Notice that for simplicity of the example, the Opponent chooses a repetition rank that is 4. This is to ensure the ability to challenge the formation of the proposed thesis by all four formation rules. We could also have developed the different formation rules in different plays and then the Opponent would only need a repetition rank of 2.

- In move 19, **O** challenges the thesis in move 0 again. The challenge is by the Analogy Challenge Rule 2, which now can be used since **O** already challenged by the Analogy Challenge Rule 1. This enables **O** to bring up a counterexample to the proposed analogy. It is now up to **O** to choose an analogy form. In this example, **O** chooses the form PAP-analogy.

- In move 20, **P** demands **O** to show that the proposed PAP-analogy is a proposition. **O** defends this in move 21.

- In move 22, **P** challenges **O**'s statement in move 21 by asking for the permission of the use of PAP-analogy for A and B. **O** defends this by stating PA_3. The precise formation of PA_3 is also left implicit.

Introducing heteronomous imperatives

In the CTT analysis, we distinguished between analogies based on characteristics and analogies based on heteronomous imperatives. The result was that we can defend stronger claims when dealing with deontic notions than we can when dealing with characteristics. This will naturally also be reflected in the dialogical implementation. Though contrary to the CTT analysis, we will not introduce a separate formalisation for these deontic analogies. It will suffice to add two definitional assumptions that enable the intended transformation. The rules introduced for analogies with properties will also hold for imperatives, though by themselves they will not be strong enough to capture all aspects of these inferences. Following previously introduced abbreviations, LA stands for law-abiding and LB stands for law-breaking.

We can establish this particular inference by including the following instances of the transmission of definitional equality 1 from Table 5.9 as general assumptions:

$\neg LB(x) = LA(x) : prop[x : A];$

$$LB(x) = \neg LA(x) : prop[x : A].$$

The first reads that A not being law-breaking is equal to A being law-abiding and the second that A being law-breaking is equal to A not being law-abiding. Generally, this seems to hold as it lies in the definition of both law-abidingness that it is not law-breaking and in law-breakingness that it is not law-abiding. They are incompatible concepts by definition. By including this definitional equality, we are able to explain the special inferences that analogies with imperatives seem to enable.

We can then treat the deontic qualifications as any other proposition when doing the analogical analysis. If the result in the target case is either that the performance or non-performance of A is not law-breaking, we can transform this result into it being law-abiding in the target case. Similarly, if the result in the target case is either that the performance or non-performance of A is law-abiding, we can transform this result into it not being law-breaking. The first might typically be used to establish the law-abidingness of A while the second might be used to establish the law-breakingness.

8.3 Dialogical example

Steamboat example

We will illustrate this approach by the steamboat example, *Adams v. New Jersey Steamboat Co.*, 151 N.Y. 163 (1896). The example is previously introduced and analysed in section 7.3. The example is a case about whether or not a certain steamboat owner is liable for a theft from a customer.

Following the previous treatment of this example, $F : prop$ stands for the proposition *refusing strict liability for the theft of valuables when the client paid for a room for some specified reasons and that the company has tempting opportunity for fraud and plunder of the client*. In the dialogical approach, we will let i represent the innkeeper case where the presence of F was law-breaking and r represent the railway case where the absence of F was law-abiding. We can here recognise this argumentative process as a case of the Proponent suggesting a PPP-analogy between F and law-breakingness, based on i, and where the Opponent attempts to utilise r as an unsuccessful counterexample by a PAA-analogy.

Formation and permissibility

The first step is to establish the formation and general permissibility of the use of the analogical argument. This means to ensure that all terms are well-typed and that the use of the particular form of analogy is legally permissible in this precise context. This is analysed in Play 10.

We can see that this play closely resembles the example in Play 9. The only difference is that we in this example discuss a particular characteristic F and its law-breakingness, rather than the characteristic B that is dependent on the characteristic A. Similar explanations of the different moves will therefore also hold here. We will simply focus the attention on the most important aspect of this constructive approach, namely the permission of the analogy. The permission of the PPP-analogy is here introduced in the initial concessions. The permission of the PAA-analogy is instead introduced by the Opponent when proposing this form as a counterargument.

In the initial concessions, we only introduce the particular permission that is needed for this particular argument, as other forms of analogy could (at least conceptually) not be permitted. There might be a discussion whether this actually can be reflected in the legal system, though we seem to safely claim that the permission of other forms of analogy might not have been *assessed*. We could have chosen to also include this second permission in the initial concessions, but by introducing it in the course of the play, our approach seems more closely connected to actual legal practice where it is the proposer of the argument that carries the burden to show that this argument is legally permitted.

8.3. Dialogical example

	O			P	
I	$F : prop$				
II	$Tar : set$				
III	$Sou : set$				
IV	$LB(x,y) : prop[$ $x : F \vee \neg F, y : Tar \vee Sou]$				
V	$PA_1(z) : set[$ $z : (x : F)LB(x)$ $\vee (y : F)\neg LB(y)]$				
				! $Analogy[F, LB]$	0
1	n:=4			n:=5	2
3	$?_{prop}$	0		$Analogy[F, LB] : prop$	4
5	? $F_{Analogy[F,LB]}1$	4		$F : prop$	6
7	? $F_{Analogy[F,LB]}2$	4		$Tar : set$	8
9	? $F_{Analogy[F,LB]}3$	4		$Sou : set$	10
11	? $F_{Analogy[F,LB]}4$	4		$LB(x,y) : prop[$ $x : F \vee \neg F, y : Tar \vee Sou]$	12
13	? $AnForm[F, LB]$	0		! $PPP\text{-}Analogy[F, LB]$	14
15	$?_{prop}$	14		$PPP\text{-}Analogy[F, LB] : prop$	16
17	? $F_{PPP-Analogy[F,LB]}$	16		$PA_1(z) : set[$ $z : (x : F)LB(x)$ $\vee (y : F)\neg LB(y)]$	18
	[Play develops normally]				
19	! $PAA\text{-}Analogy[F, LB]$	0			
21	$PAA\text{-}Analogy[F, LB] : prop$		19	$?_{prop}$	20
23	$PA_3(z) : set[$ $z : (x : F)\neg LB(x)$ $\vee (y : F)\neg\neg LB(x)]$		21	? $F_{PAA-Analogy[F,LB]}$	22
	[Play develops normally]				

Play 10: Steamboat example, formation play

Justifying the analogy

In the formation play, no justification for the analogy is established. This is done in the particle play. This justificatory process has the form of the Proponent suggesting an analogy between F and being law-breaking, on the basis of a PPP-analogy. The Opponent tries to provide a counterexample to this by a PAA-analogy, though fails since the PAA-analogy will not provide sufficient results to actually reject the PPP-analogy. The justificatory process is described in Play 11.

	O			P	
I	$f : F \vee \neg F$				
II	$t : Tar(L^{\vee}(f))$				
III	$i : Sou(L^{\vee}(f))$				
IV	$d : LB(i)$				
V	$r : Sou(R^{\vee}(f))$				
				! Analogy$[F, LB]$	0
1	n:=2			n:=3	2
3	? AnForm$[F, LB]$	0		! PPP-Analogy$[F, LB]$	4
5	! $(\forall y : \{x : F\|Sou(x)\})$ $LB(y) \supset$ $(\forall z : \{x : F\|Tar(x)\})LB(z)$	4		! $LB(p_2^t)$	12
9	$p_1^t : (\forall z : \{x : F\|Tar(x)\})$ $LB(z)$		5	$p_1^s : (\forall y : \{x : F\|Sou(x)\})$ $LB(y)$	6
7	$i : \{x : F\|Sou(x)\}$	6		$d : LB(i)$	8
11	$p_3^t : LB(p_2^t)$		9	$p_2^t : \{x : F\|Tar(x)\}$	10
13	! PAA-Analogy$[F, LB]$	0			
	[Opening of subplay]				
			13	! $(\forall y : \{x : \neg F\|Sou(x)\})$ $\neg LB(y) \supset (\forall z :$ $\{x : F\|Tar(x)\})\neg\neg LB(z)$	14
15	$p_1^c : (\forall y : \{$ $x : \neg F\|Sou(x)\})\neg LB(y)$	14		$p_2^c : (\forall z : \{$ $x : \neg F\|Tar(x)\})\neg\neg LB(z)$	16
17	$p_2^t : \{x : F\|Tar(x)\}$	16		$p_4^t : \neg\neg LB(p_2^t)$	18
19	$p_5^t : \neg LB(p_2^t)$	18		$you_{gave\ up}(21) : \bot$	22
21	$p_6^t : \bot$		19	$p_3^t : LB(p_2^t)$	20

Play 11: Steamboat example

8.3. Dialogical example

Describing the justificatory process

- I formulates the disjunction of the occasioning proposition and its negation. II states that F, the left side in I, holds in the steamboat case t. III states that the innkeeper case i is a source case and that F is present in this source case. IV states that F was law-breaking in i. V states that the railway case r is a source case and that F is absent in this source case.

- Move 0 states the proposed analogy, that there is an analogical relation between F and law-breakingness.

- In moves 1 and 2, the players choose their repetition ranks.

- In move 3, **O** challenges the proposed analogy in move 0 by the Analogy Challenge Rule 1. The Opponent here asks the Proponent to choose one analogy form that he thinks can be defended.

- In move 4, **P** chooses the analogy form to be a PPP-Analogy, where F is present in both the source case and the target case and where F was law-breaking in the source case. In terms of meaning explanations, it is here that the initial concessions III and IV are introduced.

- In move 5, **O** challenges **P**'s chosen analogy form in move 4 by the PPP-analogy Explanation Rule.

- Moves 6 to 11 show a normal development according to the rules of immanent reasoning. In move 6, **P** challenges the statement in move 5 by stating that the law-breakingness in the source cases is dependent on the presence of F. **O** challenges this statement in move 7 by stating the source case where F is present, here the innkeeper case i. In move 8, **P** defends this challenge by stating the law-breakingness in the source case from IV. In move 9, **O** defends the challenge in move 6 by stating that the law-breakingness in the target case depends on the presence of F. Move 10 establishes the presence of F in the target case by **P** challenging the statement in move 9. In move 11, **O** defends the challenge in move 10 by stating the law-breakingness in the target case.

- In move 12, **P** then defends the challenge in move 5 by stating the law-breakingness in the target case. **P** can do this because of **O**'s statement in move 11. This finishes the first analogy form.

- In move 13, **O** challenges the thesis in move 0 again. This can be done because of **O**'s choice of repetition rank in move 1. The challenge is by the Analogy Challenge Rule 2, which now can be used since **O** already challenged by the Analogy Challenge Rule 1. This enables **O** to bring up a counterexample to the proposed analogy. **O** chooses to bring in the PAA-analogy form as a proposed counterexample. This move opens up a subplay where the proposed counterexample will be brought in. It is here that the initial concession V is introduced.

- In move 14, **P** challenges the proposed analogy form in move 13, by the PAA-Analogy Explanation Rule.

- Moves 15 to 22 follow normal development according the rules of immanent reasoning. In move 15, **O** challenges the statement in move 16, claiming that an absence of law-breakingness is dependent on the absence of F in the source cases. **P** defends this challenge by stating that the double negated law-breakingness is dependent on the absence of F in the target case. **O** challenges this statement in move 17 by stating the presence F in the target case. In move 18, **P** defends the challenge in move 17 by stating the double negated law-breakingness in the target case. In move 19, **O** challenges the statement in move 18 by stating that it is not law-breaking in the target case. In move 20, **P** states that the target case

8.3. Dialogical example

is law-breaking. **P** can do this because **O** already stated this in move 11. In move 21, **O** is forced to posit $\bot$. This gives **P** the possibility to state the special play object $you_{gave\ up}(21)$ and the play terminates.

- **P** has the last word in the play and **O**'s proposed counterexample is therefore not effective and **P** wins the play.

We can see that this corresponds well together with the intended result, where the steamboat case was decided to be similar to the innkeeper case and not to the railway case.

Mortgage loan example

This section describes and analyses a particular example taken from Spanish Law, regarding Supreme Court decisions on the duty of paying the IAJD (Impuesto sobre Actos Jurídicos Documentados [Tax on Documented Legal Acts] related to the loan. The precise analysis of this particular case requires moves that go beyond the moves that are presented here and we will therefore provide only a semi-formal presentation of this example. The goal of this example is to show the role the different moves have in a concrete example taken from a contemporary civil law system.[6]

The cases

Actually, there are three main cases. However, all of them can be conceived as different plays on deciding about the interpretation of the Law concerning who must pay some particular tax specific to loans linked to a mortgage (either a mortgage loan or a credit

---

[6]The analysis and the description in this section is a modified analysis taken from «Elements for a Dialogical Approach on Parallel Reasoning. A Case Study of Spanish Civil Law» by Martínez-Cazalla, Menéndez-Martín, Rahman, and Kvernenes (2022).

warranted with a mortgage) included in the tax called *Tax on Documented Legal Acts* (Impuesto sobre Actos Jurídicos Documentados – IAJD). More crucially, they can be seen as different plays concerning the meaning of the concepts of *Mortgage Loan*, *Right* (to acquire a Mortgage Loan) and *Beneficiary of a Mortgage Loan*.

The first case

In the first case, Supreme Court Judgment 9012/2001, the appellant party, the borrower *Inmobiliaria Manuel Asín, S.A.* (IMA), submits a cassation appeal (an appeal to overturn the previous decision) against the decision that it is, themselves, the borrower; who is in charge of paying the IAJD tax involving the mortgage loan granted by the *Caja de Ahorros y Monte Piedad de Zaragoza, Aragón y Rioja* (Ibercaja). The argument of the appellant is based on the idea that though a mortgage loan is a loan, one should distinguish the two components. In other words, the point of the appellant is that mortgage loans should be understood in the divided sense – in Islamic Jurisprudence such a move is called *kasr* or breaking apart. The point is that the IAJD tax is linked to the mortgage component, not to the loan as such. In other words, according to the appellant, the property of being a loan is not the occasioning factor for determining who is in charge of the taxes at stake. The Supreme Court dismissed the appeal, based on denying the divided reading of the notion of mortgage loans and stressing the fact that this unity also leads to the unity of beneficiary, namely the borrower:

> [...] it is true that the traditional interpretation of this Chamber [3rd Chamber of the Supreme Court of Spain] has always accepted the premise that the taxable event, mortgage loan, was and is unique, and therefore, the conclusion of its subjection to AJD is, nowadays, coherent, whatever the legislative tendencies that, may be in the near future, could consecrate mortgage loan exemption in this particular tax—.

8.3. Dialogical example

> *In any case, the unity of the taxable event related to the loan produces the consequence that the only possible beneficiary is the borrower, in accordance with the provision in art. 8°.d)—.*
>
> (p. 3, para. 2-3),
> Supreme Court Judgment 9012/2001[7]

One way to put the issue of the interpretative contention concerning this case is to focus on the different ways the contenders build the meaning dependence between loan, mortgage and IAJD-duty.

Indeed, whereas the argument of IMA, the appellant party, is based on the following meaning formations, which break apart the notions of Mortgage, Loan and the Mortgage-dependent tax duty IAJD:

- $Mortgage : prop, Loan : prop,$
  $BIAJDDuty(x) : prop(x : Mortgage).$

- In words, the tax duty IAJD is dependent upon the notion of Mortgage. Accordingly, this duty is independent of the notion of Loan.

The argument of the Supreme Court in favour of Ibercaja is based on the following meaning constitution:

- $Loan : prop, Mortgage(x) : prop(x : Loan),$
  $Beneficiary(x, y) : prop(x : Loan, y : Mortgage(x)),$
  $BIAJDDuty(x, y, z) : prop(x : Loan,$
  $y : Mortgage(x), z : Beneficiary(x, y)).$

- In words, *Mortgage Loan* is a complex concept, namely it concerns those mortgages dependent upon a loan. Accordingly, the tax duty IAJD is dependent upon the complex concept Mortgage Loan, they are inseparable the notion of Loan. More-

---

[7]Sentencia del Tribunal Supremo 9012/2001, dated 19. November 2001. English summary found in Martínez-Cazalla et al. (2022, pp. 245-247).

over, the notion of Beneficiary is made dependent upon the notion of the acquirer of the Mortgage Loan. Thus, strictly speaking, the tax duty IAJD is understood as dependent upon the *Mortgage-Loan-Beneficiary*.

- Notice that the beneficiary is defined as the one that benefited of the mortgage loan. It defines the *Borrower* as the beneficiary.

Second case
The second case, Supreme Court Judgment 7141/2006, also involving mortgage and loan, yields the same juridical decision as the precedent case. However, it is interesting that the reason brought forward by the Court stresses, as relevant for the decision, an aspect of the legal feature of the transaction different to the one occasioning the decision 9012/2001. Indeed, the argument does not contest the unicity of the tax event, the credit opened by the *Caixa d'Estalvis* in *Pensions de Barcelona* (La Caixa) in favour of *Establecimientos Industriales y Servicios, S.A.* (EISSA, S.A.) and linked with a *mortgage warrant*, nevertheless, it stresses the point that the passive subject of the purchase of the *right*, namely the credit, is the beneficiary, i.e., the borrower. Thus, according to this argument of the Court, the uniqueness of the beneficiary of this kind of transaction is the relevant feature occasioning the decision that it is the borrower's duty rather than the lender's duty to pay the taxes involving the mortgage. The point is that, according to the Supreme Court, the beneficiary is the beneficiary of the main business or of the purchase of the right. The main business is the loan, the mortgage being a subject of the loan; the beneficiary of the loan is the borrower, namely EISSA; therefore, it is EISSA who has the duty to pay the due taxes:

8.3. Dialogical example

> *[...] the beneficiary is the purchaser of the good or of the right and, failing that, the persons who request notarial documents, or those in whose interest the documents are issued—.*
>
> *[...] The purchaser of the good or of the right can only be the borrower, not because of an argument such as the unity of the taxable event related to the loan, [...], but because the right referred to in the precept is the loan reflected in the notarial document, even if it is guaranteed with a mortgage and its registration in the Property Registry is the constituent element of guarantee—.*
>
> (p. 3, para. 3),
Supreme Court Judgment 7141/2006[8]

From the meaning constitution point of view, the Supreme Court adds more complexity by squeezing the notion of *right* (to acquire a loan), between the compound *Mortgage-Loan-Beneficiary* and the *IAJD-duty*. What determines the ratio legis is benefiting from the acquisition of the right implied in a loan, whatever the loan is:

- $BIAJDDuty(x, y, z, w) : prop(x : Loan, y : Mortgage(x), z : Right(x, y), w : Beneficiary(x, y, z))$.

- Under this perspective; the notion of *acquired right* is dependent upon the compound *Mortgage-Loan-Beneficiary*. In other words, the right is *the right acquired by being the Beneficiary of the Loan in any way attached to a Mortgage*, and the duty to the pay the IAJD is then made dependent upon this right.

---

[8]Sentencia del Tribunal Supremo 7141/2006, dated 31. October 2006. English summary found in Martínez-Cazalla et al. (2022, pp. 247-249).

- Hence, this alternative interpretation, that defines the right as the one acquired by the beneficiary of the loan attached to a mortgage, also leads to identifying the *Borrower* as the one who has to carry the burden of the IAJD.

Third case

The last case of our study, Supreme Court Judgment 3422/2018, also involving mortgage and loan, overturns the *ratio legis* behind the decisions deployed in the precedent cases concerning who carries the duty of paying the taxes induced by the mortgage loan. Indeed, the decision 3422/2018 establishes that it is the lender, not the borrower, who has to pay the due taxes. Moreover, it explicitly overturns juridical decisions as the ones established by Judgments 9012/2001 and 7141/2006. The argument behind the overturning indicates that if, as argued in 7141/2006, it is the case that the main business is the loan, i.e., the purchasing of a right, this right is not a *real one*, in the sense that, for example, it does induce change of ownership. A real right is the one linked to the mortgage, but this is accessory to the right acquired by the beneficiary and in fact the beneficiary of that real right is the lender, not the borrower. Hence, the due taxes must be paid by the direct beneficiary of the mortgage, namely the lender.

> The Supreme Court held that loans are not registrable, [...], as they are obviously not a real right, nor does the right have the typical real significance mentioned in the second of these precepts (since they do not modify, now or in the future, several of the rights of ownership over real estate or inherent to real rights). The mortgage, on the other hand, is not only registrable, but it is also the mortgage is a real right—.
>
> The fact that the mortgage is a real right of registry constitution makes it clearly the main business for tax purposes in public deeds in which mortgage loans or loans with mortgage guarantee are documented—.

8.3. Dialogical example

> If we still consider the loan as the main business it does not make much sense to submit to the tax a non-registrable legal business only because there is an accessory real right constituted as a guarantee of compliance with the main one.

The Supreme Court held also that:

> [...] there is no doubt that the beneficiary of the document in question is no other than the creditor, because they (and only they) are qualified to exercise the (privileged) actions that the code offers to the holders of the registered rights. They are the only party interested in the registration of the mortgage (the determining element subject to the tax analysed here), since the mortgage is ineffective if it is not registered in the Property Registry.

Thus, the conclusions were:

> 1. Based on the previous reasoning, we can now answer the question that we have considered preferential, out of the two questions raised by the First Section (Civil Chamber) of this Chamber (Supreme Court). The beneficiary of a mortgage (by loan over itself or as guarantee of a loan) is the money-lender and not the borrower. Therefore, the tax on Documented Legal Acts –when the document subject to the tax is a public deed of a mortgage (by loan over itself or as guarantee of a loan)– should be paid by the lender and not by the borrower.
>
> 2. In order to comply with the decree of admission, the above statement needs to be completed making it explicit that such a decision involves adoption of a guideline opposite to that supported by the jurisprudence of this Chamber (Third Camber – Contentious-Administrative Chamber– of the

Supreme Court) until now, as presented in the judgments (STS 9012/2001 and STS 7141/2006) among others, and therefore modifying the previous jurisprudential doctrine.

(p. 11, para. 9),
Supreme Court Judgment 3422/2018[9]

Supreme Court Judgment 3422/2018 concerns the request of the *Empresa Municipal de la Vivienda de Rivas-Vaciamadrid, S.A.* (EMVRivas, S.A.) to be exempted of the taxes required by the *Public Administration* linked to the mortgage that warranted a loan credited to EMVRivas by a bank entity. Nevertheless, as mentioned above, the decision involves a general judgment on who is the beneficiary of the mortgage linked to a mortgage loan. The argument can again here be put as concerning meaning constitution.

The main point of the Supreme Court's argument is related to distinguishing *real rights* from those acquired by taking a *loan*, and more crucially, to set as beneficiary, the beneficiary of a real right. There are several ways to implement these distinctions, but for keeping our framework as simple as possible let us compose *Loan* and *Mortgage* by a conjunction. However, the notion of *Real-Right* will be made dependent upon *Mortgage*, furthermore, *Beneficiary* will be defined as those who acquire a *Real-Right* by registering the *Mortgage* (brought forward as a warrant by the borrower). Accordingly, the *IAJD-duty* will be defined as the duty of the *R-Beneficiary*, i.e., the *Beneficiary* of the *Real-Right*.

- *Loan* : $prop$,
  $BIAJDDuty(x, y, z) : prop(x : Mortgage,$
  $y : RealRight(x), z : RBeneficiary(x, y)).$

---

[9]*Sentencia del Tribunal Supremo* 3422/2018, dated 16. October 2018. English summary found in Martínez-Cazalla et al. (2022, pp. 249-252).

8.3. Dialogical example

In order to stress the accessory feature of the Mortgage and the dependence of the notion of *R-Beneficiary* upon the concept of *Real-Right*, and the dependence of *IAJD-duty* upon the former, we can express all this as the conjunction of *Loan* with the sigma-type (the existential) expressing those dependences:

- $Loan \wedge \exists v : [(x : Mortgage, y : RealRight(x), z : RBeneficiary(x,y))BIAJDDuty(v)]$.

Presuppositions and remarks

All these cases are in fact cassation appeals and, as mentioned above, they all amount to say it bluntly to decide who of both, borrower or money-lender, is the beneficiary of either a mortgage loan or a credit warranted with a mortgage, if we are prepared (or not) to distinguish the (real) right linked to the mortgage from the right acquired with the loan.

Thus, we can see the three plays as sub-plays of a whole argument. However, for the sake of oversight in the present reconstruction, we will present each play by its own, where each relevant step is explicitly associated with a dialogical move. In order to keep stress, for the general structure of each argument, we adopt as starting point (the target case) the point of view of the Supreme Court. In the second and third play the source case refers to the precedent plays.

The given example from Spanish law is very complex and requires moves that go beyond what is introduced in this book. We will therefore provide semiformal dialogical reconstructions of the meaning explanations behind these cases. The dialogical approach, though, facilitates an integration of such moves into more general analyses of legal reasoning and argumentation. As shown in the following section, we are able to integrate the analysis into the more complex and general plays that analyse the three concrete legal cases in a very simple and effective way.

334   Chapter 8. Dialogical implementation

To facilitate reading we also assume the following definitions and abbreviations:

l	$l : Loan$
m	$m : Mortgage$
b	$b : Beneficiary$
r	$r : Right$
rr	$rr : RealRight$
rb	$rb : RBeneficiary$
d	$d : BIAJDDuty$
$r^u : Right$	This stands for u having a legal right acquired by acquiring a mortgage loan. Thus, 'r^{EISSA}' stands for EISSA in its quality of enjoying such a right.
$rr^u : RealRight$	This stands for u having a real right. Thus, 'rr^{UCE}' stands for the Unnamed Credit Entity (UCE) in its quality having a real right.
$b^u : Beneficiary$	This stands for u being beneficiary. Thus, 'b^{IMA}' stands for IMA in its quality as beneficiary.
$rb^u : RBeneficiary$	This stands for u being the Real-Right beneficiary. Thus, 'rb^{UCE}' stands for the unnamed credit entity in its quality as Real-Right beneficiary.
$d^u : BIAJDDuty$	This stands for u being the bearer of the IAJD-duty. Thus, 'd^{IMA}' stands for IMA in its quality as bearer of the IAJD-duty.

8.3. Dialogical example

For simplicity we will omit the superscript indicating the individual in the context together with the previously mentioned abbreviations. This means that

$$b^u : Beneficiary(l^u : Loan, m^u : Mortgage)$$

will be written

$$b^u : Beneficiary(l, m).$$

Fore a more detailed description and background for the analysis of the different cases, see Martínez-Cazalla et al. (2022).

Dialogical analysis

First play (9012/2001)
The first play describes a situation where the proponent uses a PPP-analogy form on the basis of some precedent cases decided in favour of the given meaning explanation. The opponent's initial counterargument fails as it cannot be given foundation in the source cases. The analyses in this section is intended to show the role the introduced rules can play in a general dialogical framework and we will therefore leave the complete run (as explicitly described for the steamboat case) of the different forms implicit. Dialogically, this situation can be described by the following semi-formal play:

	O		P	
I	Precedent-Cases decided in favour of the creditor concerning the payment of IAJD tax by a mortgage loan granted by u			
			IMA has to pay the IAJD-duty.	0
1	Why?		Because IMA is the beneficiary of the mortgage loan.	2
3	I do not agree. *Mortgage Loan* should be divided in its constituents *Mortgage + Loan*.		Develop, please.	4
	[Opening of subplay]			

	O	P	
5	If we divide the compounds of *Mortgage Loan*, we realise that the Bearer of. the IAJD-duty should be the one having the *Mortgaged* good as warranty. More precisely: $$BIAJDDuty(x) : prop$$ $$(x : Mortgage),$$ given that Mortgage Loan can be divided into $$Mortgage : prop$$ and $$Loan : prop.$$ In other words, the notion of Bearer of the tax-duty is dependent upon *Mortgage*. Hence the ratio legis for determining who has to pay is dependent of who has granted the mortgage. This also explains that though IMA is indeed the beneficiary of the mortgage, it is not the bearer of the tax-duty. The divided sense allows to define the beneficiary in the following way: $$Beneficiary(x) : prop$$ $$(x : Mortgage).$$	No. The notion of Mortgage Loan is a specific kind of loan and must be considered as a unity. In fact, it separates a class of loans. Thus, the meaning constitution of Mortgage Loan is $$Mortgage(x) : prop(x : Loan).$$ Since it cannot be divided, the beneficiary is the one to whom the mortgage loan has been granted: $$Beneficiary(x, y) : prop$$ $$(x : Loan, y : Mortgage(x)).$$ Thus, as witnessed by precedent cases, by PPP-analogy form we get the result that the beneficiary of a mortgage loan is the borrower u, right? $$b^u : Beneficiary(l, m)?$$	6

8.3. Dialogical example

	O	P	
7	I see. The PPP-analogy form has indeed foundation in the precedent cases. $b^u : Beneficiary(l, m)$	So, the borrower, u, bears the tax payment duty of the IAJD because of u's role as a beneficiary of the mortgage loan, right? $d^u : BIAJDDuty(l, m, b)$ given that $BIAJDDuty(x, y, z) : prop$ $((x : Loan, y : Mortgage(x),$ $z : Beneficiary(x, y))$.	8
9	Indeed, $d^u : BIAJDDuty(l, m, b)$.		
	[End of subplay]		
11	Yes, such a universal step seems to be grounded.	So, we can both agree that generally: *if the tax duty IAJD has to be paid by whoever is the beneficiary a mortgage loan (i.e., the borrower), then every such a borrower does?*	10
13	Yes. $b^{IMA} : Beneficiary(l, m)$	And do you also agree that the beneficiary in this case is IMA? $b^{IMA} : Beneficiary(l, m)?$	12
15	Yes, if Bearer is defined in this way, IMA is the bearer of the IAJD-duty. $d^{IMA} : BIAJDDuty(l, m, b)$	So, you also agree that IMA is the bearer of the IAJD-duty? $d^{IMA} : BIAJDDuty(l, m, b)?$	14

	O		P	
17	I give up!		This is the reason that IMA is the bearer of the IAJD-duty. $d^{IMA} : BIAJDDuty(l,m,b)$	16

Second play (7141/2006)

The second play describes a situation where the proponent initiates an argument by a PPP-analogy form and the opponent attacks this by providing an PPA-analogy form with foundation in the precedents. This forces the proponent to explain the precise meaning explanation for the analogy. By providing this precise meaning, the proponent shows that the counterargument by a PPA-analogy form of the opponent actually does not hold since this was based on another understanding than what actually was the foundation of the analogy. Dialogically, this situation can be described by the following play:

	O		P	
I	s_1 : Supreme Court Judgment 9012/2001			
			EISSA has to pay the IAJD-duty.	0
1	Why?		In the precedent case s_1, the IAJD-duty has to be paid by the borrower u in their quality of beneficiary. This can be grounded by a PPP-analogy form. Do you agree?	2
3	However, even if in the precedent case it is the borrower who had to pay the IAJD, we can form a counterargument by the form of a PPA-analogy based on other precedent cases.		Develop, please.	4
[Opening of subplay]				

8.3. Dialogical example

	O	P	
5	There are sufficient precedent cases that indicate that being the beneficiary of the loan warranted by a mortgage is not enough to determine that it is the borrower who is in charge of paying the registration tax. We can therefore provide foundation for a PPA-analogy form.	Let us see. The borrower is the one who has acquired a right. Do you agree? $$r^u : Right(l,m)?$$ given that $$Right(x,y,) : prop$$ $$(x : Loan, y : Mortgage(x)).$$	6
7	I do. $$r^u : Right(l,m)$$	Based on your endorsement, the borrower, u, is the bearer of the IAJD-duty because of u's acquired the Right of being the beneficiary of the loan, right? $$d^u : BIAJDDuty(l,m,b,r)?$$ given that $$BIAJDDuty(x,y,z,w) : prop$$ $$(x : Loan, y : Mortgage(x),$$ $$z : Right(x,y),$$ $$w : Beneficiary(x,y,z)).$$	8
9	Yes, if benefiting of a right is added, we can form a PPP-analogy form and claim its result. $$d^u : BIAJDDuty(l,m,r,b)$$		
	[End of subplay]		

	O	P	
11	Yes, such a universal generalisation can be introduced then as a rule.	So, we can both agree that generally: *if the tax duty IAJD has to be paid by the borrower, whoever this borrower is, (this borrower being the one who acquired the right associated with being the beneficiary of the loan (warranted by a mortgage) granted by the creditor), then every such borrower does*, can't we?	10
13	Yes. $b^{EISSA} : Beneficary(l,m,r)$	And you agree that the part that has acquired the right associated with being beneficiary to the loan warranted by a mortgage, in this case is EISSA? $b^{EISSA} : Beneficary(l,m,r)?$	12
15	Yes, EISSA is the bearer of the IAJD-duty. $d^{EISSA} : BIAJDDuty(l,m,r,b)$	So, you agree that it follows from your endorsements that the tax duty IAJD has to be paid by EISSA, as a result of EISSA acquiring the right associated with being the beneficiary of the loan which has been warranted by a mortgage? $d^{EISSA} : BIAJDDuty(l,m,r,b)?$	14
17	Conceded!	This is the reason that EISSA is the bearer of the IAJD-duty. $d^{EISSA} : BIAJDDuty(l,m,r,b)$	16

Third play (3422/2018)

The third play describes a situation where the proponent initiates an argument by a PPP-analogy form and the opponent attacks this by providing an entirely new analogy, that will show to be inconsistent with the originally proposed analogy. By utilising a PPP-analogy

8.3. Dialogical example

form on this new analogy, the opponent convinces the proponent of the incompatibility between the two meaning explanations and asks the proponent to provide a revised thesis based on this new analogy. Dialogically, this situation can be described by the following play:

	O		P	
I	s_1 : Supreme Court Judgment 9012/2001			
II	s_2 : Supreme Court Judgment 7141/2006			
			EMVRivas has to pay the IAJD-duty.	0
1	Why?		The point of the case 7141/2006 is that it amends the decision 9012/2001 by enriching the notion of beneficiary with the notion of right, so that it is the borrower u that is the beneficiary of the right associated with the mortgage loan. So, we should have $$b^u : Beneficiary(l, m, r)?$$ Do you agree?	2
3	I do. $$b^u : Beneficiary(l, m, r)$$		By a PPP-analogy form, this leads to the 7141/2006-conclusion that it is the beneficiary of the right associated with the mortgage loan that is the bearer of the IAJD-duty, right? $$d^u : BIAJDDuty(l, m, r, b)?$$	4
5	No, I do not agree. This is inconsistent with another meaning explanation for this notion, and this indicates that advocated *ratio legis* must be revised. I therefore propose an entirely new analogy and I will show that a based on a PPP-analogy form, we will get a new result, incompatible with the your point in step 4.		Develop, please.	6
	[Opening of subplay]			

	O	P	
7	The creditor v is the one who has the real right being associated with the mortgage itself. Do you agree? $rr^v : RealRight(m)?$	Yes, I do. $rr^v : RealRight(m)$	8
9	Do you also agree that the creditor v is the beneficiary as a result of having acquired the real right associated with the mortgage itself? $rb^v : RBeneficiary(m, rr)?$	Yes, they are the beneficiary of the real right. $rb^v : RBeneficiary(m, rr)$	10
11	So, since the beneficiary is the creditor, and the beneficiary is the bearer of the IAJD-duty, then it follows that it is the creditor who is in charge of paying the due taxes, right? $d^v : BIAJDDuty(m, rr, rb)?$	Yes, that does indeed seem to be following from this notion of beneficiary of the real right. $d^v : BIAJDDuty(m, rr, rb)$	12
13	And you also agree that the money-lender and the borrower cannot both be bearers of the IAJD-duty, so that your statement in step 4, corresponding to the conclusions contained in the cases 9012/2001 and 7141/2006 is incompatible with your statement in step 12?	Yes, my statement in step 4 corresponding to the conclusions contained in the cases 9012/2001 and 7141/2006 is incompatible with my statement in step 12. My statement in step 4 must be given up and the meaning explanations must be overturned.	14

8.3. Dialogical example

	O	P	
15	The occasioning factor determining the ratio legis is being the beneficiary of the real right associated to warranting a mortgage. Recall that the beneficiary of a real right is the one who benefits of a change of property. Do you agree now that the appropriate meaning explanation of beneficiary is one who acquired a real right associated with the mortgage? $$RBeneficiary(x,y) : prop$$ $$(x : Mortgage,$$ $$y : RealRight(x))?$$	I agree. $$RBeneficiary(x,y) : prop$$ $$(x : Mortgage,$$ $$y : RealRight(x))$$	16
17	Do we furthermore agree that the meaning explanation for the bearer of the IAJD-duty is the beneficiary that acquired the real right associated with the mortgage? $$BIAJDDuty(x,y,z) : prop$$ $$(x : Mortgage,$$ $$y : RealRight(x),$$ $$z : RBeneficiary(x,y))?$$	Indeed. $$BIAJDDuty(x,y,z) : prop$$ $$(x : Mortgage,$$ $$y : RealRight(x),$$ $$z : RBeneficiary(x,y))$$	18
19	I ask you therefore to revise your original statement, based on an overturning of the meaning explanations in the precedent cases 9012/2001 and 7141/2006 as argued for from step 7 to 19.		
	[End of subplay]		
		Based on your new analogy I will defend the following revised thesis: UCE has to pay the IAJD-duty.	20

	O	P	
21	I agree. Though, please develop your justification for your revised thesis.	Recall, since the beneficiary of the real right associated with the mortgage is the creditor, and this beneficiary is the bearer of the IAJD-duty, then it follows that is the creditor who is in charge of paying the due taxes, right? $$d^v : BIAJDDuty(m, rr, rb)?$$	22
23	Yes, it does. $$d^v : BIAJDDuty(m, rr, rb)$$	Do you agree on the following general formulation: *If the tax duty IAJD has to be paid by the moneylender, whoever this creditor is (this creditor being the one who acquired the real right associated with being the (real) beneficiary of the registration of the mortgage linked to the loan granted by this creditor), then every such creditor does?*	24
25	Yes, the generalisation is now grounded.	Do you agree then that it follows that the meaning explanations that provide the conclusions of the precedent cases have to be overturned? And further, in the particular case of the UCE, having the real right of the mortgage, do you agree that it is also the bearer of the IAJD-duty? $$d^{UCE} : BIAJDDuty(m, rr, rb)?$$	26
27	Yes. I concede both the overturning and the conclusion. $$d^{UCE} : BIAJDDuty(m, rr, rb)$$	This is the reason that you demanded in step 21 for my revised thesis that UCE is the bearer of the IAJD-duty. $$d^{UCE} : BIAJDDuty(m, rr, rb)$$	28

Results

Dialogues, counterexamples and interactions

In the dialogical approach we might distinguish between material and formal dialogues. We are here in the context of *material* dialogues. This means that the plays will be reasoning with content, rather than being purely formal or logical. This is reflected in the way the players interact with each other, in the sense that their ability to win a play is dependent on some material facts about the source and target cases.

Interacting rules

This dialogical analysis introduces different rules that together provide a way to deal with the notion of analogical reasoning. There is here a distinction between what is called *challenge rules* and *explanation rules*. In addition, there is also a structural rule regarding the use of the challenge Rules, namely the *Analogy Challenge Rule Restriction*. We argue that by combining these rules, we can provide an analysis of analogical reasoning for the legal context. As previously described, the idea is to let the player proposing the analogy first explain the foundation for the proposed analogy, namely to suggest one analogy form that holds for the source cases. At this step we are still only speaking about an *unrestricted* analogy, as the player can choose any analogy form that can be confirmed by at least one source case. The next step is to let the other player suggest a counterexample to the proposed analogy form. The second player must then assure two things on the choice of counterexample, first that the proposed analogy form actually can provide a claim that is incompatible with the first players claim, and second that this proposed analogy form can be confirmed by at least one source case. In the steamboat example, the Opponent looses because of the first requirement, namely that the proposed analogy form did not provide an actual counterexample even though it had a confirmation in the source cases. This means that even when the railway case provided justification for the PAA-analogy, the PAA-analogy form is not sufficient to provide a counterexample to a PPP-analogy.

The idea behind this analysis of analogical reasoning is that the different explanation rules can provide counterexamples to each other, based on how they affect the entailed characteristic in the target case. An analogy form that provides justification for $\neg B$ in the target case can be used as a counterexample to an analogy form that provides justification for B in the target case, and opposite. Also, an analogy form that provides justification for $\neg\neg B$ in the target case can be used as a counterexample to an analogy form that provides justification for $\neg B$ in the target case, and opposite. This enables us to categorise the different analogy forms, based on how they provide counterexamples to each other, shown in Table 8.4.

B	$\sim$	$\neg B$	$\sim$	$\neg\neg B$
PPP		PPA		PAA
AAP		PAP		APA
		APP		
		AAA		

Table 8.4: Analogy forms, counterexamples

'$\sim$' should simply be understood as incompatibility. We see from this table that the forms PPP and AAP can be used as counterexamples to the forms PPA, PAP, APP and AAA and opposite. PAA and APA can be used as counterexamples to the last ones mentioned, though they do not produce justification for B, only for $\neg\neg B$, which are not intuitionistically equivalent. This means that these particular analogy forms cannot provide justification for B, but still can provide justification for a counterexample to $\neg B$. The reason for this is that they are *negative analogies*, namely that they are based on a difference in the source case and the target case. In

8.3. Dialogical example

terms of the Proportionality-principle, they provide justification for not treating the cases similarly, which is not the same as to provide justification for how the cases should be treated. This corresponds to a distinction between what we might call direct and indirect justification. We claim here that indirect justification (showing that the alternatives are unjustified) is not sufficient for establishing justification for the initial claim and that this is the reason for not enabling these negative analogies to provide justification for B instead of only $\neg\neg B$.

Player independence and creativity
All rules are described player independently. This means that none of them are specific for either the Proponent or the Opponent. The advantage of this is first that it provides natural meaning explanations where both agents are described as equals and second that it can be used as a foundation to describe more complex argumentative processes. In the steamboat example, the Opponent provided a counterexample by the same analogy as was proposed by the Proponent, namely between F and LB. However, because of the player independent rules, the Opponent could also have responded to this by providing an entirely new analogy. For the Opponent to succeed in doing this, he must of course choose an analogy that will actually be incompatible with the initial analogy form by the Proponent. Such move would open up a subplay in a very similar manner as with the Analogy Challenge Rule 2. In the steamboat example, an alternative analysis would be to consider that the Opponent proposes a new analogy between F and LA, and justifies it by a PAP-analogy. This will yield the same result as in the described play because of the definitional incompatibility between LA and LB.

We could have included the proposal of a new analogy as a ninth way of challenging in the Analogy Challenge Rule 2, though this threatens the finiteness of the plays, as every play could be potentially infinite. From the perspective of meaning, it is not sure that this is unwanted as it provides a natural way to understand legal discourse as a never-ending discussion of specification, interpretation and re-interpretation. However, from the point of view of dialogues and strategies, we do want to ensure the possibility to settle on a, even if temporary decision. This is the reason for leaving the question on introducing new analogies into a play rather open. Proposing a new analogy in this way seems to demand an aspect of *creativity* that resists thorough logical description. It corresponds closely to what Brewer (1996) calls *the abductive step* and seems then also related to the argumentative move of *inference to the best explanation*.

We do not intend to provide an analysis of such creativity, though simply note that if such move were to be introduced in a play, it might directly be implemented into the analysis as a potential counterexample (or eventually a counter-counterexample and so on), in the same way as any other example. We claim then to be able capture by the introduced rules, the assessment of the move after its introduction, but because of its creative aspect, not the introduction of the move itself.

Combining notions

A common challenge for many logical analyses of juridicial phenomena is the combination of deontic and modal notions, which in many frameworks gives rise to a number of paradoxes.[10] In immanent reasoning this is avoided by precisely allowing both the modal and the deontic notions to be based on a type-theoretical foundation.

The deontic imperatives (also the modal notions of possibility and necessity) are defined by a type-theoretical formulation and are not introduced as distinct operators. This allows for a framework where are free of most common paradoxes of deontic logic.[11] The

---

[10] See for example Navarro and Rodríguez (2014) for a detailed account of many standard paradoxes.

[11] See Rahman and Granström (2019) for comments on how many paradoxes simply do not occur when depending on a type-theoretical definition of deontic imperatives.

8.3. Dialogical example

most important reason for this is that the framework interprets the performance of actions directly in the object language, rather than considering them in a model or higher order predicate. What allows for this is the particular notion of dependent types, found only in CTT and closely related extensions.

With this analysis of analogical reasoning, we have also included deontic imperatives directly into our description of analogical reasoning. This is a rather unconventional strategy as many theories would consider these questions separately. However as mentioned, these questions become interconnected in CTT as we consider actions in the object language. For analogies, this first enables us to see the particular aspect of analogical reasoning. Second, it shows how analogies might be used for reasoning with actions, not only propositions. We can thereby explain how a conclusion of an analogical argument might be the performance of some action, not simply a proposition describing a rule. This apprehends the point of Jørgensen's dilemma, by showing how analogical reasoning can occur not only with truth and falsity, but also with actions, rules and principles.

Initial permission of analogy

One of the core features of this analysis is its ability to represent initial conditions concerning the permission of the use of an analogical argument. This seems to be feature newly introduced here, not found in other contemporary logical analyses or representations of analogical reasoning. Even though other analyses do not include such permission, it is frequently highlighted as an essential aspect in the utilisation of analogical argumentation, especially related to Civil Law and European legal systems. A particular advantage in the given analysis in immanent reasoning is that the the initial permissions can be assessed in the same play as the content of the analogy. This kind of interplay between higher- and lower-order notions is a particularity of CTT that we do not find in other frameworks.

Legal restrictions
In many civil-law inspired systems, there might be situations or areas where the use of analogical arguments is limited because of for example constitutional restrictions or for going against some fundamental values. Most contemporary legal systems incorporate some variant of the principle of legality, or *nulla poena sine lege*. This principle is often interpreted as prohibiting the use of analogies in penal law for imposing sanctions. An analogy is in this sense understood as an extension of the present legal framework and such extension can thereby not be used for grounding punishment, as the action was not illegal at the time of the crime. This corresponds to what by Langenbucher (1998) is called a *rule-based analogy*. The use of *principle-based analogies* on the other hand might be permitted also in penal law as it provides what is considered to be a precision or interpretation of an already existing rule, rather than an extension of the present legal framework. The distinction between the two variants and their permissibility in different legal contexts might vary, both between different legal systems and between particular cases or situations.

There might also be restrictions on the basis of some fundamental values. We might consider the use of analogical argumentation as impermissible if it breaks or goes against some values that are considered to be essential for the state, the legal system or individuals as such. An example is the Norwegian Constitution (Grunnlova) that states:

> Verdigrunnlaget skal framleis vere den kristne og humanistiske arven vår. Denne grunnlova skal tryggje demokratiet, rettsstaten og menneskerettane.
>
> Our values will remain our Christian and humanist heritage. This Constitution shall ensure democracy, a state based on the rule of law and human rights.
>
> Grunnlova (The Constitution), 1814 §2

8.3. Dialogical example

If the use of an analogical argument goes against human rights or undermines the democracy or the rule of law, it should not be permitted. In EU law, the use of an analogical argument that threatens the goals of the union might for example also be impermissible.

One might consider the condition of *being in a context of doubt* or *lacuna* as an initial condition on the use of analogy. However, in the dialogical approach we can understand this condition in two ways. First, it can be an initial condition. Second, it can be a way to challenge the analogy in the play by providing some explicit rule on the matter. The difference between the two is whether we allow for the analogical argument to be introduced before challenging it by a rule, or whether we reject the introduction of the analogy in the first place because of a lacking context of doubt. These two ways of understanding the context of doubt are not incompatible and we might very well consider both to be present in the framework.

The mentioned restrictions for the use of analogical arguments should be considered as examples, and surely not as an exhaustive list of requirements. The effect these restrictions have on analogical arguments seems to depend heavily on the particular legal framework we operate within and legal practice within that framework. The goal here is not to enter into the discussion on the content of these requirements for permitting analogical reasoning, as this would demand a proper logical treatment in itself. It is rather to enable analysing these restrictions as prohibiting the use of analogical arguments. The analogy is then not rejected by the quality of the analogy, but rather because of the context that this argument is used within.

Structure of permission
The analysis provides four different variants of the permission of analogies, where the form resembles:

$$PA_1(z) : set[z : (x : A)B(x) \lor (y : A)\neg B(y)].$$

This statement is a condition for the formulation of a particular analogical form. Each formulation assesses analogies of two forms, which is why we are provided with four formulations of a permission of an analogy, rather than eight. In this example, we permit analogy forms that provide justification for

$$(x:A)B(x)$$

and

$$(x:A)\neg B(x).$$

Generally, their structure permits an analogy based on some A to infer some B or its negation. They formulate what we can call *direct* counterexamples. If one accepts an analogical argument between some A and some B, one must also accept the possibility of providing a direct counterexample, $\neg B$, to this argument. If each permission of analogy only consisted of one part, we could risk ending up with a *unrestricted* analogy simply because of lacking permission. Such analogy should be given very little consideration in terms of justification. This is the reason for making this condition twofold, so that the permission of the analogy always ensures the ability of providing a counterexample. By connecting them with a disjunction, we represent the possibility of either side to fulfil. The permission of the analogy, $PA(z)$, is formulated as a set on the basis of the given disjunction. When permitting the analogy, we therefore do not commit to any given result in the target case.

Permission and dialogues

In the CTT analysis, the permitted analogies are all provided as conditions for the formulation of the analogy itself. This means that one has to accept the permission of *all* analogy forms when providing an analogy of *one* form. In the dialogical approach, this gets more refined. Here we connect the permission of the analogy not to the analogy in itself, but rather to the particular analogy form. This seems to be closer to actual legal practice as one would not have to explicitly permit analogies of all forms when using only a few. It avoids so to speak to assess the permissibility of "irrelevant" analogy forms. There is no logical reason for this not to be done also in the CTT analysis, but the dialogical approach offers a way to this in a natural and comprehensible way without entering into overly complex formulations.

The goal here is to show how the given analysis of analogies can provide a way to formulate the initial conditions imposed on the use of analogical reasoning. Such condition is commonly found in the contemporary literature, though usually left implicit or unexplained in the theoretical analyses. By the higher-order notation of dependent types, the framework of CTT enables us to formulate such restriction explicitly and thereby provide further descriptions of the meaning explanations regarding the use of analogies in legal reasoning.

Proportionality and dialogues

Compounds

In section 6.3, we argued for considering analogical reasoning as a question of *similar relevancy*, in line with Aristotle's conception of proportionality. In this dialogical analysis, we consider the transfer from the source case to the target case by means of a hypothetical, represented in the formalisations as an intuitionistic implication. This hypothetical is what represents the notion of similar relevancy in this analysis. In both the source case and the target case, we have a formulations of relevance from A to B and the hypothetical captures how these relevancies are similar and how one can transfer such dependency in the target case, based on a similar dependency in the source case. Note that this is not a material conditional so it captures the transference of the content of the source case to the content of the target case, not simply their truth value. Contrary to other analyses[12] we see here that such formalisation really captures the

---

[12] An exception is the Islamic model by Rahman and Iqbal (2018), which is also based on immanent reasoning.

important interaction found between the similarity and the relevancy found in analogies by not simply considering them separately as two distinct imposed requirements. By considering analogies in CTT, we are able to reason with content, not only with truth and therefore capture such inference as directly related to proportionality.

This analysis captures analogical reasoning with single properties and compound conjunctive and hypothetical properties. This means that the occasioning characteristic that the analogy is based upon can have the form of either a single predicate or as a complex predicate consisting of a conjunction or a hypothetical. We have seen how this play out in the Steamboat example where we had a conjunctive property that was analysed as a single predicate. However, this approach has certain limits in the sense that it cannot analyse interpretations of the content of *disjunctive compounds*. A legal concept can be said to consist of a disjunctive compound when something falls under that concept if it is A or B, but not necessarily both. This analysis can account for using such properties as a foundation for further reasoning, but not for interpreting the precise content of this compound. Say that there is a question whether something that has the property C falls under a certain concept. The question is then whether this concept is a disjunction of three properties, $A \vee B \vee C$, or whether it is a disjunction of a conjunction, $A \vee (B \wedge C)$. This requires an analysis of the interpretation of the content of this particular concept. In order to capture such interpretation, one will need to depend on some extension of the presented framework that can give an account of the content of such disjunctive compounds, not only use them to show some further property. To also include an analysis of disjunctive compounds would then seem like a natural, future extension to the present project.

8.3. Dialogical example

Multiple analogies
In chapter 3, the way different theories of analogy handled multiple analogies was heavily emphasised. The introduced analysis is very much in line with the approaches by Rahman and Iqbal (2018) and Brewer (1996). We have therefore not introduced a higher-order operator that deals with ranking as in Bartha (2010) and Prakken and Sartor (1996), but we rather consider multiple analogies by means of *new moves* in a play. A competing analogy in this sense can either be a regular counterexample with a new analogy form or as a newly introduced analogy. As described previously, the introduction of a new analogy seems to depend on a *creative* aspect that is difficult to capture logically. Though, as soon as any new analogy is introduced, we can describe its precise interaction with any previously introduced analogy in the same way as the approach handles regular counterexamples. Since the analysis recognises the introduction of both a new analogy and an analogy form as a *proposition*, the framework also enables reasoning with analogies as with any other proposition. This includes considering an analogy as a characteristic in another analogy. We might in this way have an analogy of analogies (or an analogy of an analogy of analogies and so on). This is done without leaving the object language. It is a significant feature when representing legal reasoning as it enables the analysis of interpreting interpretations in a direct and natural way, without assuming any hierarchy of the interpretations. This important feature seems absent in the approaches of Bartha (2010) and Prakken and Sartor (1996) as their object language only permits interpretations and analogies of a single level.

Policy and psychology
As described in section 2.2, there seems to be a tension between what might be called a psychological view of analogies and a policy-based view. In the psychological view, the characteristics that ground the analogy are determined by some psychological or epistemological state. In the policy-based view, these characteristics are rather

determined by a rule or policy. This analysis does not intend to take any standpoint in this discussion as the meaning explanations given here seem able to capture both views. However, it does seem to engage in the conflict as the dialogical approach can be used to resolve parts of this tension.

The motivation for developing a contemporary dialogical approach to logic is to bring back the ancient tradition of dialectics by uniting logic, argumentation and rhetoric. The main idea in a simple dialogical framework is that one agent, the Proponent, tries to convince another agent, the Opponent, of a certain claim. In this analysis of analogies, the Proponent tries to convince the Opponent of the quality of an analogical argument. It is not based on rules or similarities as such, but on giving and accepting *reasons*. A reason here can be understood both as providing some consistent rule or policy that can explain the analogy, or as some relevant aspect that grounds the notion of relevant similarities. In this sense, the dialogical approach opens up for both views and do not take a standpoint in what these reasons should consist of.

However, because of its game-theoretical foundation, the ultimate goal for the dialogical approach relates to the notion of *accept*. The precise content of these reasons might vary, as long as they are reasons that can be rationally accepted by both players. Something counts as a reason insofar it can be mutually recognised as such. Furthermore, we might say that something counts as a *good* reason insofar it can be *rationally* recognised as such. Reasoning can then be understood in terms of rational rhetoric.

The reluctancy towards rules and policies found in Weinreb (2005) is based on the lack of explicitly formulated rules in practical argumentation, while Posner's (2006) scepticism to Weinreb's psychological view comes from the lack of requiring general understanding. Weinreb and Posner do not disagree on the logical requirements we impose on good analogies, as both presuppose rational guidelines for analogical reasoning. By representing analogical reasoning as a rational game of giving and accepting reasons, we

8.3. Dialogical example

seem to resolve parts of this tension. In a game, agents (players) bring forward and accept reasons, which explains the psychological aspect that these reasons have. In the same time, for these reasons to be good, they must contain some general aspect that explains the how these reasons should be rationally accepted. As mentioned, we do not claim to have resolved this debate, only to have highlighted how answering seems less pressing when the goal is to provide the meaning explanations behind analogical reasoning. The important aspect is then not the precise content of the given reasons, but how they can be used practically for resolving disagreements in a rational way.

Chapter 9

Theoretical Considerations

9.1 Logical, actual and real assumptions

When I go to the supermarket, I suppose that they are open. Furthermore, I suppose they might have the things I need and that if I have sufficient amount of money, I will be able to buy these things. Also, I suppose that the supermarket has a floor, that the number indicating the price is meaningful and that physical objects have an objective existence. However, some of these assumptions I usually do not even consider. They form a basis of my habit or tradition and I will only be aware of them if I am confronted with something challenging them, for example when entering a supermarket that does not have a floor or that does have a skeptical philosopher at the front door, proclaiming the fallibility of our senses.

Similarly in sciences, legal reasoning, or any other pursuit of knowledge, we suppose a large amount of things. Political science, sociology and history suppose the existence of societies. Physics, economics and architecture suppose mathematics. Mathematics and computer science suppose set theory and logic. Most fields suppose a notion of truth and the existence of language. Every tradition or even study within a particular field will also suppose many other particular things that are not necessarily shared by the whole field. A political scientist might suppose the rationality of agents and a historian, a particular publishing date of a particular book. It provides the context that is used as a background for acquiring further knowledge, and we are for a great part not aware of our dependence before we are confronted with something challenging it.

This section argues for the identification of three kinds of assumptions, logical assumptions, actual assumptions and real assumptions. It will do so by presenting the debates regarding meaning/content and actuality/potentiality, continue with a description of propositions, before showing how the Kantian distinction between logical and real possibility can provide a 'synthesis' of the mentioned discussions and show us how three forms of important judgments can easily be formalised in the constructive type-theoretical framework by Martin-Löf (1984). This discussion will focus on assumptions regarding concepts related to propositions, namely claims of truth and falsity. This is not to say that all assumptions can be reduced to propositions (mathematics being an obvious example), nor to say that similar arguments might not hold outside of propositions, but is a practical constraint to keep the discussion at reasonable length.

Potentiality and actuality

For a historian to suppose the existence of societies, she will first have to suppose that the notion of societies is a meaningful one and second to suppose that there actually are such things. Let us therefore (if we dare to say) suppose a distinction between meaning and content of a concept. In this sense, the meaning seems to come before the content of the concept, as a historian supposes the concept of societies and then that there actually are such things. But already here we seem to enter into a problematic area.

9.1. Logical, actual and real assumptions

A modern analogy to this distinction is the distinction between type and token. To say that we have a type does not entail that we have a token of that type, though for us to meaningfully speak about a token, we need to suppose a type that this token belongs to. (Wetzel 2018) In this way, the content of a concept will depend on its meaning. A concept must be meaningful for it to have any content, though the reverse might very well not hold. That a concept is meaningful does not imply that it has content. We all understand the word '*unicorn*', though (as long as we exclude fictional objects) there are no such things. This makes it clear that we actually speak about some kind of conditional in the following way:

$$\text{Meaning} \Rightarrow \text{Content.}$$

This however, must not be confused with the logical notion of implication. As mentioned, that a concept has meaning does not entail that it has content. However, for a concept to have content, it must have meaning. In epistemological terms, meaning provides a necessary, though not sufficient conditions for content. To give a practical example; for us to know whether there are such things as societies, we need to have an idea of what societies are, or what it means for something to be a society. This does not require us to have a real definition of the concept that will act as a function, so that for all things we can discretely decide whether that thing is a society or not. For many or maybe most concepts, this will be an unattainable requirement. We simply, for some things have to be able to recognise whether that thing is a society or not. To go back to mathematical terms, for a concept to have meaning, it must be describable by a function, partial or total, that decides whether something belongs to that concept or not. We might consider this as a requirement of recognisability. The concept is meaningful if it is recognisable whether some things falls under that concept. This clearly brings up some further questions. Recognisable by whom? And how? These questions will be (partially) assessed by bringing forward some historical remarks.

Studies of the notion of meaning has a long history in the history of philosophy of language that might be traced back to different works of Aristotle, and particularly to *De Interpretatione* which gives us an early detailed account of language and meaning. In this work we are provided with an example of the word '*goat-stag*' which clearly has a meaning, but since it is simply a name, neither truth nor falsity can be attached to it without adding anything further. For Aristotle, written marks is a representation of spoken sounds which in turn represent affections in the soul. These affections are then what both spoken sounds and written marks represent and the affections are common for all, while both the sounds and marks are solely conventions and might differ between people. (De Interpretatione, I.I,16a4-16a18) The meaning of a concept is then a convention; it might differ. And we might have a representation or symbol of an affection in the soul that is the same for all, which are like actual things and therefore provide content to the concept. Written signs represent spoken sounds which represent affections in the soul. We then have something that looks like the following hierarchy for the representation of the notion of meaning:

Affections in the soul

⇓

Spoken sounds

⇓

Written signs.

At least from a contemporary point of view, both *spoken sounds* and *written signs* are then expressions of language. Though Aristotle holds that written signs are representations of spoken sounds and therefore also subordinate of the spoken sounds, both express the affections in the soul and therefore also language. For the present purpose it does not seem to be essential to maintain a distinction between written and spoken language. The structure of the language for Aristotle seems therefore to have to the following form:

9.1. Logical, actual and real assumptions

Affections in the soul

Expressions of language.

As it stands, the notion of affections in the soul seems rather unclear. The discussion related to the soul is presented in *De Anima (On the Soul)*. And relevant notions for this particular purpose is found in book III, chapter 8 (431b20-432a14), where the two first sentences of chapter 8 state:

> Let us now summarize our results about soul, and repeat that the soul is in a way all existing things; for existing things are either sensible or thinkable, and knowledge is in a way what is knowable, and sensation is in a way what is sensible: in what way we must inquire. Knowledge and sensation are divided to correspond with the realities, potential knowledge and sensation answering to potentialities, actual knowledge and sensation to actualities.
>
> Aristotle (De Anima, III.8,431b20-26)

Aristotle provides us here with a distinction between potentiality and actuality, along with a distinction between sensible and thinkable things. Here, it is the first distinction that will play the prominent role. The distinction between potential and actual is thoroughly discussed in the Aristotle's *Metaphysics*. Aristotle applied this distinction to many different areas and fields like physics, ethics and ontology, but as mentioned earlier we will here be occupied with the notion of propositions and therefore the distinction between actual and potential knowledge.

Aristotle includes a discussion on the relation of priority between actuality and potentiality and it is clear that actuality has priority over potentiality in the following way:

Actuality $\Rightarrow$ Potentiality.

Let us leave this particular discussion to Aristotle and come back to a variant at a later stage. For us to continue this investigation, we will concentrate the discussion on propositions and we therefore have to introduce a more precise understanding of what a proposition is.

Propositions

A proposition is a bearer of truth or falsity, but for now we have not said anything about what is needed for a proposition to be true (or false). The BHK-interpretation (Brouwer-Heyting-Kolmogorov) of a proposition will be taken for granted. This states that a proposition is true when there is a proof or demonstration of it. The meaning of a proposition is what counts as a proof or demonstration of its truth. In the light of the BHK-interpretation, the notions of proof, demonstration, method of realisation and method of solvability can be used interchangeably. (Martin-Löf 1984, p. 5) The interpretation links propositions to sets, so that a true proposition corresponds to a non-empty set. A proposition is false when there is a proof that it leads to a contradiction. In logical terms, a proposition P is true when we have a proof p, so that p is a member of P; a proposition P' is false when we have proof p', so that p' is a member of $P' \to \bot$. (Martin-Löf 1984, pp. 5-6)

That the truth of a proposition is actual means simply that the proposition has been proved, that there is an actual and specific proof of that proposition. That the truth of a proposition is potential means that it can be proven. (Martin-Löf 1991, p. 142) A proposition can therefore be actually true or potentially true. As Aristotle has showed us, actuality is prior to potentiality. For propositions this might seem intuitively wrong, as surely a proposition can only be actually true if it was already potentially true. However, if we recall our conceptions of truth and proposition, we see that it really is about acting. A proposition is actually true when there has been an actual proof or demonstration of it. The actual proof or demonstration surely involves an actual action of an agent. It

9.1. Logical, actual and real assumptions

is the act of proving or the act of demonstrating that will give us an actually true proposition. Since there must be a subject that performs this act of demonstration, we seem entitled to consider the notion of actual truth of propositions to be about knowledge.

We noticed that the actual truth of a proposition must assume that the proposition is potentially true. However, that a proposition is true potentially can only be established after a demonstration of its actual truth. If we think in terms of inferences, we seem entitled to infer the potentiality from the actuality, but not the other way around. This principle has been described by the scholastics as *Ab esse ad posse valet consequentia*, which is an inference from actual to potential, or in modal terms, from existence to possibility. (Kenny 2014, pp. 71-72) An inference the other way around, from potentiality to actuality, does seem to be more controversial. However, by accepting certain interpretations of the principle of plenitude, one might also consider oneself entitled for this other inference. The principle of plenitude states that all potential things will be actual throughout the course of time, though there seems to be reason to think that this principle cannot hold, at least for propositions. (Martin-Löf 1991, p. 143) There does not seem to be any good reason to think that all potentially true propositions will receive an actual demonstration throughout the history or in the future. The inference from actual truth to potential truth seems therefore to be a good rule of inference, while the opposite seems not. We can then safely claim:

$$\frac{\text{Actual truth}}{\text{Potential truth.}}$$

Assumptions, possibility and actuality

As discussed, it is the actual that makes a proposition true. By using an example from Heidegger (1927, §44), it is the actual askew picture that makes the proposition "`The picture on the wall is hanging askew`" true. This is what is meant by the proposition itself, not some mental reconstruction. This reflects the priority of actuality over potentiality, introduced by Aristotle as the assertion itself is a result of the real thing in itself, not the other way around. For the proposition "The picture on the wall is hanging askew", the actual (or Real in Heidegger's terms) askew picture is what makes that proposition true, thereby its truthmaker,

 : "The picture on the wall is hanging askew".

The askew picture [1] is the proof that makes the proposition "The picture on the wall is hanging askew" true, namely its content. However, it is not what makes the proposition meaningful. Based on the two discussions on meaning-content and actual-potential we seem to arrive into some trouble as it is clearly the content that is the actual, not the meaning. If the actual has priority over potential, would not content have priority over meaning? How then can it be dependent on meaning? We will here suggest a solution of this where we distinguish between two different kinds of judgment. This issue was highlighted by Immanuel Kant in his *Kritik der reinen Vernunft* (*Critique of Pure Reason*) (A244/B302, 1781), and our distinction here will reflect his distinction between the logical possibility of a concept and the real (or transcendental) possibility of things. That a concept is logically possible means that it does not contradict itself. For propositions this should simply be understood as recognising the concept of being a proposition. For a thing to be really possible it has to correspond to an object, which for propositions means that it can be judged to be true. We are then provided with two notions of possibility, a logical and a real, and we will explain how the actual seem to conceptually end up somewhere in the middle of these two notions. (Martin-Löf 1991, pp. 143-144)

---

[1]Magritte, R. (1928) *Les charmes du paysage*

9.1. Logical, actual and real assumptions

Based on our previously mentioned definition, we can link meaning to logical possibility since it is the recognition of the concept of being a proposition which essentially decides what counts as making the proposition true or false. If a proposition is meaningful, it is logically possible and if a proposition is logically possible, it is meaningful. We can also link real possibility to potentiality. That a proposition is really possible is implied from the proposition's actuality, while still for a proposition to be actual, it would seem to depend on being really possible. We then arrive at the following conceptual order of propositions:

$$\text{Meaning/Logical possibility}$$
$$\Downarrow$$
$$\text{Actuality}$$
$$\Downarrow$$
$$\text{Potentiality/Real possibility.}$$

Based on this representation, we can see that we have three corresponding judgments for propositions. We can judge a proposition as meaningful, actual or potential, and we see that these judgments have a hierarchical relationship between each other. For a proposition to be judged actual it has to be meaningful, and for it to be judged potential it has to be both meaningful and actual. Since we have three different kinds of judgments, we also have three different kinds assumptions that can be used as grounding knowledge. And all three different kinds of assumptions might play a different role. (Martin-Löf 1991, pp. 143-144)

This becomes clearer by an example. Heidegger says to Husserl, `"The picture on the wall is hanging askew"`. We first establish the type that this statement belongs to. Since it is either true or false, it is a proposition. In logical terms, this is to say that it is of the type *proposition*,

`"The picture on the wall is hanging askew"` : *proposition*.

This however, does not yet say anything about whether it is true or not that the picture is askew. It simply states that what Heidegger said was meaningful. We do not yet know whether it is true that the picture is hanging askew and the 'proof' or truthmaker of this proposition is the actual askew picture,

 : "The picture on the wall is hanging askew".

When we see the actual askew picture, we can know that what Heidegger said was true. For assumptions, we might not have a 'proof' or truthmaker of the assumptions that we take. If Husserl later tells Sartre, he will not have seen the askew picture and will therefore not have a truthmaker for Heidegger's claim. Instead, he will take Husserl's word for it. Sartre will give the responsibility of its truth to Husserl. This is a dialogical process of giving responsibility that would seem to be essential in discussions within scientific communities. (Martin-Löf 2017a,b). Since we do not have a particular truthmaker, we can represent Sartre's assumption that the picture is hanging askew by a hypothetical, which is a variable,

x : "The picture on the wall is hanging askew".

The three kinds of judgments correspond to three kinds of assumptions and we can categorise them into the following:

Logical assumption

$\Downarrow$

Actual assumption

$\Downarrow$

Real assumption.

9.1. Logical, actual and real assumptions

Logical assumptions describe the meaning of a concept. For example, a sociologist supposing that 'society' is a meaningful concept and that it can be used in propositions with truth or falsity; a historian supposing that "The plague came from China." is meaningful; or if we step outside propositions, a mathematician supposing numbers.

Actual assumptions describe the existence of a particular object referred to by the concept. Here we are of course not restricted to physical objects, but anything that would make the proposition true, which could be amongst others physical objects, mental constructions or deductive proofs. Examples might be an archeologist supposing that a specific thing actually is a golden ring from the middle ages, or a sociologist supposing the existence of the French society.

Real assumptions describe the existence of an object referred to by the concept, but without the specification of any individual. It is the kind that we would normally call 'assumption' in both everyday life and scientific argumentation. It occurs when a researcher depends or refers other works, but also when making general qualifications to frame the discussion. Examples can be a sociologist supposing the there actual exist societies, or a philosopher referring to the distinction between actual and potential in Aristotle's Metaphysics.[2]

We can clearly see that both actual assumptions and real assumptions seem to depend on some logical assumptions. The dependency of real assumptions on actual assumptions seems intuitively more unclear. This can however be explained in terms of justification in the sense of *ab esse ad posse valet consequentia*, so that the real assumptions are only properly justified when depending on some actual assumption. Justification in this sense has to be understood epistemologically, not practically. It would seem practically unattainable to exclude all real assumptions that do not depend on

---

[2] These real assumptions correspond to what Sundholm (2019) has identified as *epistemic* assumptions. We choose to call them *real* assumptions in order to stick both with the original Kantian terminology and Martin-Löf's (1991) analysis of these concepts.

any actual assumption, but in order to provide proper justification for the real assumptions in the sense of Aristotle and Heidegger, actuality should be strived for. And this seems to reflect the present goals for research quite well, namely to provide actual foundations for the assumptions made.

Assumptions in scientific and legal reasoning play an important role and we seem to be able to distinguish between three different kinds. The first is the logical assumption that relates to the meaning of a concept. The second is the actual assumption that connects the concept to an individual object. The third is the real assumption that connects the concept to a hypothetical object.

In this section we have presented a distinction between three different kinds of assumptions, where all three seem to play an important role in legal reasoning. The kinds are based on both the Aristotelean distinction between actuality and potentiality and the Kantian distinction between logical and real possibility.

9.2 Distinction of steps and future contingency

Throughout the history of logic and philosophy, at least since Aristotle, there has been a debate about the status of the truth for future events. This discussion entered the field of legal reasoning by Leibniz's work *De Conditionibus*, where he provided a thorough analysis of what we call *conditional rights, suspensive conditions* or *moral conditionals*. We will use Leibniz's own example that *Primus is committed to pay 100 dinars to Secundus, provided a ship arrives from Asia*. One aspect of conditional rights is that they must be about future and contingent events, which will be discussed here in the light of Aristotle's example: *There will be a sea-battle tomorrow*.

9.2. Distinction of steps and future contingency

The given analysis of analogical reasoning is based on a formalisation of the notion of moral conditionals, as analysed by Leibniz. This work describes analogical reasoning as a special kind of complex conditional that we argue has much in common with the notion of moral conditionals. One might in some sense consider analogical reasoning to be a special, complex case of a moral conditional.

Characteristics of a conditional right

Leibniz developed his analysis of the notion of conditional right in two academic dissertations, *Disputatio Juridica (prior) De Conditionibus* (A VI, I, 1665) and *Disputatio Juridica (posterior) De Conditionibus* (A VI, I, 1965). Together they provide a detailed account of the logical structure that lies behind such conditional. Leibniz points out that it has the form of a hypothetical judgment where the truth of the *jus* (the consequent) is made dependent on the truth of the *fact* (the antecedent). This dependency relation then has the form of being introduced by the will of the arbiter and as Leibniz points out, this gives the conditional also a *moral* aspect. (Rahman and Kvernenes 2021, p. 8)

Based on Leibniz's work, Magnier (2015, p. 73) provides a description of the different requirements that should be imposed on conditional rights. These can briefly be summarised in eight points:

1. *The consequent cannot be true if the antecedent is not true;*

2. *The consequent cannot be its own condition;*

3. *The truth value of the consequent cannot be known as long as the truth value of the antecedent is not certified (i.e., not known to be true);*

4. *If it is known that the antecedent is true, then the consequent is also true;*

5. *If it is known that the antecedent is false, then the consequent is also false;*

6. The antecedent cannot be a contradiction;

7. The consequent cannot be a tautology;

8. The antecedent is not known to be true.

The 8th requirement describes what is known as the *suspensive clause* that defines the conditional right. Together with the notion of suspension, also the *convertibility* of the moral conditionals has received very much attention in the literature. Leibniz seems to consider the notion of conditional right as some kind of logical biconditional, rather than a conditional. This seems to follow from the requirements 1, 4 and 5. This biconditional reading of the conditional right and its convertibility has been extensively studied in Armgardt (2001, 2010), Boucher (2008), Koch and Rüßmann (1982), and Thiercelin (2008, 2009, 2010). The convertibility seems to on the surface to undermine the difference between the *fact* and the *jus*, so we might consider the dependency that the *jus* has on the *fact* as analogous to the dependency that the *effect* has on its *cause*, namely that the condition starts to exist first. This however, might challenge what distinguishes moral conditionals from other conditionals. The difference can then be said to lie in the nature of this dependency. While the dependency that grounds the relation between the *cause* and the *effect* is some natural necessity, the dependency that grounds the relation between the *fact* and the *jus* is the will of the arbiter, recognised by competent authorities. What distinguishes moral conditionals from other conditionals is then not the dependence itself, but rather the meaning of this relation. (Rahman and Kvernenes 2021, p. 9)

The convertibility of the notion of conditional right has received a large amount of attention in the contemporary literature. Since it clearly does not have the form of a material conditional, different authors have attempted to interpret it as a bi-conditional (Armgardt) or in terms of connexive logic (Thiercelin). By interpreting the conditional right as a bi-conditional, we quickly end up with blurring the difference between the *jus* and the *fact* as mentioned in the

9.2. Distinction of steps and future contingency

previous paragraph. The connexive-logic approach solves to a great extent this problem and seems to give a precise description of conditional rights without reducing it to a regular biconditional. It describes both the quasi-causal link between the *jus* and the *fact* and how both of these must be contingent propositions. However, this logical approach departs significantly from a standard classical approach. (Magnier 2015, p. 78)

Another important feature of the conditional right is the epistemic nature of suspension. One of the main contributions of Leibniz for the understanding of conditional right is precisely to link epistemic uncertainty to the conditional structure that produces the conditional right. According to this analysis, the fulfilment of the condition of the conditional right must be *uncertain*. Its fulfilment must not have been known at the moment of its formulation. This clearly introduces challenges regarding the determination of truth for such formulation and its status in regard of non-fulfilment. Leibniz's solution to this challenge is to let the truth of the conditioned be dependent on the truth of the condition and in the same time include uncertainty regarding the truth value of this condition. The conditional right as such should then be considered as true, even though its condition is not yet known to be true. Leibniz further connects this issue to the problem of future contingents. Based on Leibniz's solution, we can therefore consider two relevant aspects for the introduction of suspension in conditional rights:

1. *The truth of the conditioned should be dependent on the truth of the condition;*
2. *The truth of the condition should be uncertain.*

Together, these two aspects form what Leibniz understands as the suspensive clause of the conditional right. The first aspect seems to be a logical feature of conditionals while the second aspect connects this issue to the problem of the uncertainty regarding future events and its temporal structure, a problem known since antiquity and famously explained by Aristotle. (Rahman and Kvernenes 2021, pp. 12, 15)

Magnier (2015) provides an analysis of conditional rights by utilising *public announcement logic*. This framework manages to capture several important aspects regarding suspensions in conditional rights. The condition is considered uncertain at the moment of its formulation. The conditioned is epistemically triggered after the condition has been fulfilled and the temporal aspect is thereby also included. It also includes a requirement for the evidence of the fulfilment of the condition to be of public knowledge.

However, one problem with this approach is that it struggles to explain other conditions without leaving the object language. This means that for example requirement 6 (*The antecedent cannot be a contradiction*), can only be described in this approach by a metalogical definition. The meaning of the proposition can therefore not be checked at the object language level. These kinds of requirements have not received very much attention in the literature about Leibniz and conditional right, even though these so-called ridiculous conditions were thoroughly studied by Leibniz himself. (Rahman and Kvernenes 2021, pp. 12, 15)

There will be a sea-battle tomorrow

In *De Interpretatione* (I.9,18b17-19a39), Aristotle introduces an example, a claim about future events. His example is the following two statements:

> *There will be a sea-battle tomorrow*

and

> *There will not be a sea battle tomorrow.*

9.2. Distinction of steps and future contingency

The challenge occurs when attempting to provide a truth value for these propositions. Neither of them seem true at the moment of the utterance. Though in both classical and Aristotelean logic, if the propositions are combined by a disjunction, it would seem to be a clear instance of the valid principle of the excluded middle. This would then indicate that they indeed should be assigned a truth value and that the disjunction should hold with *necessity*. However as noticed by Aristotle, neither of the disjuncts seem to hold with necessity. It is neither necessary that there will be a sea-battle tomorrow nor that there will not be a sea-battle tomorrow. (De Interpretatione, I.9,19a30-35) Though when time passes and *tomorrow* has become *today*, the truth of one of the propositions should be established. The question still stands regarding the status of the truth for each proposition, as neither can be asserted as true nor false at the time of utterance.

Future contingents

Following Aristotle, the same problem was analysed by Diodorus Cronus (340-280 B.C.E.) as a trilemma, where three seemingly innocent propositions cannot all be true. The dilemma can then be represented by the following three propositions:

1. *Every proposition true about the past is necessary;*

2. *An impossible proposition cannot follow from a possible one;*

3. *There is a proposition which is possible, but which neither is nor will be true.*

For the problem of future contingents, it here takes the form of the Master Argument. The precise reconstruction of this argument has been discussed through the history of logic, philosophy and theology and has received many sophisticated formulations. In the middle ages, the problem was connected to the question about divine foreknowledge. A divine being was often assumed to have the knowledge about all future events and this clearly connects to the question regarding the necessity of such events. (Øhrstrøm and Hasle 2020)

If we go back to the legal context, the challenge of future contingents is relevant, precisely since the uncertainty of the condition in a conditional right is of the same form as what we find in future contingents. One feature of the conditional right is that its condition is a contingent, future event.

Time and probability

Leibniz introduces the notion of time in his analysis and also combines it with the notion of probability, which enables the condition not only to be uncertain, but as something that might come gradually,

> *Nam uti fractio inter 0 et integrum media est, ita jus Conditionale inter nullum et purum, et uti fractiones variant, quae infra ½ est propius accedit 0, quae supra propius accedit 1, ita jus Conditionale aestimatione variam recipit, et modo puro modo nulli variis gradibus accedit.*

> Since (in a similar manner) as a fraction is the middle between 0 and the unity, so is conditional right in between the inconditional (or pure) right and the nullification of a right. And as fractions vary, so that when they are below ½, they are closer to 0, and when they are above ½, they are closer to 1; [in a similar manner], the conditional right receives a variable estimation, in such a way that it admits various gradations, sometimes closer to the inconditional (pure), and sometimes closer to its nullification.

> Leibniz, *Specimen certitudinis* (A VI, II, 1665)

9.2. Distinction of steps and future contingency

In this way, conditional rights might vary so that their probability is sometimes closer to 1 (a pure right) and sometimes closer to 0 (a nullification). A pure right in this sense is a right that can be claimed straightforward, without any qualification. A nullification of a conditional right amounts to the removal of the right, so that it is a right that cannot be claimed. A conditional right is then considered to be in the middle of these two extremes. The probability distributions then describe how probable it is for the beneficiary to have access to the specified right, agreed to by the benefactor. This also means that the probability of the access to the specified right depends on the probability of the truth of the conditioned. (Leibniz, A VI, II, 1665) The combination of time parameters and probability allows Leibniz to formulate the condition as a suspension, which can be understood as a probability of ½. This aspect was pinpointed by Armgardt (2001).

Based on these notions of time and probability, we can explain the following relevant results regarding the conditional right:

- If, at t_j, we come to know that the probability of the fulfilment of the condition is ½ (*conditio incerta*), then we are in the case of conditional right, and so the probability of having access to the legal claim is ½.

- If, at t_k (where t_k is after t_j), we come to know that the probability of the fulfilment of the condition is 1 (*conditio est necessaria*), then the legal claim of the conditional right is immediately (and inconditionally) efficient.

- If, at t_k (where t_k is equal to t_j), we come to know that the probability of the fulfilment of the condition is 1, then the legal claim is immediately efficient, but then we are in presence of an inconditional or pure right.

- If, at t_k (where t_k is after t_j), we come to know that the probability of the fulfilment of the condition is 0 (*conditio defecit*), then the legal claim is immediately nullified.

- If, at t_k (where t_k is equal to t_j), we come to know that the probability of the fulfilment of the condition is 0, then the legal claim is nullified from the very start. (Rahman and Kvernenes 2021, p. 24)

Establishment of contract

The conditional right is a contract between a benefactor and a beneficiary, granted by competent authorities. By introducing a time aspect about future contingency, we also oblige ourselves to specify the moment of formulation. We can therefore list four notions that need some specified content for a conditional right to be put in place:

1. the benefactor,
2. the beneficiary,
3. the legal norm granting the transference and
4. the time of the agreement.

Leibniz then introduces the following example:

> Primus is committed to pay 100 dinars to Secundus, provided a ship arrives from Asia.

In this example *Primus* should be understood as the benefactor that grants the conditional right to the *Secundus*, the beneficiary. This conditional right should then be grounded in some legal norm. In this context, such legal norm can be that it should be *neither illegal nor against boni mores*. In short, it must be a legally acceptable agreement. The last notion to be specified is the time dimension. The time of agreement must precede the potential fulfilment of the condition in time. (Rahman and Kvernenes 2021, p. 21)

CTT and moral conditionals

The advantage of the CTT approach regarding the formalisation of Leibniz's analysis of conditional rights lies mostly in its overall capacity to implement all the mentioned aspects without leaving the object language and relying on metalogical definitions regarding the meaning and interpretation. We can therefore give an account of the meaning of such contract in the same language as we would assess the truth of such contract. The present analysis of analogical reasoning relies heavily on this interpretation of the conditional right as it considers analogical arguments to be a special and complex kind of moral conditional. We will provide a short explanation of the implementation Leibniz's analysis of conditional rights in CTT.[3]

A particularity of the CTT approach is its ability to express dependency, introduced by a hypothetical judgment. Truth is then directly connected to the notion of proof, though in empirical contexts we would rather speak about evidence which acts as proof objects.[4] Since truth is directly linked with proof and therefore also evidence, Leibniz's example can be expressed by the following hypothetical:

> Primus is committed to pay 100 dinars to Secundus, provided there is some evidence x for that a ship arrives from Asia.

This again can be understood in the following way:

> The evidence p for a payment obligation that instantiates the proposition *Primus must pay 100 dinar to Secundus* is dependent on some evidence x for a ship arrival,

---

[3]For a more thorough-going explanation, see Rahman and Granström (2019). This explanation is based on Rahman and Kvernenes (2021).

[4]See Rahman, McConaughey, et al. (2018) for details regarding empirical quantities.

which clearly leads us into a CTT hypothetical, where P is the payment obligation and S is the set of ship arrivals,

$$b(x) : P(x : S).$$

This provides the logical structure that is present behind conditionals (moral conditionals included) in the sense that it shows how the truth of the payment obligation (*jus*) is dependent on the truth of the ship arrival (*fact*). However, this formulation does not include any notion of suspense or contingency in relation to the ship arrival. Since we are in an intuitionistic and constructive framework, this can be achieved by simply introducing a disjunction of S and its negation as a condition. It is not assumed to be true as such, and its truth requires to know whether it is the left or the right that obtains. The contingency can then be represented by the following disjunction:

$$x : S \lor \neg S.$$

In order to represent this contingency, we also need to describe the precise dependency that the payment obligation depends on, as it depends on a ship arrival and not on there not being a ship arrival. This also enables us to implement the convertibility, namely that if we were to know that there would be no ship arrival, we are able to infer that *Primus* does not have any payment obligation. This means that we in fact have two dependencies, one for each side of the disjunction in the following way:

> If there is some evidence for a ship arrival and this arrival solves the uncertainty (S or not S) underlying the conditional right, (i.e., if the ship arrival provides evidence for the left side of the disjunction), then the beneficiary is entitled to the payment agreed by the terms of the contract;

9.2. Distinction of steps and future contingency

> If there is some evidence for no ship arrival and this solves the uncertainty (S or not S) underlying the conditional right, (i.e., if the evidence for no ship arrival provides evidence for the right side of the disjunction), then the beneficiary is not entitled to the payment agreed by the terms of the contract.

This formalisation of this conditional right then becomes:

$$b(x) : ((\exists y : S)left^\vee(x) =_H y) \supset P)$$
$$\land ((\exists z : \neg S)right^\vee(x) =_H z) \supset \neg P(x : S \lor \neg S).$$

This formalisation explains both the suspensive feature and the convertibility of conditional right. Though as mentioned earlier, Leibniz's analysis also includes the formulation of the legal conditions and the time parameters related to the formulation.[5] (Rahman and Kvernenes 2021, pp. 19-21)

In the introduced example, $b(x)$ stands for the contract which is distinct from the content of the conditional right itself, expressed by the propositional structure. This distinction is a particularity of the CTT framework that enables us to describe properties with the contract itself, not only its propositional content. It is then $b(x)$ that should satisfy the legal requirements, represented in two parts. The first part is the establishment of the contract between the benefactor and the beneficiary,

$$Entered\text{-}into(b(x), Primus, Secundus).$$

This means that $b(x)$ is in a triadic relation with *Primus* (benefactor) and *Secundus* (beneficiary). The second part is that $b(x)$ should follow a legal norm granting the contract. This can consist of multiple requirements of both legal and logical character, for example that the benefactor actually possesses the goods that could be

---

[5]For details regarding the inferential structure related to this formalisation, see Rahman and Granström (2019).

transferred or that the condition is neither a tautology nor an inconsistency. This part can be represented by a property $N(y)$, so that we in this example have:

$N(b(x))$.

If we allow **fact** and **jus** to stand for the condition and the conditioned, the explicit dependency of the contract on the conditional right can be formalised as:

$Entered\text{-}into(b(x), Primus, Secundus)$
$\qquad \land N(b(x)) : set(x : \textbf{fact}, b : (v : (\textbf{fact})\textbf{jus}).$

We can also go from the lower-level formalisation to the higher-level formalisation when there is reason to question the formation of the contract. In the dialogical approach, this is done in a very subtle way by the move of formation request.[6] (Rahman and Kvernenes 2021, pp. 21-22)

The last aspect of the conditional rights is the temporal one. The introduction of time parameters in CTT was first done by Ranta (1994, pp. 101-108). In this approach there are multiple ways to introduce the notion of time, depending on what kind of concepts we would like to introduce. Generally, time is introduced as propositional functions over a set *time*,

$B(t) : prop(t : time)$.

Though instead of defining a set such as *time*, Ranta (1994) suggests to introduce sets based on a particular calendar, in his case the Gregorian calendar. This means that the sets defining time will not be a universal set *time* as suggested above, but rather have the

---

[6]Notice that this kind of interplay between the higher level and the lower level is a particularity of certain type-theoretical frameworks that includes a notion of dependent types.

9.2. Distinction of steps and future contingency

following forms:

    $year : set;$
    $month : set;$
    $day : set.$

The canonical elements of $year$ will then be natural numbers as in the following example:

    $1647 : year.$

$month$ consists of the twelve months,

    $\{January, February, ..., December\} : month.$

day consists of a family of sets, comprising the numerals from 1 to between 28 and 31, depending on x and y,

    $day\text{-}of(x, y) : set(x : year, y : month).$

A particular day can then be introduced in the following way:

    $(1646, July, 1) : day.$

Minutes and seconds (or other units of time) can be introduced in a very similar way as days. (Ranta 1994, pp. 102-103) To provide specific time expressions, Ranta introduces an @-operator[7]. This operator enables us to attain a certain precision intended in this particular context. The previously introduced time parameters do not refer to a particular point in time as it will always be possible with further specification. It is an intuitionistic insight that all of these points are merely approximations. The @-operator then enables us to provide a specification precise enough for the particular context. With this operator, one can form expressions such as:

    @(1646)

---

[7] This is written 'AT' in Ranta's (1994) original work

and

$$@(1646, July, 1).$$

This again can be used to form propositions regarding particular historical or future events. By assuming

$$x\ born@(y) : prop(x : philosopher, y : day),$$

we can form the expression of Leibniz's birthday,

$$\text{Leibniz } born@(1646, July, 1).$$

We can express uncertainty regarding the fulfilment of the **fact** (condition) at a specified time $@(t_j)$ and that the **jus** (conditioned) depends on this uncertainty. This is done by utilising the @-operator so that under the assumptions:

$$\mathbf{jus}@(t) : prop(t : time, x : \mathbf{fact});$$
$$S@(t) : prop(t : time);$$
$$\neg S@(t) : prop(t : time),$$

we can formulate the uncertainty in the following way:

$$\mathbf{jus}@(t_j) : prop(x : (\exists t : time)(S@(t) \vee \neg S@(t))).$$

Following Ranta (1994, p. 120), future can then be expressed

$$t_k > t_j.$$

which is an abbreviation of

$$t_k : time, n : N, t_k = t_j + s(n) : time.$$

In the example, a situation where it is known at t_k that a ship does arrive at t_k can then be formulated as:

9.2. Distinction of steps and future contingency

if, at some @(t_k) after the moment of the contract t_j, we come to know that a ship arrived, then from this very moment, *Secundus* can claim for the money,

$$(\exists y : S@(t_k))left^\vee(x) =_{S@(t_k)} y@(t_k) \supset P@t_k(t_k > t_j).$$

Contrary, a situation where it is known at t_k that no ship will arrive can be formulated as:

if, at some t_k after the moment of the contract t_j, we come to know that no ship will ever arrive, then from this very moment *Secundus*' claim for the money will be nullified,

$$(\exists z : \neg S@(t_k))right^\vee(x) =_{\neg S@(t_k)} z@(t_k) \supset \neg P@t_k(t_k > t_j).$$

The framework also enables to place other or further time constraints on the contract, such as a deadline for fulfilling the condition. (Rahman and Kvernenes 2021, pp. 26-27)

With the introduction of time parameters, we can see that CTT provides a way to handle most of the relevant aspects regarding conditional right, or moral conditionals. However, the notion of probability still stays largely simplified. As mentioned earlier, this approach takes account of probabilities of three kinds,

- the case that the probability of the condition is 1/2 and we speak about a conditional right,

- the case that the probability of the condition is 1 and we speak about a pure right and

- the case that the probability of the condition is 0 and we speak about a nullification.

We can clearly see the limits of this approach as it cannot account for precisely the gradual notion given by probability.[8]

---

[8] Such notion of probability is currently being developed in Rahman and Kvernenes (2021), where a gradual notion of probability is being introduced regarding the certainty of satisfying the disjunction in the head of the hypothetical.

9.3 PERFORMANCE AND DEONTIC QUALIFICATION

The constructive type-theoretical framework is built to avoid keeping form and meaning apart. This particular understanding is what enables this theory to provide such fine-grained analysis of hypothetical judgments. This theory is, with a few and closely related exceptions, the only framework that enables analyses of hypotheticals where form is dependent on some content by the utilisation of dependent types. (Martin-Löf 1984, p. 3) We can therefore capture the hypothetical nature of not only linguistic meaning, but also relevant legal notions and their relation to each other in a way that cannot be explained in other logical systems. Because of the particular notion of hypotheticals that are utilised in the constructive type theory, we are able to analyse complex notions which legal and deontic reasoning depends heavily on in a more refined way than what is the case with most other logical frameworks.

Good Shoemakers

The challenges of analysing complex notions are very well described by Aristotle in *De Interpretatione* (I.11,20b31-21a6), where he also provides us with the typical example in the literature, namely the good shoemaker. It does not follow from a person, let us call him Simon, being both good and a shoemaker, that Simon is a good shoemaker. Nor does it follow from Simon being a good shoemaker, that Simon is good. However, we can infer from Simon being a good shoemaker, that Simon is a shoemaker. This poses problems to the classical, modern conception of logic. In the classical, modern framework, there are two straightforward ways of dealing with this. The first way is to consider 'good shoemaker' as a single predicate which characterises the individual 'Simon'. This can be written, when GS means 'good shoemaker' and s means 'Simon', in the

9.3. Performance and deontic qualification

following way:

$$GS(s).$$

In this classical conception of logic, the transition from an individual to an existential, to go from "Simon is a good shoemaker" to "Some shoemakers are good", can be done by simply replacing the individual with a variable bound by an existential quantifier. The quantified variant, "Some shoemakers are good", is then formalised in this way:

$$\exists x(GS(x)).$$

However, this formalisation does not enable us to infer that Simon is a shoemaker. The second way is to consider 'good shoemaker' as two predicates characterising 'Simon', bound together by a conjunction. This can be written, when G means 'good', S means 'shoemaker' and s means 'Simon', in the following way:

$$G(s) \land S(s).$$

We are now able by conjunction elimination, to infer that Simon is a shoemaker, $S(s)$. However by the same rule, we are also able to infer that Simon is good, $G(s)$. None of these analyses provide a satisfactory solution to the mentioned problem. One way to solve this is to introduce a higher-order system, for example Montague grammar.[9] Such approach would evidently invoke the standard challenges related to higher-order logic.

There have been attempts to solve this problem in classical first-order predicate logic by amongst others Kitcher (1978) and Ben-Yami (1996). Common for these approaches is that they analyse the predicates either by comparing the subject in respect to the predicate to the general class that the subject belongs to, or by comparing the subject to some standard. Our example with the

---

[9] See Kamp (2013) for a comparison of two higher-order approaches based on Geach (1956).

shoemaker is then analysed in the following way by the approach of Ben-Yami, where $B(x,y)$ means 'better than' and SSG means the 'standard shoemakers goodness':

$$S(s) \wedge \forall x(SSG(x) \to B(s,x)).$$

We are here provided with an analysis of the example "Simon is a good shoemaker" as "Simon is a better shoemaker than the standard shoemaker". The similar, though more sophisticated analysis by Kitcher analyses the example in respect to some average goodness of shoemakers. This full-fledged analysis by Kitcher also requires substantial extensions of standard predicate logic. There are several problems with these approaches and the first two are also discussed by the respective authors.

The first problem is that there is a challenge involved when comparing the good shoemaker Simon with the not very good shoemaker Rachel, who happens instead to be a very good politician. The analysis is not able in a simple way to describe how Simon is a better shoemaker than Rachel, but not better *tout court*.

The second problem is related to what happens if there are *no other shoemakers* than Simon, for example that all other shoemakers suddenly disappeared from the face of the earth, or just happened to synchronisedly close their practice. Simon would still seem to be a good shoemaker because of the emptiness of the antecedent in the universally quantified conditional. This seems fine, but the problem is that a similar point also holds if it happened not with Simon, but with Rachel. Rachel would suddenly become a good shoemaker, and maybe if we accept a negated variant of the analysis, in the same time also a bad shoemaker. An attempted solution to this, proposed by Kitcher (1978, p. 9), is to consider the comparison to be related not with actual things, but with possible things. We would then consider these predicates as modal. For Simon to be a good shoemaker, he should not be compared to the actual shoemakers, but to a class of possible shoemakers, or shoemakers in some or all possible worlds.

9.3. Performance and deontic qualification

The problem here would be to choose which shoemakers and which possible worlds that should be used to construct our notion of a standard or average shoemaker as there would seem to exist infinite amounts of both possible worlds and possible shoemakers.

The third problem is related to what is *meant* by the proposition "Simon is a good shoemaker". As mentioned, both approaches analyses the proposition in respect to some standard or average shoemaker. When this proposition is uttered by an agent, let us call him Socrates, it might be the case that Socrates meant something along these lines and that the analyses offer a plausible explanation of the proposition. However, this does not seem to be the only way this proposition can be understood. In these analyses we seem committed to have at least two shoemakers, where one might be merely possible. This cannot reasonably be the only way that this proposition could be understood. When Socrates utters that Simon is a good shoemaker, Socrates made a claim about a single shoemaker, namely Simon, and there is nothing obviously present in this utterance indicating that there must be a second shoemaker (actual nor possible) used for comparing Simon. If presenting the present analyses of Socrates' asserted proposition, Socrates might very well object, claiming that it is not what he meant by his assertion. The third problem is then that the proposition might be reasonably interpreted as not saying anything about any other shoemaker than Simon. The interpretation that these analyses rely on should be considered only as plausible specifications, rather than a description of its meaning. In light of this, one might say that the analyses might provide a reasonable analysis of the notion 'better ... than', but that these approaches do not capture the notion of 'good' as it is used in the proposition "Simon is a good shoemaker". Aristotle himself would also seem very likely to object to this kind of analysis, based on his teleological understanding of goodness.

Aristotle solves this problem by distinguishing terms into subjects and predications, and in particular distinguishing predications that are non-accidental (predications already contained in the thing) from the accidental (predications that are not contained in the thing). 'Good' is then an accidental predication that belongs to some particular shoemaker, namely Simon. According to *De Interpretatione* (I.11,21a7-18), 'good' is accidental for 'shoemaker' and they should therefore not be considered as *one*. This also holds between 'Simon' and 'shoemaker', as the second is an accidental predication. The analysis of the proposition would then for Aristotle consist of two analyses. Aristotle does not introduce a formal framework to represent these notions, though we would categorise these propositions as singular or particular affirmations. Let S be 'Simon' and M be 'shoemaker'. The first part of the proposition would then by Aristotle be analysed as "Simon is a shoemaker",

S is M.

Let G be 'good'. The second part of the proposition would then be analysed as "Good is said of the shoemaker",

M is G.

It seems evident that these two analyses must be connected, so that the shoemaker in the second analysis is the very same shoemaker as the shoemaker in the first analysis, namely Simon. Aristotle's point here would be to say that the proposition actually contains two parts and our analysis would have to be dependent on what information we intend to pull out from the proposition. If we are interested in whether Simon is a shoemaker or not, we would need the first analysis and if we are interested in whether he is good, we would need the second analysis. The Aristotelean approach is even simpler for the quantified variant, "Some shoemakers are good", as this only requires a single affirmation. This sentence is analysed as "Good is said of some shoemakers" in the following way:

Some M are G.

9.3. Performance and deontic qualification

In the these analyses, we are not able to infer that Simon is good *tout court*, which is what we wanted. We are also able to infer that the shoemaker is good and that Simon is a shoemaker. However, a problem with this analysis is precisely the connection between the first part and the second part. It does not analyse how the good shoemaker in the second part is precisely Simon from the first part. This is connected to a more general problem that seems to partially motivate the popularity of modern Fregean logic. An assertion in Aristotelian logic contains a single subject and a single predication that is either affirmed or denied of that subject. This has shown to be insufficient both for analysing even simple mathematical arguments, but also for representing everyday reasoning. (Smith 2020) The Fregean approach to logic did solve many of the problems with Aristotelean logic, particularly regarding mathematical reasoning and the analysis of relations. It also solved some problems related to linguistic analysis. However, the Fregean approach also has some restrictions, both for mathematics and for linguistics. The relation between Fregean logic and mathematics has been thoroughly discussed in the literature since Frege's *Begriffsschrift* from 1879, both by Frege himself and by many commentators. We have here shown an example of a problem in the linguistic context, though examples with nested quantifiers have also received very much attention in the literature regarding the logical analysis of linguistic phenomena.

CTT and hypotheticals

The CTT approach for analysing complex notions and hypotheticals is fundamentally different from the Fregean approach and does actually seem closer to Aristotle's own analysis. In the previously described approaches, the form of both 'shoemaker' and 'good' were introduced at the syntax level and therefore taken for granted in the analysis of the meaning. In CTT, we introduce the form explicitly on the same level as its meaning, namely the object level. The following analysis was introduced by Ranta (1994, p. 24). The general predicate *Good* is defined as a proposition over a set A where 'goodness' is defined,

$Good(A, x) : prop(x : A)$.

In some notations, A as it occurs in the argument position of the function is left implicit, so that *Good* is defined in the following way:

$Good(x) : prop(x : A)$.

To highlight the meaning of this example, we will use the first notation. Here, *Good* is a proposition defined on a set *Shoemaker* and the second step is therefore to introduce this set,

$Shoemaker : set$.

This is given as a basis for the introduction of 'good' as a proposition defined over this set,

$Good(Shoemaker, x) : prop(x : Shoemaker)$.

The meaning explanations for 'Good shoemaker' then reads that "*Good* is a proposition for x, when x is a *Shoemaker*". To say that the individual *Simon* is a good shoemaker can be analysed as:

$Good(Shoemaker, Simon) true(Simon : Shoemaker)$.

This reads: "It is true that good is said of the shoemaker Simon". The existentially quantified sentence "Some shoemakers are good" may be formalised as follows:

$(\exists x : Shoemaker) Good(Shoemaker, x) true$.

The quantified analysis is based upon a logical analysis of the sentence in predicate calculus, though the more general type-theoretical analysis will use the disjoint union,

$(\Sigma x : Shoemaker) Good(Shoemaker, x) true$.

9.3. Performance and deontic qualification

Here we do not pay attention to this distinction as we are anyway interested in the logical aspect, though in a linguistic or computational context this distinction would seem more important. In CTT, the sentence is made true by a proof object and in the case of "Some shoemakers are good", this a pair of elements (a, b) so that

$$(a, b) : (\exists x : Shoemaker) Good(Shoemaker, x),$$

where a is an element of $Shoemaker$ and b is a function that takes a and verifies $Good(Shoemaker, a)$. Since propositions are interpreted as sets, we might also say that b is a function that yields an element of the set or proposition $Good(Shoemaker, a)$. This corresponds to the following instance of the Σ-formation rule:

$$\frac{Shoemaker : set \quad Good(Shoemaker, x) : prop}{(\exists x : Shoemaker) Good(Shoemaker, x) : prop,} \quad (x : Shoemaker)$$

together with the following instance of the Σ-introduction rule:

$$\frac{a : Shoemaker \quad b : Good(Shoemaker, a)}{(a, b) : (\exists x : Shoemaker) Good(Shoemaker, x).}$$

The formation and introduction rules provide descriptions for how to build the judgment. The elimination rules provide descriptions for what inferences we might do based on that judgment. If we have a proof object c for the proposition so that

$$c : (\exists x : Shoemaker) Good(Shoemaker, x),$$

we know that c must be a complex proof object, consisting of a pair. The elements of this pair is given by projections, which are functions that gives a proof object for accordingly the first and the second element of the pair. $p(c)$ is a left projection that gives a proof object for the first element of the pair. $q(c)$ is a right projection that gives a proof object for the second element of the pair. This situation then corresponds to two instances of the elimination rules. The left projection gives an element for the set *Shoemaker* in the following way:

$$\frac{c : (\exists x : Shoemaker) Good(Shoemaker, x)}{p(c) : Shoemaker.}$$

The right projection gives a proof for $Good(Shoemaker, p(c))$ in the following way:

$$\frac{c : (\exists x : Shoemaker) Good(Shoemaker, x)}{q(c) : Good(Shoemaker, p(c)).}$$

The elimination rules provide proof objects that are linked with the first and the second element of the pair, by accordingly the left and the right projections. Formally, this is described by two evaluations. The first evaluation connects the left projection to the first element of the pair,

$$p(a, b) = a : Shoemaker.$$

The second evaluation connects the right projection to the second element of the pair,

$$q(a, b) = b : Good(Shoemaker, p(c)).$$

This means that we can infer two things from this formalisation of "Some shoemakers are good". We can infer a certain shoemaker and we can also infer that this shoemaker is a good shoemaker. We cannot infer that this shoemaker is good tout court. This seems to be precisely what we wanted, without relying on a particular meaning explanation of neither 'shoemaker' nor 'good'.

Deontic logic and hypotheticals

The analysis of hypotheticals, based on the notion of dependent types seems to be a particularity for Martin-löf's constructive type-theoretical framework and some extensions of it. It is an important feature for the analysis of deontic imperatives and legal reasoning generally, as we are able to precisely explain the connection between an action and its legal qualification.

Deontic qualifications and actions are tightly connected to each other. If we say that an action is law-abiding or law-breaking, we want to express that it is the action itself (or eventually the agent performing the action) that is law-breaking or law-abiding. In the CTT framework, when defining an action A as law-breaking, we make the law-breakingness explicitly dependent on the action or kind of action,

$LB_A.$

This is an abbreviation of the following:

$LB(A, x)(x : A).$

Following common notational practice, we omit A in the argument place of LB and end up with the following notation:

$LB(x)(x : A).$

This is the same form as we find in the analysis of 'Good shoemaker'. As with the shoemaker example, CTT connects the deontic qualification to the performance of the action so that it is the action that is law-abiding or law-breaking. If we introduce an agent in the example, it is not so that the agent performed A *and* was law-breaking. It was precisely the agent's *performance* of A that was law-breaking. This connects closely to the example of the shoemaker and is a very important motivator for the utilisation of CTT in analysing deontic imperatives particularly and legal reasoning generally.

The CTT analysis provides a fine-grained view on the connection between the performance of the action and the deontic qualification of that action. This is done explicitly by the identity statements linking the proof object of the choice to the proof object of the qualified action, by providing an injection with expressions of the forms $left^\vee(y) = x$ and $right^\vee(y) = x$. When a choice has been made, the variable x will be substituted. The variable y is only substituted as a result of imposing a deontic qualification of an action, and the injections $left^\vee(y)$ and $right^\vee(y)$ then provide the connection between the choice made and the deontic qualification of that choice.

We consider first that the decision regarding the legality of the action only occurs after the choice of performing or not performing the action. Second, that it is the particular action (performed as a result of the choice) that is object for deontic qualification. Considering the choice of performing the action as a distinct step from the decision regarding the deontic qualification seems to provide a natural and apprehensible way to understand the future contingency of the deontic qualification. The performance (or non-performance) of the action is neither law-abiding nor law-breaking before the action is actually performed. As mentioned, this also enables us to consider actual and particular actions, and not only kinds of actions to be law-abiding or law-breaking. This seems important for the explanation of precedents and cases. Even though we universally quantify over the source cases, it is a particular action that caused the law-abidingness or law-breakingness, not a general kind of action.

We do not claim that legal rules involve particular actions, as that would seem to go against a principle of equality. The point is to highlight the particular nature of case-based or analogical reasoning, which really is about the application to a particular case, based on some other particular cases. Analogy is considered to be argumentation from a particular to a particular and we would like to specify this particularity in the qualification of the action. Case-

9.3. Performance and deontic qualification

based reasoning is called upon for the application to a particular case and is in the same time based upon a particular application of another case. This aspect seems often to be overlooked by many present analyses of case-based or analogical reasoning that only consider kinds of, and not actual individual actions.

Conclusion

Project

The present project is twofold. First, it gives a thorough representation of the concept of analogical reasoning in law by introducing and comparing contemporary theories. Second, it provides an independent analysis of analogical reasoning in the framework of immanent reasoning.

The first part explained and compared six contemporary theories of analogical reasoning in law. These theories were categorised into *schema-based* theories and *inference-based* theories. Schema-based theories of analogical reasoning capture the notion of analogy by a description of a rule or schema. Inference-based theories on the other hand explain analogical reasoning as a distinct way of reasoning. We identified the theories by Brewer (1996), Alchourrón (1991) and Woods (2015) to be schema-based and the theories of Bartha (2010), Prakken and Sartor (1996) and Rahman and Iqbal (2018) to be inference-based. We then compared the theories by how they handle the notions of *horizontal* and *vertical* relations and by how they analyse *multiple, competing* analogies.

The second part of the project was to provide an independent analysis of reasoning by analogy by utilising the framework of immanent reasoning. Immanent reasoning was described, together with an informal explanation of the other relevant notions of *case*, *relations* and *initial conditions*. The project then introduced two kinds of analogical reasoning, *general precedent-based reasoning* and *precedent-based reasoning with heteronomous imperatives.* These kinds were first analysed in the general formulation of constructive type theory and then given an alternative formulation in the dialogical interpretation. Following this, we introduced a discussion on the advantages of utilising immanent reasoning as a framework for analysing legal reasoning in general and analogical reasoning in particular.

Results

The first goal is to describe analogical reasoning by introducing and comparing different contemporary theories of analogical reasoning in law. The second goal is to provide an independent analysis of analogies.

Even though the different contemporary theories had greatly different starting points, they all provided thorough and deep analyses of the concept of analogy. The schema-based theories provided explanations of both the horizontal and the vertical relations as either explicit or implicit *formal structures*. The inference-based theories on the other hand reduced the question of the horizontal relations to be a question of *identity* or *similarity*. The vertical relations were then described by a particular form of logical *dependency*. Across the categorisations of schema-based and inference-based theories, the theories differed in how they handled multiple, competing analogies. Two leave this notion *unexplained*, two introduce a particular *higher-order* operator on the different analogies and two consider multiple competing analogies as something that should motivate a *change* of the original analogy.

Based on a variant of the principle of *proportionality*, the present project provided an analysis of analogy in the framework of immanent reasoning. By utilising the formalisation of moral conditionals where one formulation is embedded in another formulation, we showed how we could represent analogical reasoning. Because of the particular notion of dependent types in CTT, this approach also allowed for formalising *initial conditions* by an explicit notion of *permitted analogies*. This is a new feature, not previously known to have been introduced in any contemporary analysis of analogy. The dialogical interpretation takes this one step further, as this does allow for representing this feature as an individual condition for the particular *form* of the introduced analogy. This was done by distinguishing in total eight different forms of analogies. The dialogical interpretation also enabled the unification of general precedent-based reasoning and precedent-based reasoning with heteronomous imperatives in a simple way. We have shown that the framework of immanent reasoning is a powerful tool to handle analogical reasoning, which also seem capable of analysing inferences in law more generally.

FURTHER RESEARCH

In the contemporary legal discourse, a notion that is often considered to be closely connected to reasoning by analogy is *balance of interests*. This is an aspect that is often given considerable practical attention when solving a legal issue, a point highlighted by Armgardt (2022). Here, we have not attempted to include interests in the analysis. Though because of its close relationship with interpretation of precedents and analogical reasoning, it would indeed seem to be an aspect worth considering in an extended analysis of legal reasoning.

One of the particularities of the present analysis is its ability to express initial conditions in the formalisation. However, the precise *content* of these conditions stays to a large extent unexplained. A natural continuation of this project would then be to analyse the exact content of the initial conditions. This could then show the effects the no-answer question and the requirement of no-constitutional restraints could potentially have on the analysis.

Furthermore, the present project briefly described the notion of *precedent*. It identified the conditional structure found in legal cases, though a precise analysis of precedents and cases would seem valuable not only for the understanding of analogies in law, but generally for all kinds of legal reasoning. Precedents and legal cases provide a significant aspect of most contemporary legal systems and a thorough analysis of such notions in CTT could provide a deeper understanding of the logical interactions that take place between reasoning, logic and law.

BIBLIOGRAPHY

Alchourrón, Carlos E (1991). «Los Argumentos Juridicos a fortiori y a pari». In: *Carlos E. Alchourrón y Eugenio Bulygin, Análisis lógico y derecho*. Madrid, Centro de Estudios Constitucionales.

Aristotle (1984). *Complete works of Aristotle, volume 1: The revised Oxford translation*. Ed. by Jonathan Barnes et al. Vol. 96. Princeton University Press.

Armgardt, Matthias (2001). *Das rechtslogische System der" Doctrina conditionum" von Gottfried Wilhelm Leibniz*. Elwert.

— (2010). «Zur Rückwirkung der Bedingung im klassischen römischen Recht und zum stoischen Determinismus». In: *Tijdschrift voor Rechtsgeschiedenis/Revue d'Histoire du Droit/The Legal History Review* 78.3-4, pp. 341–349.

— (2022). «A formal model for analogies in civil law reasoning». In: *New Developments in Legal Reasoning and Logic*. Springer, pp. 171–183.

Bartha, Paul F. A. (2010). *By Parallel Reasoning: The Construction and Evaluation of Analogical Arguments*. Oxford University Press, p. 356.

Ben-Yami, Hanoch (1996). «Attributive Adjectives and the Predicate Calculus». In: *Philosophical studies* 83.3, pp. 277–289.

Boucher, Pol (2008). «Leibniz: What Kind of Legal Rationalism?» In: *Leibniz: What Kind of Rationalist?* Springer, pp. 231–249.

Brewer, Scott (Mar. 1996). «Exemplary Reasoning: Semantics, Pragmatics, and the Rational Force of Legal Argument by Analogy». In: *Harvard Law Review* 109.5, p. 923.

Clerbout, Nicolas and Shahid Rahman (2015). *Linking Game-Theoretical Approaches with Constructive Type Theory: Dialogical Strategies, CTT Demonstrations and the Axiom of Choice*. Springer, p. 99.

Frege, Gottlob (1879). *Begriffsschrift, Eine Der Arithmetischen Nachgebildete Formelsprache Des reinenDenkens*. Halle: Verlag von Louis Nebert.

Geach, Peter T (1956). «Good and Evil». In: *Analysis* 17.2, pp. 33–42.

Gentzen, Gerhard (1935). «Untersuchungen über das logische Schließen. I». In: *Mathematische zeitschrift* 39.1, pp. 176–210.

Hart, Herbert Lionel A (1958). «Positivism and the Separation of Law and Morals». In: *Harvard law review*, pp. 593–629.

Heidegger, Martin (1927). *Sein und Zeit*. Halle : M. Niemeyer.

Hesse, Mary (1965). *Models and Analogies in Science*. University of Notre Dame Press.

Kamp, Hans (2013). «Two Theories about Adjectives». In: *Meaning and the Dynamics of Interpretation*. Brill, pp. 225–261.

Kant, Immanuel (1998). *Critique of Pure Reason*. Trans., eds. Paul Guyer, and Allen Wood. Cambridge: Cambridge University Press.

Kenny, Anthony (2014). *Five Ways: St Thomas Aquinas Vo*. Routledge.

Kitcher, Philip (1978). «Positive Understatement: The Logic of Attributive Adjectives». In: *Journal of Philosophical Logic* 7.1, pp. 1–17.

Koch, Hans-Joachim and Helmut Rüßmann (1982). *Juristische Begründungslehre: eine Einführung in Grundprobleme der Rechtswissenschaft*. Beck.

Kvernenes, Hans Christian N (2021). «Approaching an Analysis of Reasoning by Analogy». In: *New Developments in Legal Reasoning and Logic: From Ancient Law to Modern Legal Systems*. Logic, Argumentation and Reasoning, Springer.

Langenbucher, Katja (1998). «Argument by Analogy in European Law». In: *Cambridge Law Journal* 57.3, pp. 481–521.

Lorenzen, Paul (1961). «Ein dialogisches konstruktivitätskriterium». In: *Infinitistic Methods*, pp. 193–200.

Magnier, Sébastien (2015). «La Logique Au Service Du Droit: L'analyse de La Signification Du Terme "Incertain" Dans La Définition de La Condition Suspensive Du Droit Civil Français». In: *International Journal for the Semiotics of Law* 28.3, pp. 647–660.

Martin-Löf, Per (1984). *Intuitionistic Type Theory*. Vol. 9. Bibliopolis Napoli.

— (1991). «A path from logic to metaphysics». In: *Atti del Congresso Nuovi problemi della logica e della filosofia della scienza*. Vol. 2. Editrice CLUEB, pp. 141–149.

— (2017a). «Assertion and Request (Oslo Lecture)». In: *Unpublished*.

— (2017b). «Assertion and Request (Stockholm Lecture)». In: *Unpublished*, pp. 1–9.

Martínez-Cazalla, Maria Dolors et al. (2022). «Elements for a Dialogical Approach on Parallel Reasoning. A Case Study of Spanish Civil Law». In: *New Developments in Legal Reasoning and Logic*. Springer, pp. 217–254.

Navarro, Pablo E and Jorge L Rodríguez (2014). «Deontic Logic and Legal Systems». In: *Tijdschrift Voor Rechtsgeschiedenis*. Ed. by 2-3. In Matthias Armgardt/Fabian Klinck/Ingo Reichard 13(14). Vol. 63. 3. Cambridge University Press, pp. 498–511.

Øhrstrøm, Peter and Per Hasle (2020). «Future Contingents». In: *The Stanford Encyclopedia of Philosophy*. Ed. by Edward N. Zalta. Summer 2020. Metaphysics Research Lab, Stanford University.

Posner, Richard A (2003). *Law, pragmatism, and democracy*. Harvard University Press.

— (2006). «Reasoning by analogy (reviewing Lloyd L. Weinreb, Legal Reason: The Use of Analogy in Legal Argument (2005)». In: *91 Cornell Law Review* 76.

Prakken, Henry and Giovanni Sartor (1996). «A Dialectical Model of Assessing Conflicting Arguments in Legal Reasoning». In: *Logical Models of Legal Argumentation*.
— (1998). «Modelling Reasoning with Precedents in a Formal Dialogue Game». In: *Judicial Applications of Artificial Intelligence*. Dordrecht: Springer Netherlands, pp. 127–183.
— (2016). «A logical analysis of burdens of proof». In: *Legal evidence and proof*. Routledge, pp. 237–268.
Rahman, Shahid and Johan Georg Granström (2019). «Legal Reasoning and Some Logic after All. - the Lessons of the Elders». In: *In D. Gabbay, L. Magnani, W. Park and A-V. Pietarinen (eds.) Natural Arguments. A Tribute to John Woods. London: College Publications, pp. 743-780*. I, pp. 1–46.
Rahman, Shahid and Muhammad Iqbal (2018). «Unfolding Parallel Reasoning in Islamic Jurisprudence (I) epistemic and dialectical meaning in Abu Ishaq al-Shirazi's system of co-relational inferences of the occasioning factor». In: *Arabic Sciences and Philosophy* 28.1, pp. 67–132.
Rahman, Shahid and Hans Christian N Kvernenes (2021). *Conditional right, Legal Reasoning and Games of Why and How*. P. 265. Forthcoming.
Rahman, Shahid, Zoe McConaughey, et al. (2018). *Immanent reasoning or Equality in Action*. Logic, Argumentation and Reasoning, Springer, p. 265.
Ranta, Aarne (Feb. 1991). «Constructing Possible Worlds*». In: *Theoria* 57.1-2, pp. 77–99.
— (1994). *Type-Theoretical Grammar*. Oxford Science Publications.
Smith, Robin (2020). «Aristotle's Logic». In: *The Stanford Encyclopedia of Philosophy*. Ed. by Edward N. Zalta. Fall 2020. Metaphysics Research Lab, Stanford University.
Sundholm, Göran (2019). «The Neglect of Epistemic Considerations in Logic: the Case of Epistemic Assumptions». In: *Topoi* 38.3, pp. 551–559.

Thiercelin, Alexandre (2008). «On two argumentative uses of the notion of uncertainty in Law in Leibniz's juridical dissertations about conditions». In: *Leibniz: What Kind of Rationalist?* Springer, pp. 251–266.
— (2009). «La théorie juridique leibnizienne des conditions: ce que la logique fait au droit (ce que le droit fait à la logique)». PhD thesis. Lille 3.
— (2010). «Epistemic and practical aspects of conditionals in Leibniz's legal theory of conditions». In: *Approaches to legal rationality*. Springer, pp. 203–215.
Thomson, Judith Jarvis (1971). «A Defense of Abortion». In: *Philosophy and Public Affairs* 1.1, pp. 47–66.
Weinreb, Lloyd L (2005). *Legal reason: The use of analogy in legal argument*. Cambridge University Press.
Westen, Peter (1981). «On Confusing Ideas: Reply». In: *Yale LJ* 91, p. 1153.
Wetzel, Linda (2018). «Types and Tokens». In: *The Stanford Encyclopedia of Philosophy*. Ed. by Edward N. Zalta. Fall 2018. Metaphysics Research Lab, Stanford University.
Woods, John (2015). *Is Legal Reasoning Irrational?: An Introduction to the Epistemology of Law*. College Publications.

INDEX

abduction, 30, 32, 35, 38
action
    facultative, 47, 202
    forbidden, 202, 203, 206, 211–213, 215, 266, 268, 279, 280
    obligatory, 47, 202, 203, 206–215, 267, 268, 281
    permissible, 55, 56, 202, 203, 205–207, 211–213, 215, 266–268, 279, 320, 350, 351
        evenly, 204, 211
        recommended, 203, 211
        reprehended, 204, 211
    permitted, 44, 45, 47–49, 53, 213
    prohibited, 47, 49
actuality, 11, 360, 363–367, 370
Adams v. New Jersey Steamboat Co., 151 N.Y. 163 (1896), 37, 227, 275, 319

Alchourrón, Carlos E, 3, 7, 29, 43–49, 108, 110, 111, 113, 115, 117, 232, 399
analogia, 17
analogy
    form, 290–293, 295–299, 302, 304–311, 313, 314, 317, 318, 323, 324, 335–341, 345–347, 352, 353, 355
    multiple, 1, 4, 8, 62, 73, 74, 114–118, 355, 399, 400
    negative, 60, 61, 68, 71, 106, 240, 243, 251, 268, 280, 303–306
    permitted, 2, 9, 248, 264, 265, 315, 352, 401
    positive, 60–63, 65, 66, 68, 69, 71, 73, 112, 240, 242, 251, 259, 267, 274, 280, 301, 302, 307, 308

410   Index

  principle-based, 18, 21, 23,
    26, 222, 350
  rule-based, 18, 19, 25, 26,
    221, 222, 350
argument
  a fortiori, 29, 43, 46–48,
    108, 111
  a pari, 29, 43, 47, 48, 108,
    111
  Aristotle, 2, 6, 12, 18, 43, 187,
    229, 230, 238, 239,
    353, 362–364, 366,
    369, 370, 374, 375,
    386, 389–391
Armgardt, Matthias, 372, 377,
    401
assumption
  actual, 360, 368–370
  epistemic, 104
  logical, 360, 368–370
  real, 359, 360, 368–370

Bartha, Paul F. A., 4, 8, 29,
    57–59, 62–64, 66, 67,
    69–73, 75–78, 99,
    107–109, 112, 114–117,
    217, 226, 231, 355, 399
Ben-Yami, Hanoch, 387, 388
benefactor, 215, 216, 377, 378,
    381
beneficiary, 215, 216, 326–344,
    377, 378, 380, 381
Boucher, Pol, 372

Brewer, Scott, 3, 7, 29–38,
    40–42, 107, 108, 110,
    111, 113, 114, 117,
    221, 222, 227, 232,
    241, 275, 276, 348,
    355, 399

characteristic
  entailed, 217, 226–228,
    237, 240–244, 246,
    247, 259, 290,
    300–308, 310, 313,
    314, 346
  occasioning, 217, 226–228,
    231, 237, 240–243,
    259, 290, 300–308,
    311, 354
Civil Law, 18, 19, 21, 22,
    25–27, 83, 210, 221,
    222, 325, 349
Clerbout, Nicolas, 156, 177
Common Law, 3, 18, 19,
    23–27, 50, 52, 221,
    222, 277, 281
conditional right, 11, 213, 215,
    216, 370–374, 376–382,
    385
counterexample, 7, 106, 227,
    293, 298, 310, 311,
    314, 315, 318, 320,
    322, 324, 325,
    345–348, 352, 355
deontic
  category, 206, 260, 263,
    264, 266–268, 274, 281

Index

  imperative, 204, 206, 207, 265, 348, 349, 395
  logic, 201, 202, 348, 395
  qualification, 11, 203, 206, 207, 214, 291, 319, 386, 395, 396
  status, 261, 266–268, 277, 281
dependent types, 2, 8, 11, 13, 349, 353, 382, 386, 395, 400
dialogue
  formal, 179, 187–189, 191, 345
  material, 178, 179
  tree, 87–89, 93, 94
Donoghue v. Stevenson, A.C. 562 (1932), 23, 24

al-Fārābī, 203
Frege, Gottlob, 391

Geach, Peter T, 387
Gentzen, Gerhard, 128
Granström, Johan Georg, 201–204, 207–211, 213, 215, 216, 254, 348, 379, 381
Grant v. The Australian Knitting Mills, A.C. 85 (1936), 23, 24

Hart, Herbert Lionel A, 230
Hasle, Per, 376
Heidegger, Martin, 365
Hesse, Mary, 2

heteronomous imperatives, 1, 9, 201–203, 208, 210, 213, 237, 260, 318
Hoffmann, 230

Ibn Ḥazm, 202–204, 260
immanent reasoning, 1, 2, 5–8, 10–13, 145, 147, 177, 178, 180, 181, 186–189, 195–197, 201, 220, 244, 246, 289, 309, 313, 314, 323, 324, 348, 349, 353, 399–401
inference-based theory, 1, 3, 4, 7, 8, 29, 30, 108–110, 112–115, 399, 400
inheritance, 45–49, 111, 113
initial conditions, 2, 6, 11, 18, 221, 222, 295, 300, 315, 349, 353, 399, 401
intelligibility, 202
Iqbal, Muhammad, 4, 8, 29, 100, 101, 103–106, 109, 113, 114, 116, 117, 201, 227, 233, 353, 355, 399
Islamic Law, 4, 100, 104, 210, 326

Kamp, Hans, 387
Kant, Immanuel, 366
kasr, 326
Kenny, Anthony, 365
Kitcher, Philip, 387, 388
Koch, Hans-Joachim, 372

Kvernenes, Hans Christian N, 206, 219, 260, 325, 371, 372, 374, 378, 379, 381, 382, 385

lacuna, 20, 27, 221, 248, 351
Langenbucher, Katja, 18–27, 221, 222, 350
Leibniz, Gottfried W, 11, 202, 215, 216, 370–374, 376–379, 381, 384
Lorenzen, Paul, 12

Magnier, Sébastien, 216, 371, 373, 374
Martin-Löf, Per, 5, 8, 121–123, 129, 131, 132, 134, 135, 137, 360, 364–369, 386
Martínez-Cazalla, Maria Dolors, 325, 327, 329, 332, 335
Matadeen v. Pointu, (1998) 1 AC 98, 109), 230
McConaughey, Zoe, 5, 8, 126, 128, 129, 131–133, 135–137, 139, 145, 147–154, 156, 158–160, 163–165, 167, 171, 174, 175, 177–181, 183, 185, 187, 188, 195, 197, 200, 201, 219, 379
meaning
    as use, 5

explanation, 2, 11, 12, 233, 291, 295, 313, 316, 323, 333, 335, 338, 341–344, 347, 353, 356, 357, 392, 394
    global, 155, 179, 187
    local, 179, 181, 185, 187, 189
Menéndez-Martín, Tania, 325
modality, 47, 48, 61, 140, 201–203, 207, 348, 365, 388
moral conditional, 2, 11, 215, 370–372, 379, 380, 385, 400

Navarro, Pablo E, 201, 348

Plato, 12, 187
policy, 25, 41, 42, 84, 355, 356
Posner, Richard A, 41, 42, 356
potentiality, 11, 360, 363–367, 370
Prakken, Henry, 4, 8, 29, 78–99, 109, 112, 114–117, 218, 231, 355, 399
principle
    alike, 238–240, 242
    differently, 238–240, 243
probability, 72, 376–378, 385
proportio, 17
proportio, 17, 18
proportionalitas, 17

Index

proportionality, 2, 6, 7, 18, 229–231, 238, 239, 242, 291, 293, 311, 347, 353, 354, 400

R. v. Morgentaler, 1988. 1 S.C.R. 30, 51
Rahman, Shahid, 4, 5, 8, 29, 100, 101, 103–106, 109, 113, 114, 116, 117, 126, 128, 129, 131–133, 135–137, 139, 145, 147–154, 156, 158–160, 163–165, 167, 171, 174, 175, 177–181, 183, 185, 187, 188, 195, 197, 200–204, 207–211, 213, 215, 216, 219, 227, 233, 254, 325, 348, 353, 355, 371, 372, 374, 378, 379, 381, 382, 385, 399
Ranta, Aarne, 126, 134, 140, 141, 143, 382–384, 391
ratio
  decidendi, 23–25, 52, 56, 90
  legis, 21, 25, 329, 330
reasoning
  case-based, 21–23, 396, 397
  exemplary, 17
  parallel, 17, 49, 55, 106, 201

relation
  horizontal, 58–60, 75, 76, 98, 107–111, 113, 217, 223–225, 228, 229, 400
  horizontal vertical, 229, 231–233
  hypothetical horizontal, 59, 217, 229
  vertical, 1, 8, 32, 57–59, 76, 98, 110–114, 217, 222–229, 231–233, 400
relevancy, 24, 41, 42, 110, 113, 217, 226–228, 231, 233, 291, 353, 354
relevant similarity, 20, 21, 25, 42, 43, 50, 52, 277
requirement
  co-exclusiveness, 101–104, 113, 227, 228, 237
  co-extensiveness, 101, 102, 104, 113, 227, 237
  efficiency, 7, 101–104, 106, 113, 118, 227, 228, 232, 237–239, 242, 246, 293, 311
restrictions
  constitutional, 20, 27, 222, 350
  legal, 350
reward, 202–205, 208–212, 261, 264
Rodríguez, Jorge L, 201, 348
Roman Law, 215
rule

analogy-warranting, 30,
    31, 34–36, 111, 113
challenge, 291–295,
    309–311, 313, 314,
    317, 318, 323, 324,
    345, 347
explanation, 291, 295–299,
    301–310, 313, 314,
    323, 324, 345, 346
formation, 6, 11, 128, 129,
    131–134, 136, 137,
    139, 145, 179–182,
    189, 190, 196, 291,
    297, 298, 301–308,
    317, 393
particle, 6, 146–156, 158,
    165, 167, 181, 183,
    189, 190, 199
structural, 147–149, 155,
    156, 158, 159,
    187–190, 294, 345
Rüßmann, Helmut, 372

sanction, 202–204, 208–212,
    261, 350
Sartor, Giovanni, 4, 8, 29,
    78–99, 109, 112,
    114–117, 218, 231,
    355, 399

schema-based theory, 1, 3, 4,
    7, 29, 30, 107,
    109–111, 113, 114, 232
Sentencia del Tribunal
    Supremo
    3422/2018, 330, 332, 340
    7141/2006, 328–330, 332,
        338, 341–343
    9012/2001, 326–328, 330,
        332, 335, 338, 341–343
Smith, Robin, 391
stare decisis, 23, 50, 52, 238,
    277, 281
Sundholm, Göran, 369

Thiercelin, Alexandre, 372
Thomson, Judith Jarvis,
    52–55

Weinreb, Lloyd L, 41, 42, 356
Westen, Peter, 41
Wetzel, Linda, 361
Wittgenstein, 5, 145, 177
Woods, John, 3, 4, 8, 29,
    49–52, 54–57, 108,
    110, 111, 113, 115,
    117, 221, 232, 399

Øhrstrøm, Peter, 376

www.ingramcontent.com/pod-product-compliance
Lightning Source LLC
Chambersburg PA
CBHW051032160426
43193CB00010B/909